International Peace Conferences

Nijhoff Law Specials

VOLUME 86

The titles published in this series are listed at *brill.com/nlsp*

International Peace Conferences

By

Bertrand G. Ramcharan

BRILL
NIJHOFF

LEIDEN | BOSTON

Library of Congress Cataloging-in-Publication Data

Ramcharan, B. G.
International peace conferences / Bertrand G. Ramcharan.
pages cm. -- (Nijhoff law specials ; v. 86)
Includes bibliographical references and index.
ISBN 978-90-04-24589-1 (pbk. : alk. paper) -- ISBN 978-90-04-24590-7 (e-book) 1. Pacific settlement of international disputes. 2. Peace. I. Title.
JZ5597.R36 2015
341.7'3--dc23

2014039927

This publication has been typeset in the multilingual "Brill" typeface. With over 5,100 characters covering Latin, IPA, Greek, and Cyrillic, this typeface is especially suitable for use in the humanities. For more information, please see www.brill.com/brill-typeface.

ISSN 0924-4549
ISBN 978-90-04-24589-1 (paperback)
ISBN 978-90-04-24590-7 (e-book)

This book is printed on acid-free paper.

Peacemaking, 1496

This led to the envoys of both parties...talking of peace. At first, heralds went over and concluded a truce, by virtue of which the Duke of Orleans was permitted to leave Novara and received food for his troops. Hereupon negotiations were opened as to the peace itself. There sat in Lodovico's chamber, himself, his wife, and the envoys of the League, on one side of the table, and on the other the French; at the end were two secretaries for the two parties and the two languages, and the negotiations were carried on between them. When one, two, or three Frenchman all began talking at once, Lodovico interrupted them with 'Ho, ho! One at a time' and thereupon himself carried on the conversation. He brought it about that, at the expiration of fourteen days, on the 9th October (1496) all parties were agreed.

LEOPOLD VON RANKE, *History of the Latin and Teutonic Nations from 1494 to 1514*. London, George Bell and Sons, York Street, Covent Garden, 1887, pp. 85–86.

Contents

Foreword

This is an important and innovative book. It presents a unique historical study of international peace conferences and performs a helpful service in highlighting the many achievements of the United Nations in its largest ever peacekeeping operation, in the former Yugoslavia, which, at its peak, had an authorised strength of up of 50,000 peacekeepers. It also shows that where success eluded the UN this was not because of a lack of heart but because of the non-cooperation of parties on the ground or of great powers pursuing their own agendas instead of those they had agreed upon in the Security Council.

The United Nations, even with its limitations, has special characteristics that are quite different to those of a Great Power. This is why it enjoys the trust of most Governments and peoples the world over. The fact that it is an Organization representing the whole of humanity requires it to act as a servant of the peoples of the world, even when dealing with reprehensible factions. The United Nations engages in cooperative diplomacy. Without the cooperation of parties and of powers directly concerned it can achieve little. A Great Power can resort to what some American writers have termed 'coercive diplomacy'.

The United Nations had good peace plans for Bosnia and Herzegovina, including the Vance-Owen plan which I helped negotiate. But the plan, as other UN-EU plans, could not stick because leading powers chose to arm some of the parties and to encourage them to fight. How could the UN achieve a negotiated peace when some of the parties were being armed and pushed to fight?

When the major powers were ready, they used coercive diplomacy and brought the conflict in Bosnia and Herzegovina to an end with the conclusion of the Dayton Accord on 21 November, 1995. From the spring of 1993 to the autumn of 1995, UN-EU negotiators strived with guts and determination to help end the war but could not clinch a deal because the pre-eminent power was not yet ready. When it was, coercive diplomacy brought the conflict to an end. In the intervening period, many tens of thousands of people died during the continuing conflict. This is a salutary lesson that scholars and historians will hopefully reflect upon.

While the Bosnian conflict dragged on because of the policies of major powers, the International Conference on the Former Yugoslavia, a joint enterprise between the United Nations and the European Union, helped, as this book shows, to contain conflict in Croatia, prevent conflict in Macedonia – with the first ever preventive deployment of UN peacekeepers, contain the dispute between Greece and the Former Yugoslav Republic of Yugoslavia (FYROM), negotiate an Interim Agreement between Greece and the FYROM that resolved the bulk of their differences except for the disagreement over the name of the FYROM, negotiate a peace agreement for the Danube region of Croatia, provide humanitarian assistance to some three million people in the most difficult circumstances, highlight human rights violations, conduct peacekeeping in harrowing circumstances, with parties seeking to use the presence of the peacekeepers for their own advantage, and neogotiate cooperative relations with the North Atlantic Treaty Organization (NATO).

The United Nations did, as this book shows, practice the Art of the Possible in Peacemaking, Peacekeeping and Humanitarianism. The author is in a unique position to marshal the evidence for this. For three and a half years he supported the peacemakers of the ICFY, including myself, and served as Director of ICFY. For the better part of 1993 he also served simultaneously as the Director of the Office of the Special Representative of the UN Secretary-General, my good friend Thorvald Stoltenberg, who led all UN operations on the ground, peacemaking, peacekeeping and humanitarian. The author is in a unique position to tell about the UN contributions and tribulations.

During the better part of a year that I served as Chairman of ICFY's Working Group on Bosnia and Herzegovina it was my good fortune to have enjoyed the support and friendship of the author and it therefore gives me great pleasure to commend this historic book on International Peace Conferences, and on the Art of the Possible in UN Peacemaking, Peacekeeping and Humanitarianism.

Martti Ahtisaari
Helsinki

Preface

This book has emerged out of our experience as Director of a rather innovative peacemaking, peacekeeping and humanitarian initiative, the International Conference on the Former Yugoslavia, between 1992 and 1996. What was particularly striking about this conference was the experiment of two full-time Co-Chairmen, one from the United Nations and one from the European Union, who laboured tirelessly for peace in different parts of the former Yugoslavia for three and a half years.

We were fortunate to have been part of the Secretariat from the outset, in September, 1992, and witnessed its efforts throughout, until its closure at the end of March, 1996. At the beginning, there were few historical insights to draw upon. The London Conference on Yugoslavia, held in August, 1992, had been more in the nature of a classical, deliberative peace conference. It was the London Conference that had decided on a full-time International Conference on the Former Yugoslavia, with two full-time Co-Chairmen, both former Foreign Ministers, and with six Working Groups, essentially negotiating groups, some of whom served full-time, such as the Chairman of the Working Group on Bosnia-Herzegovina and the Working Group on Ethnic Communities, Nationalities and Minorities.

But the strategies and organization of the conference had to be pieced together from start by the Co-Chairmen and their colleagues. Over the years we have found ourselves reflecting on whether there might have been experiences of international peace conferences that might have been useful at the beginning of this process. This has led us to research and to offer, in Part One of this book, a conspectus on the role of international peace conferences in history.

In Part Two we offer a case study of the strategies and experiences of the International Conference on the Former Yugoslavia. We found that however hard the negotiators tried, they could not clinch peace agreements without the support of major powers, especially the pre-eminent power of the time, the USA. We discuss this experience through the lens of the art of the possible in UN peacemaking, peacekeeping, and humanitarianism.

At the end there are two selected bibliographies for further guidance.

We are grateful to President Martti Ahtisaari, Nobel Peace Laureate and Former President of Finland, and a respected friend and colleague in the Yugoslav peace efforts, for writing a generous Foreword to the book.

PART 1

International Peace Conferences

Introduction

Appearing on the 'Charlie Rose' current affairs programme on public television in New York on 6 August, 2012, former US Secretary of State Henry Kissinger discussed the conflict in Syria and the stalemate in the search for a settlement. When Mr Rose asked him what he thought might be a way forward, he thought aloud that an international conference of the USA, Russia, and China, together with other powers, might be able to work out the elements of a solution. It remained to be seen whether it would succeed, but he thought that the option was worth considering.

Mr Rose then asked him whether Iran should be invited to such a conference as a country with interests and influence in the conflict. He recognized that Iran had the capacity to influence developments on the ground but alluded to political difficulties that would arise, having regard to international sanctions that had been imposed on it on account of its nuclear policy. If an agreement were reached beforehand with Iran on the issue of its nuclear ambitions then it could be invited. As will be seen in this book participation and procedure in international peace conferences can be problematic.

Five weeks earlier, in an effort to support the implementation of Special Envoy Kofi Annan's six point plan for Syria, a one-day international conference had been convened in Geneva on 30 June, but there had been differences between the USA, on the one hand, and Russia and China on the other hand, on the future of Syrian President Bashar Assad. Iran and Saudi Arabia, two countries with interests in the conflict, had not been invited to participate in the meeting.

Were another international conference to be held, as suggested by Secretary Kissinger, it would not be the first time that the international community had resorted to the idea of an international conference in a desperate situation. This approach has been tried time and time again. The London Conference of 1992 on Yugoslavia was a case in point. It had been called in a desperate effort to come up with ideas for peace in the deadiest conflict in Europe since the end of World War II. And, as we shall see later in this book, after the US-led coalition had invaded Afghanistan in 2001, the method used for charting the way forward was to convene the Bonn Conference on Afghanistan at the end of 2001. The Bonn Conference of 2001 and a follow-up conference a decade later, in 2011, helped put together building blocks for rebuilding Afghanistan as a country.

For many centuries now, international peace conferences have been used to help in the search for peace in a variety of situations. Yet, international peace

 | DOI 10.1163/9789004245907_002

conferences, as a genre – as opposed to individual conferences, have not been considered much in the literature even though, taken together historically, they represent a substantial component of institutions for global governance. There are notable studies on particular conferences such as those of Westphalia, Vienna, Paris, and San Francisco.[1] But there have been few attempts to draw insights from them that might be helpful in the quest for peace in our times. And there are powerful insights indeed.

It is little known, for example, that the Vienna Congress of 1814–15 laid the foundations for the abolition of slavery and gave us the first recorded agreement for the protection of minorities. Earlier, the Congress of Westphalia had, in the Treaty of Osnabruck, recognised some rights for religious minorities. The strategies of the Vienna Congress provided building blocks for preventive diplomacy and for the peace and security systems of the League of Nations and the United Nations. The Central American peace processes of the 1980s gave a strategic role to confidence-building and to human rights strategies that the international community is still seeking to emulate in dealing with conflict situations in our times. This book seeks to draw together some strands from international peace conferences of the past that might be helpful in the quest for peace in the future.

Starting during the period of the Renaissance and continuing during the Westphalian, Vienna, post-Vienna, League of Nations, and United Nations orders, one finds numerous examples of international peace conferences – buffetted by competing political perspectives, and by the interests of major powers, global and regional.

Taken together, it will be submitted in this book that international peace conferences have made foundation contributions in at least seven areas: first, in arranging for regional or international orders: Westphalia provided a regional order for Europe that would be extended later to the rest of the world. Paris, 1919 and San-Francisco, 1945, gave us the League of Nations and United Nations experiments. Second, it has been suggested that there is a straight line running from the balance of power system in Europe in the seventeenth and eighteenth centuries to the collective security experiments of the twentieth century. Third, international peace conferences have performed as instruments of global governance. One could see this with great conferences that led to peace settlements, such as that of Dayton in 1995, which ended the most serious conflict in Europe since the Second World War. Fourth, international peace conferences have contributed to post-war settlements, as in the case of the peace treaties concluded at Versailles in 1919 and the 1920s and at Paris in

1 See the bibliography at the end of this book.

1946–47. Fifth, international peace conferences have given us experiences in arrangements for conflict prevention and preventive diplomacy. The concert system introduced after the Vienna Congress of 1815 is an example of this. Sixth, international peace conferences have contributed to confidence-building – or what would be considered peacebuilding in our times. The Central American Peace Conference of 1907 is a good example of this, as are the Contadora and Esquipulas peace processes. And, seventh, starting from Westphalia to our times, international peace conferences have contributed to efforts for the promotion and protection of human rights.

It will not always be straightforward to distinguish between a peace process and a peace conference and some flexibility is needed on this point. The oldest surviving peace treaty,[2] concluded between Ramses II of Egypt and the Hittite King, Hatti Hattusili III in 1280 BC[3] followed wars between the two countries, and diplomatic negotiations by their representatives. We do not know the format of the negotiations and whether they might have had conference dimensions. After the conclusion of the treaty the Hittite King visited his Egyptian counterpart in what one source claims might have been the first summit meeting in history of the leaders of two countries.[4]

Charlemagne convened periodic assemblies of representatives of the territorial units under his sovereignty, but these were probably not peace conferences as such.[5] However, the Contadora/Esquipulas processes in the 1980s involved successive meetings of leaders of Central American and other nations who adopted broad declarations of policy and facilitated the conclusion of treaties. As far as we know there was no organized conference structure as such but what took place involved, essentially, successive regional peace conferences.

A clear early initiative for a peace conference was the proposal of September 1443 by Filippo Maria Visconti for joint action by Florence, Venice and Milan to end the war between Francisco Sforza and the Pope. Visconti proposed, among other things, a peace congress, which did meet, but came to little result. However Pope Nicholas V followed up by convening a peace congress eleven

2 Some accounts consider it a treaty of alliance.

3 Some accounts give it the date of 1259 BC. See "Egyptian-Hittite Peace Treaty (1259 BCE)". Commentary by P.J. Brand, University of Memphis, http://www.milestonedocuments.com/view/egyptian-hittite-peace-treaty/i, consulted on 25 June, 2012.

4 S.M. Arab, MD., "The Pharaoh Who Made Peace with his Enemies and the First Peace Treaty in History," http://www.arabworldbooks.com/ramses.htm, consulted on 25 June, 2012.

5 See http://history-world.org/charlemagne.htm: Holy Roman Empire. Author: Guizot, Francois P.G., consulted 24 September, 2012.

years later, in 1454, which produced significant peace agreements. One can find subsequently in the historical records peace conferences and treaties at Calais and Bruges in 1521, at Cercamp in 1558, at Le Cateau in 1559, and at Munster/Osnabruck/Westphalia between 1644 and 1688.

Thereafter, there was the Vienna Congress in 1814–15, the Congress of Berlin in 1878, the Hague Peace Conferences of 1899 and 1907, the Central American Peace Conference held in Washington in 1907, the Paris Peace Conference of 1919, the Paris Peace Conference 1948, the Round Table Conference on Indonesia 1949, the Japanese Peace Conference held in San Francisco, 1951, the Geneva Conference on Indo-China, 1954, the London Conference on Cyprus, 1959, the Geneva Conference on Laos, 1962, the Geneva Conference on the Middle East, 1973, the Paris Talks on Vietnam, 1969–73, the International Conference on Kampuchea, 1981, the Contadora/Esquipulas Central American peace processes of the 1980s, the International Conference on Kampuchea, 1989, the European Community Conference on Yugoslavia, 1991, the London Conference on Yugoslavia, 1992, the International Conference on the Former Yugoslavia, 1992, various Middle East Peace Processes such as the Quartet of the present time, and international conferences on Afghanistan and Syria. One could also possibly include some Camp David talks on the Middle East as international peace conferences.

There have been peace negotiations that have resembled international peace conferences, such as the peace processes on Vietnam, South Africa and Afghanistan. Some of them had features well worth remembering. As we have already said, the dividing line is not a clear-cut one.

The international peace conferences of primary interest in this book are those that provided frameworks for peace, or involved negotiations for peace, as opposed to the promotion of peace generally.[6] However, the Hague Peace conferences of 1899 and 1907, are in a special category inasmuch as they led to major codifications of the Laws of War and to the establishment of the Permanent Court of Arbitration.

Historically, aside from the peace process between Egypt and the Hittites in 1280 BC, we have not come across any other recorded example of an international peace conference in non-European experiences. The origins of the concept of an international peace conference are to be found mainly in the

6 See, for example, http://peace.maripo.com/p_conferences.htm, "145 International Peace Conferences over the years." Consulted on 18 October, 2011. See also http://histclo.com/essay/war/peace/war-peace.html: War and Social Upheaval: Peace Conferences, consulted on 24 September, 2012.

European diplomatic experience, starting in the period of the Renaissance, but the concept has been applied to non-European situations susequently.

We should, however, note some Native North American traditions of peace and peacemaking that we are not able to date or count among international peace conferences, though the rationale of some of their practices is somewhat similar. Antony Adolf in his recent book, Peace. A World History[7] writes that native North Americans had their own longstanding peace and peacemaking traditions:

> Three prominent examples are the calumer, the League of Peace and Power, and Condolence Councils. The calumer or peace pipe may have originated with the Pawnee of Nebraska, but by the time Europeans arrived it was in use across the continent...Many tribes recognized peace chiefs and war chiefs, and non-violent codes of intra-tribal conduct were widespread, such as the Cherokee Harmony Ethic by which tribesmen were required to walk away from a conflict and resolve it through generosity rather than bellicosity. But the League of Peace and Power was one of the first and few inter-tribal bodies Europeans encountered whose sole aim was to promote *cooperative peace* among its otherwise autonomous communities....Each tribe had its own council. ...The Grand Council of these tribal councils convened as necessary to debate, resolve and pronounce on pressing or ongoing issues and popular proposals....Rites and rituals sometimes referred to as 'Forest Diplomacy' served to widen bases of Great Council deliberations. Among them were Covenant Chains, in which weapons were linked in symbolic circles of friendship and Condolence Council rites, in which the dead were mourned, new chiefs named and inter-tribal ties and histories celebrated by storytelling, song and dance. Although for the most part lost to Europeans, many of these native North American peace traditions survived their colonialism and imperialism.[8]

Philosophically, the great religious and belief systems of the world do have ancient doctrines on the concept of peace and on the relationship between peace and war. Judiaism has the concept of shalom. Christianity blesses peacemakers. Islam has the concept of Salam, Hinduism the concept of shanti, Buddhism the concept of ahimsa (non-violence). African and other traditional beliefs have concepts akin to peace. Judaism, Islam, Hinduism and Christianity

7 Cambridge, Constable, 2009.

8 Ibid, pp. 150–151.

all accept, however, that in certain circumstances it is permissible to engage in warfare.[9]

Politically, as Sir Michael Howard discusses in his insightful book, *The Invention of Peace*, war was an inherent feature of the prevailing world orders during the time of the Roman Empire, the Holy Roman Empire, and the Westphalian order. It was during the Enlightenment period that war was challenged as part of the natural order. Immanuel Kant was the leading philosopher heading the charge against war. The Congress of Vienna 1814–15 was the first diplomatic occasion when the major powers marked a break in the belief that war should be tolerated as an inherent part of the prevailing order. The Congress of Vienna sought to build on the balance of power idea and on the idea of a concert of the great powers that could hopefully be used to prevent war. As mentioned above, the Vienna Congress also saw accords for the abolition of slavery and for the protection of minorities.

The political currents at Vienna involved, in the analysis of Howard, three schools of thought: the Conservative, the Liberal, and the Nationalist. The Conservatives sought to entrench the balance of power. The Liberals sought to build on the notion of moral and legal values and on institutional arrangements, and the Nationalists sought to incarnate the concept of the Nation state (as opposed to the state simpliciter that had been provided for under Westphalia). Henry Kissinger, in his book, Diplomacy, has fascinating accounts of the grand strategies being pursued at Vienna and Paris.[10]

The order installed by Vienna would see refinements in the 1870s, when the concept of the nation-state registered gains, and would go on to the First World War. The three schools of thought, Conservative, Liberal and Nationalist would continue at the Paris Peace Conference in 1919 but 1919, Howard found, would also see the introduction of two contending visions of world order that would go down to 1989: the liberal and the communist. The former sought to build on universal values while the latter sought victory for the working classes world-wide. During the Second World War the Hitlerian concept of world order considered war as the natural order of things and Hitler's aim was global conquest.

The United Nations was built on a combination of the conservative and liberal perspectives, "with the Communists holding their powder dry." The United Nations scheme, Howard noted, would never work as conceived and military alliances such as NATO would help keep the peace until the fall of communism

9 See, generally, A. Adolf, Peace. A World History. Cambridge, Polity Press, 2009:

10 H. Kissinger, Diplomacy, New York, Simon & Schuster, 1994.

in 1989. In 2001 the world, in Howard's assessment, changed dramatically with the terrorist attacks in the United States and the consequent "war on terror."

Part One of this book seeks to consider the major international peace conferences historically, with an approach that, hopefully, would make the book relevant to the present and the future. At a time when the UN is putting much emphasis on developing its capacity for supporting mediation, the book would hopefully make a contribution when it comes to the organization and conduct of international peace conferences.

Chapter 1, A Historical Overview, provides snapshots of some of the major conferences. It seeks to offer some insights into different ways in which international peace conferences were used to respond to problems and situations of conflict.

Chapter 2, Institutional Architectures, presents the main types of institutional architecture of the different conferences, taking a thematic approach. At Vienna and Paris the major powers held sway while the International Conference on the Former Yugoslavia had a Steering Committee, two Co-Chairmen, and six Working Groups focusing on Confidence Building, Economic Measures, Succession Issues, Humanitarian Issues, Nationalities and Minorities, and on Bosnia and Herzegovina. By presenting the different institutional architecture a practitioner about to set up a future international peace conference might hopefully be reminded of some experiences to draw upon.

Chapter 3, Conflict Prevention, seeks to identify the experiences of some conferences that sought to head off future conflicts. For example, the Congress of Vienna decided that in the event of a threat to the order established by the Congress, the major powers would come together and seek to head off the threat. Practitioners setting up a future peace conference or engaged in one might be able to draw upon insights into conflict prevention and preventive diplomacy.

Chapter 4, Peacemaking, seeks to identify the main peacemaking strategies pursued by the different conferences and to draw insights from them. Approaches or techniques of particular merit will be highlighted for the benefit of future practitioners.

Chapter 5, Peacekeeping, presents the experiences of key conferences, such as they exist, in the deployment of observers or peacekeepers (in the case of the later conferences). Regarding the Former Yugoslavia, for example, it was the ICFY that proposed the establishment of what became the preventive deployment in Macedonia. Again, the aim will be to analyse the practice and offer insights for the future practitioner.

Chapter 6, Peacebuilding, seeks to identify what might be considered peacebuilding efforts of outcomes of the different conferences. This should be of particular interest to the UN Peacebuilding Commission and to scholars and practitioners of peacebuilding.

Chapter 7, Human Rights, will attempt to show how some past conferences sought to deal with minority or human rights issues and to draw lessons from them. The topic of minorities featured in a number of the international peace conferences. More recently, human rights issues have been central to the efforts of some of the conferences.

Chapter 8, Justice, seeks to discuss how some conferences addressed the issue of justice (or did not). Since an emphasis on justice is of more recent experience, one finds such materials mainly in the recent conferences.

The Conclusion draws together some of the main findings of the book. We will suggest that having regard to the common problems facing humanity at the start of the twenty first century, and mindful of the difficulties facing the United Nations, the time might be opportune to convene an international peace conference to modernise the architecture of peace and security in the twenty first century.

There is a separate Introduction below to Part Two of the Book on the International Conference on the Former Yugoslavia.

CHAPTER 1

International Peace Conferences

A Historical Overview

Introduction

Students of war and world history paint a picture of endemic violence within, and among, human communities,[1] how major military powers emerged, evolving weaponry, internal conflicts, wars against neighbours and rivals, conquests and reversals, near-world empires, historic rivalries, e.g. among the Assyrians, Egyptians and Hittites, and the consolidation of great empires such as the Roman, the Mauryan, and the Chinese, the rise of the Persians, the Turks and the Mongols, and the ever presence of wars in human history.[2] For the most part, wars were settled by victory/defeat, and there were few peace treaties as such.

Two notable exceptions in antiquity were the treaties between Ramses of Egypt and the Hittitite King, Hatti Hattusili in 1280 BC, and the Treaty of Nicias between Athens and Sparta in 421 BC. There were negotiations leading to the conclusion of both treaties. Envoys met in conference to negotiate the peace of Nicias. Whether these could be considered peace conferences or peace negotiations is open to discussion. The latter is probably more accurate., but, as we saw in the Introduction to this book, the first evidence of an international peace conference as such is to be found among the Italian States of the Renaissance. One can find on the Internet a list of some 145 peace conferences convened over the years to promote peace generally.[3] We will not be looking at these promotional conferences. Our focus will be on international peace conferences convened in the face of, during, or in the aftermath of conflicts.

---

1 See R. Overy, "The State of the World," Introduction to The Times History of the World, London, Times Books, 2008, pp. xxiv–xxv: "...throughout human history both death and pain have been inflicted unnaturally, the product of deliberate violence on the part of human communities. Man, and almost always the male of the species, is a uniquely aggressive and punitive creature....There is single answer to the question of why violence should be such a hallmark of world history, but it can be found on almost every page. ... Civilizations, however sophisticated, have indulged in violence of every kind. Religions have often led the way in devising grotesque ways to seek out heresies and exorcise devils."

2 See The Teaching Company, Great Courses: War and World History. Taught by Professor J.P. Roth. Course Guidebook. Chantilly, Virginia, 2009.

3 See, for example, http://peace.maripo.com/p_conferences.htm, "145 International Peace Conferences over the years." Consulted on 18 October, 2011.

 | DOI 10.1163/9789004245907_003

In his notable work, Peace and War: Conflicts and International Order 1648–1989[4] K. Holsti asked: What do men fight about? How have their attitudes toward war changed? And to what extent have they succeeded in creating international orders and institutions that manage, control, or prevent international conflicts and crises from breaking out into war?[5] He concluded that war-making had been essentially a rational activity, a means designed to protect or achieve certain known ends. Men did not go to war for the sake of battle, but to resolve issues that could not be reconciled by other means. The Clausewitzian approach did not regard war as a form of deviant behaviour. War, rather, was characterized in instrumental terms as a rational, if not desirable, means of achieving or defending known purposes. According to Clausewitz, war is an 'act of violence intended to compel our opponent to fulfil our will…War is not merely an act of policy but a true political instrument, a continuation of political intercourse, carried on with other means'.

Wars, Holsti continued, did not occur 'because' but 'in order to'. The emphasis on purpose steers us at least part of the way around the hurdle of the assumed explanatory powers of ecological, genetic, and relational variables. The underlying problem for investigation was not why did nations fight, but what they were fighting about.

But how did they make peace? International peace conferences were one way. Historically, one might say that the origins of international peace conferences lay in one or more of the following categories: Friendly intercessions by third powers; interventions by self-interested powers such as the Holy See; interventions by major powers individually or acting in concert to prevent or stop wars; conferences organized by victors after major wars, such as after the Napoleonic wars or the First World War; pressure of public opinion on third powers to act to stem wars; and, from the twentieth century, peace conferences organized by international or regional organizations.

We offer later in this chapter a review of key international peace conferences, with brief snapshots of what they were convened to discuss. As will be seen, they vary much in character, composition, and results. An illustration of the complexities involved in classifying an event as international peace conference is provided by an event convened in Geneva on 30 June, 2012 on the conflict then raging in Syria.

Towards the end of June, 2012, as his efforts to promote his six point peace plan for Syria were coming up against increasing difficulties on the ground,

---

4 K. Holsti, Peace and War: Conflicts and International Order 1648–1989 Cambridge University Press, 1991.

5 Ibid, p. xvi.

former UN Secretary-General Kofi Annan, the UN/Arab League peace Envoy, carried out consultations on the idea of an international conference in Geneva involving « governments and countries with influence on one or the other parties ».[6] In the light of his consultations he invited leading powers to a Ministerial conference on Saturday 30 June 'to endorse a political transition plan'. A statement from Mr Annan's office said that the 'Action Group's' objectives were to 'identify steps and measures' that would secure full implementation of his peace plan, including a ceasefire and 'guidelines and principles' for a transition.[7]

The Foreign Ministers of China, France, Iraq, Kuwait, Qatar, Turkey, Russia, UK, USA, along with UN Secretary-General Ban Ki-moon and Arab League Secretary-General Nabil El-Araby, attended a meeting on the situation in Syria at the United Nations office in Geneva on Saturday 30 June, 2012. Iran and Saudi Arabia, two countries reportedly supporting different sides in the conflict, were not invited to attend. The meeting adopted a statement calling on the parties to the conflict to recommit to a ceasefire; to work for a transitional government; to pursue a Syrian-driven peace process; to aim for a consitutional review; and to engage genuinely in the quest for peace.

Mr Annan said after the conference that there was international agreement that a transitional government should be set up in Syria, which could include both members of the government and opposition. But US Secretary of State Hilary Clinton commented to the media that Syrian President Bashar al-Assad could not remain in power, 'given the blood on his hands'. Russian Foreign Minister Sergei Lavrov said, however, that there were no preconditions to the proposed transition that dictated who should or should not be in the transitional government.[8] Diplomats defended the Geneva conference as the 'start of a process' to revive Mr Annan's faltering plan.[9] In the end the conference did not save Annan's peace plan and he resigned. He was succeeded by the veteran peacemaker Lakhdar Brahimi.

Could one consider this an 'international peace conference'? It was called by the Special Envoy, after consultations, to endorse his proposals, met on a single day, did not involve the participation of two countries with strong interests in the confict, and adopted an exhortatory statement the interpreatation of parts of which was immediately disputed by the Foreign Ministers of Russia and the USA.

---

6 Financial Times, 25 June, 2012.

7 Financial Times, 28 June, 2012.

8 BBC News, 30 June, 2012.

9 Financial Times, 2 July, 2012.

If one compares this meeting with more formal events one might be tempted not to consider it an international peace conference as such. But then, if one pauses for a moment, why would one deny it the label of an international peace conference. We saw, in the Introduction to this work, former US Secretary of State Henry Kissinger suggesting the idea of an international conference of China, Russia, and the USA to help come up with an approach that could help end the conflict. On balance, one is probably better advised to take a flexible and pragmatic approach to what is an international peace conference.

Keeping this in mind, one might ask whether there are historical insights that could be suggested from the conferences of the past. Any such distillation is necessarily subjective, but one could offer the following:

In the first place, we might note the role of such conferences in the development of regional and global public orders – one might even say of global governance. The Italian city states pioneered a practice that was to become common after the Congress of Westphalia, of convening periodic conferences to deal with problematic situations.

In the second place, we might note the role of the Great Powers that sought to concert their efforts for the prevention, management, and resolution of problem situations and generally to secure the peace. Preventive diplomacy began here. Recognition of the role of the Great Powers would extend directly to the League of Nations and the United Nations, *vide* the Permanent members of the Security Council.

In the third place, we might note the role of individual great powers who took it upon themselves to convene international gatherings to discuss problematic situations or issues. The Hague Peace Conferences of 1899 nd 1907 are examples of this, as was the Central American conference of 1907, convened in Washinton by the USA.

In the fourth place, we might note the role of a group of States, such as in the Contadora and Esquipulas peace processes in Central America in the 1980s.

In the fifth place, we might note the role, in the more recent era, of regional organizations, or of a combination of efforts of regional and international organizations. ...The 'Carrington Conference' or the EU conference on Yugoslavia is an example of the former. The International Conference on the Former Yugoslavia was a good example of a joint effort by the European Union and the United Nations.

In the sixth place, we might note the role of the United Naions and its Security Council in initiating peace conferences.

In the seventh place, we might note the role of international peace conferences after major international wars in endeavouring to establish public orders of the future. The Versailles peace conference of 1919 and the San Francisco conference of 1945 are examples of this. The San Francisco conference of 1945, of course, had a particular purpose and had been preceded by war-time meetings of the leaders, mainly, of the UK, USA and USSR.[10]

In the eighth place, we might note the role of international peace conferences in in ratifying previously negotiated peace treaties. The San Francisco conference of 1951, where the post-war peace treaty with Japan was concluded, was an example of this.

In the ninth place, we might note the role of international peace conferences in laying down a framework of principles for negotiations for particularly difficult conflicts or where peacemaking is protracted. The London Conference of 1992 on Yugoslavia is a case in point.

In the tenth place, we might note the brainstorming role of some international peace conferences. Henry Kissinger's suggestion of an interntional conference on Syria, to which we referred earlier, is an example of this.

Keeping in mind the foregoing ten historical perspectives on international peace conferences, we think that it would be justified to consider such conferences as a useful part of the processes of global governance in our times, and more particularly when it comes to the prevention, management, and resolution of conflicts. Thomas Weiss and Ramesh Thakur have offered a presentation of global governance that sees it as referring to concrete cooperative problem-solving arrangements, many of which increasingly involve not only the United Nations of states but also other UNs', namely interntional secretariats and other nonstate actors. These cooperative problem-solving arrangements may be formal, taking the shape of laws or formally constituted institutions for a variety of actors (such as state authorities, intergovernmental organizations (IGOs), non-governmental organizations (NGOs), private sector entities, other civil society actors, and individuals) to manage collective affairs. They may also be informal (as in the case of practices or guidelines) or *ad hoc* entities (as in the case of coalitions). They define global governance as the complex of formal and informal institutions, mechanisms, relationships, and processes between and among states, markets, citizens and organizations, both inter- and non-governmental, through which collective interests on the global plane are articulated, duties, obligations and privileges are established, and differences are mediated through educated professionals.[11]

In the remainder of this chapter we note the Egyptian/Hittite peace treaty of 1280 BC and the Peace of Nicias, and then proceed to provide some snapshots

10 See, generally, H. Kissinger, Diplomacy, New York, Simon & Schuster, 1994.

11 T.G. Weiss and R. Thakur, The UN and Global Governance: An Idea and its Prospects, Indiana University Press 2007.

of international peace conferences since 1443. For historical purposes we have opted for a chronological rather than a thematic presentation, keeping in mind the ten thematic perspectives we have already offered. We devote more space to some of the conferences than others. For some, such as the 1712 Congress of Utrecht and the 1870 Congress of Berlin, the idea is to record their occurrence. For others, such as the Congress of Westphalia/Munster, we go into greater detail because of their precedential or historic value. In a few instances, we pass over some meetings that would formally qualify as international peace conferences/congresses but which are of little interest from the perspective of drawing insights for future peace efforts.

Egyptian-Hittite Peace Treaty, 1280 BC

There is no historical record to suggest that the concept of an international peace conference existed in the Near-East or in any part of the world in this historical epoch. But although this peace treaty was not the outcome of a peace conference as such, it did follow negotiations by plenipotentiaries and it is worth noting for its historical significance as the oldest surviving peace treaty, as well as for its contents.

In the wake of some two centuries of wars between Egypt and the Hittites, and with "another round of war…on the horizon," "(D)iplomatic negotiations took place for two years and a peace treaty was concluded in the 21st regal year of Ramses' reign with 'Hattusili III' in 1280 BC"[12] Two copies of the treaty were recorded, one in hieroglyph and the other in Akkadian, and both still survive. The treaty consisted of 18 articles one of which had a clear preventive rationale:

> Reamasesa (Ramses), the great king, the king of the country of Egypt, shall never attack the country of Hatti to take possession of a part (of his country). And Hattusili, the great king of, the king of the country of Hatti, shall never attack the country of Egypt to take possession of a part (of that country)

12 S.M. Arab, MD., "The Pharaoh Who Made Peace with his Enemies and the First Peace Treaty in History," http://www.arabworldbooks.com/ramses.htm, consulted on 25 June, 2012. See also, T. Bruce, The Kingdom of the Hittites. Oxford, Oxford University Press, 1999. H. Klengel, "From War to Eternal Peace: Ramesses II and Khattushili III," Canadian Society for Mesopotamian Studies 37 (September 2002). E.H. Cline, "Hittites," The Oxford Encyclopaedia of Ancient Egypt. Ed. D.B. Redford, Oxford, Oxford University Press 2001, 2005.

Other articles provided for mutual assistance against external and internal enemies and for the extradition of wanted persons. "During the next 46 regal years of Ramses II, peace continued and the treaty was respected until the fall of the Hittite Empire."[13]

Peace of Nicias, 421 BC

This peace treaty between Athens and Sparta, although also not issuing from a peace conference, is again worth noting briefly as one of the oldest surviving of which there is a good historical account by Thucydides in his History of the Peloponnessian Wars. It was concluded in 421 BC and intended to last for fifty years. It did bring about a brief end to the fighting but did not survive long. According to Thucydides it lasted for six years and ten months, during which period neither side invaded the other's territory.[14] However, in actual fact, war broke out between the two sides after about a year and a half, in 418 BC.

The opening negotiations for the treaty had begun in 425 BC as Sparta suffered losses in the war. When Athens also suffered losses in 424 BC the two sides agreed to a one year truce. After this truce broke down and the fighting continued, the two sides succeeded in concluding the treaty, which Thucydides named after the Greek negotiator Nicias, in 421 BC. Like the Egyptian-Hittite treaty, it consisted of eighteen articles. According to Adcock and Mosley, "Representatives of both Athens and Sparta met several times in conference before producing the terms for approval. A conference of the allies of Sparta met and accepted the peace..."[15]

Also like the Egyptian-Hittite peace treaty, the Peace of Nicias had a preventive rationale: the treaty was to be in force between the Athenians and their allies, and the Spartans, with their allies, for fifty years 'without fraud or damage by land or sea'. It would not be lawful to take up arms with the intent to do injury either for the Spartans and their allies against the Athenians and their allies, or for the Athenians and their allies against the Spartans and their allies, 'in any way or by any means whatever'. 'If disputes should arise between them, they are to deal with it by law and by oath, as may be agreed between them'. The words

13 Ibid. Antony Adolf writes that the treaty was negotiated by plenipotentiaries about fourteen years after the battle. See A. Adolf, Peace. A World History. Cambridge, Polity Press, 2009, p. 34.

14 Thucydides, The Peloponnesian War. Oxford World Classics, Oxford, OUP, 2009, with introduction by P.J. Rhodes and M. Hammond.

15 F. Adcock and D.J. Mosley, Diplomacy in Ancient Greece. New York. St. Martin's Press, 1975, pp. 51–52.

of the oath taken upon conclusion of the treaty were: 'I shall abide by the terms of the treaty honestly and sincerely'. This oath was to be renewed annually by both sides. 'If any point connected with any subject at all has been overlooked, alterations may be made, without any breach of oath, by mutual agreement and on due consideration by the two parties, the Athenians and the Spartans'.[16]

It would take almost a thousand years after the Peace of Nicias, for us to see the first evidence of an international peace conference as such, first at the end of the Hundred Years War between England and France, and then in the experience of the Italian city states as the Roman Empire was faltering.

Congress and Treaty of Arras, 1435

After almost a hundred years of war between England and France a Congress was convened in Arras in 1435 involving representatives of England, France and Burgundy and representatives of Pope Eugene IV and the Council of Basel. The Congress produced the Treaty of Arras,[17] which was facilitated by representatives of the Pope and the Council of Basel. From a historical point of view the Congress was one of the earliest, and provided the model of third party facilitation. It also provided the precedent of legal opinions on contested issues, provided by the Council of Basel. The details of the Treaty of Arras need not detain us further here.

Peace Congresses of 1443 and 1454: The Peace of Lodi

In September, 1443, Filippo Maria Visconti of Milan made a proposal for joint action by Florence, Venice and Milan to end the war then ongoing between Francisco Sforza of Florence and the Pope, and for this action to be followed by a Congress of the major Italian powers for the settlement of all outstanding political questions and the exchange of mutual guarantees. The Congress, when it finally convened, was poorly attended and came to nothing.[18] However, in 1454 a peace congress was summoned by Pope Nicholas V. After initial difficulties, the Peace of

16 Text taken from « The Peace of Nicias », http://www.livius.org/pb-pem/peloponnesian_war/war_t04.html, consulted on 26 June, 2012. For a brief summary of the agreement, see J. Rikard (22 June 2011), Peace of Nicias 421 BC, http://www.historyofwar.org/articles/peace_nicias.html, consulted on 26 June, 2012.

17 See J.G. Dickinson, The Congress of Arras, 1435. A Study in Medieval Diplomacy. New York, Biblio and Tannen, 1972.

18 G. Mattingly, Renaissance Diplomacy. Jonathan Cape, London. 1955, p. 83.

Lodi was concluded, after which the first general pacification of Italy quickly followed, the Most Holy League. It was entered into, with the full concurrence of Pope Nicholas V, by the three chief northern belligerents, Florence, Venice and Milan, for the purpose of stabilizing the *status quo* and guaranteeing the existing Italian powers against aggression from within or without the peninsula.[19]

The treaty was signed at Venice on 30th August, 1454. It provided for a defensive alliance for twenty-five years, with provisions for subsequent renewals. The signatories promised to defend each other's territories in Italy against any and all aggressors, and for this purpose agreed on a schedule of military forces which they were severally to maintain, and a programme for joint military action in case of emergency. Each signatory reserved the right of its allies to be included. The Peace of Lodi is considered to have established, in respect of the Northern Italian city-states a system of balance of power and collective security similar to that which the Congress of Westphalia would establish in 1648 in respect of Western Europe.

Peace Conferences at Calais/ Bruges, 1521; Peace Negotiations at Cercamp, 1558; Peace Negotiations at Le Cateau, 1559 : The Treaties of Cateau-Cambresis, 2 and 3 April 1559.

Joycelyne G. Russel, in her book on Peacemaking in the Renaissance,[20] writes at some length about the peace negotiations between, mainly, England and France at Calais and Bruges, in 1521. These involved negotiations among ambassadors and other representatives. Similarly, she goes into considerable details about the peace negotiations, again mainly involving England and France at Le Cateau in 1559 leading to the Treaties of Cateau-Cambresis of 2 and 3 April, 1559.

The conferences and negotiations themselves do not need much discussion here. However, the Treaties of Cateau-Cambresis, of 2 and 3 April, 1559 themselves have many features that are worth noting. Ms Russel, in Appendix B to her book provides useful summaries of the treaties from which we might note the following points: The treaty between King Philip II and Henri II (3 April 1559) provided that Arbitration shall take place on the claims of the Princes over the Abbey of S. Jean-au-Mont and its lands in French and Spanish dominions. There were to be arbiters on each side, plus a super-arbiter, if necessary. The same treaty agreed, as a preventive measure, upon a marriage between the Duke of Savoy and Madame Marguerite de France, sister of the King of France.

---

19 Ibid, p. 88.

20 Philadelphia, University of Pennsylvania Press, 1986. Ms Russel, under the name Dickinson, had earlier written the study cited earlier on the Congress of Arras, 1435.

The treaty between King Henri II and Queen Elizabeth I (2 April 1559) provided, as a preventive measure that no armed vessel would leave any of the ports of France or England without giving previous security to the Admiral of France or England that the peace would not be violated. In the same spirit, during a period of eight years it would not be lawful either for the King of France, or the King and Queen of Scotland, or the Queen of England, to make any hostile attempt upon the realm or subjects of the other.

The treaty of Cateau-Cambresis further provided for a number of restitutions that are summarised in Appendix C to Ms Russel's book.

Congress of Westphalia/Munster/Osnabruck, 1648

The Congress of Westphalia, in the assessment of Peter Wilson,[21] was a groundbreaking event. Medieval church councils had been the closest precedent, but this was the first truly secular gathering. It drew on established protocol and negotiating styles, but its sheer scale and the complexity of the issues compelled innovation and dissemination of common guidelines. First and foremost, the congress eroded the medieval principle of hierarchy. The presence of so many representatives from rulers of different rank required a new, simpler form of interaction. It was agreed that all kings had the title of 'majesty' and that all royal and electoral ambassadors were to be addressed as 'Excellency' and could arrive in a coach pulled by six horses. Such matters were far from trivial. They represented a major step towards the modern concept of an order based on sovereign states interacting as equals, regardless of their internal form of government, resources, or military potential. The Congress established a new way to resolve international problems through negotiations among all interested parties. Attempts to resolve later European wars drew directly on this precedent, notably the Congresses of Utrecht (1711–13) and Vienna (1814–15), and the method was extended, in line with the changing global order, at the Peace Conference of 1919 and, ultimately, with the United Nations.

Altogether, 235 official envoys and representatives attended, but the total number of participants was far larger, since all were accompanied by additional staff.

The proceedings attracted wide public interest, which the delegates deliberately cultivated and manipulated. The Congress broke new ground in that it

21 P.H. Wilson, The Thirty Years War. Europe's Tragedy. Cambridge, Mass., The Belknap Press of Harvard University Press, 2009. p. 672.

dispensed with an official chair or mediator. There were no plenary sessions. Instead, negotiations proceeded through bilateral talks, often held in parallel with multiple partners. Talks with the Swedes were held in Osnabruck, while those with France took place in Munster. Mediation was restricted to that by Chigi and his able Venetian colleague Alvisi Contarin acting as go-between for France with the Hapsburgs, who had refused formal direct talks. Religious differences mattered little and Protestants and Catholics were present in both venues.

The two treaties agreed upon concluded the Thirty Years War. The Emperor and Empire settled their own problems, and those with Sweden, in the Peace of Osnabruck (IPO) that simultaneously served as a new statement of the imperial constitution applying across the Empire. The parallel Peace of Munser (IPM) with France was less complete, because it excluded the Burgundian Kreis, as well as the Duchy of Lorraine, which remained occupied by French troops. It covered Austria's territorial concessions to France, as well as articles confirming the constitutional arrangements agreed with Sweden and the imperial Estates in the IPO.

Both treaties were formally sworn on 24 October accompanied by a seventy-gun salute. Two copies of each were prepared for the ceremonies, followed by further copies over the subsequent days that were witnessed by the envoys to ensure no changes were slipped in. These were despatched to the relevant courts, while at least another 42,000 copies were printed for an eager public over the coming year.

According to Wilson, Westphalia's significance lay not in the number of conflicts it tried to resolve, but in the methods and ideals it applied. The first article of both the IPO and IPM stated they were instruments of a 'Christian, general and permanent peace' intended to establish lasting friendship across the continent. This was more than merely a statement of good intentions. The Congress offered a new charter for European relations. The sections on the imperial constitution did refer to the Empire's earlier settlements of 1552 and 1555, but otherwise the documents made no mention of other European treaties, instead offering a new framework for peace. The treaties ending other wars were regarded as extensions to Westphalia, pacifying additional parts of the continent. The Westphalian treaties continued to be invoked in major European settlements up to the Congress of Vienna in 1814–15, which ended the Napoleonic Wars. These later settlements rested on the same understanding of international law as a voluntary contract superior to all existing secular and religious law.[22] Only the Pope rejected the entire settlement.

22 Ibid, p. 753.

The positive interpretation of Westphalia regards it as the birth of the modern international order based on sovereign states interacting (formally) as equals within a common secularized legal framework, regardless of size, power or internal configuration.

Utrecht, 1712

The Peace of Utrecht followed the War of Spanish Succession and consisted of various treaties concluded after negotiations on different occasions. At one stage a Congress was convened in Utrecht in January, 1712 where a leading subject of discussion was about guarantees that France and Spain would not be merged into a single entity. The maintenance of the balance of power was a key issue during the negotiations. This congress need not detain us further in the present context.

Vienna, 1814–15

David King has written that "The Congress of Vienna was indeed quite unlike any other peace conference in history. It was to be the first large peacemaking venture in almost 175 years, and it has been controversial ever since. In addition to the many issues and tensions, one of its most fascinating features is the explosive mix of delegates sent to the decadent Habsburg capital."[23] Some 215 Heads of state, including principalities and grand duchies attended, backed up, according to one source, by some one hundred thousand support staff of various kinds.[24]

The proceedings of the conference were not straightforward and have been criticised by Harold Nicholson, who similarly made trenchant criticisms of the organization and conduct of the Paris Peace Conference a hundred years later.[25] Prior to the arrival of the other delegations, the four principal powers constituted themselves as a committee to decide important questions. They decided that, as a courtesy, they would inform France and Spain of their decisions and the plenary Congress would then assemble to endorse their decisions. In the

23 D. King, Vienna, 1814. New York, Harmony Books, 2008, p. 3.

24 F. Stanton, Great Negotiations. Agreements that Changed the Modern World. Yardley, Pennsylvana, 2010, p. 246.

25 H. Nicholson, The Congress of Vienna. A Study in Allied Unity 1812–1822. London, Constable, 1946, p. 134.

end result, the skilful diplomacy of Talleyrand brought France into the inner circle of five. The Congress established a number of committees, including a Statistical Committee, which undertook information-gathering and checking on particular situations and communities. The Final Acts of the Congress were signed on 9 June, 1815.

The results of the Congress were quite remarkable. It re-established a balance of power in Europe, brought together multiple German entities into a German confederation, re-created a Kingdom of Poland, provided for the neutrality of Switzerland, decided that Norway would henceforth belong to Sweden, and adopted a declaration calling for the abolition of the international slave trade. Henry Kissinger, in his book on the Congress, and in his later book on Diplomacy, provides fascinating insights into the strategies of the major powers. Great Britain, for example, was keen on the balance of power as an arrangement to head off future conflicts, but it would not endorse the idea of preventive strategies in the abstract. It was only with the advent of the twentieth century, with the arrival of growing German power following its unification, that Great Britain came to be interested in preventive arrangements as a genre. The power dimensions of this were striking. Great Britain recognized that German power at the beginning of the twentieth century could surpass those of France and Great Britain and thus started to search around for general preventive strategies – which it would not countenance at Vienna![26]

Congress of Berlin, 1878

In the Russo-Turkish War of 1877 and 1878, Russia had defeated Turkey and obliged it to accept the Treaty of San Stefano, which created a greatly-expanded Bulgaria under Russian protection. Britain feared that Russia might spread its control to Constantinople (now Istanbul) and to the Suez Canal. Great Britain and Austria demanded a revised treaty. This led to the Congress of Berlin (13 June - 13 July), a diplomatic meeting of the major European powers. Russia, weakened by war, consented to a revised treaty. The Treaty of Berlin thus replaced the Treaty of San Stefano.[27] The Congress of Berlin

26 H. Kissinger, Diplomacy, New York, Simon & Schuster, 1994, p. 88.

27 http://www.britannica.com/EBchecked/topic/62090/Congress-of-Berlin, consulted 26 June, 2012. See further, W.N. Medlicott, The Congress of Berlin and After. A Diplomatic History of the Near Eastern Settlement, 1878–1880 (1963); M.H. Yavuz and P. Sluglet (Eds.), War and Diplomacy: The Russo-Turkish War of 1877–1878 and the Treaty of Berlin. University of Utah Press, 2012.

provided for guarantees of religious beliefs, an important watershed in international relations.

Hague Peace Conferences, 1899 and 1907

The two Peace Conferences had as their fundamental aim to contribute to the avoidance of war through the development of international law, the promotion of peaceful methods for the settlement of disputes, the advancement of international arbitration, and the lessening of human suffering in war by codifying and developing the rules of warfare.[28] The idea of the prevention of war through resort to good offices or mediation, expressed for the first time in Protocol 23 of the Declaration of Paris was picked up explicitly at The Hague Peace Conferences of 1899 and 1907. Out of The Hague Peace Conferences came the Permanent Court of Arbitration and the Hague provisions on the laws of war.

In Article 2 of The Hague Convention on the Pacific Settlement of International Disputes, of 18 October, 1907, the contracting powers agreed, in the event of a dispute, to have recourse to the good offices or mediation of one or more friendly powers before resorting to arms. Article 3 gave the right to Powers not involved in a dispute to offer good offices, even in the course of hostilities. The exercise of this right was not to be considered an unfriendly act.

The ideas for the peaceful settlement of disputes and, thereby, the prevention of war, elaborated upon at the Hague Peace Conferences would be picked up after the devastation wrought by the First World War and inserted into the Covenant of the League of Nations.

Central American Peace Conference, 1907: General Treaty of Peace and Amity[29]

The Central American Peace Conference held in Washington in 1907 grew out of a friendly initiative taken in the summer of 1907 by the Presidents of the USA and Mexico, "in an endeavour to secure an adjustment of pending disputes between several of these Republics in some form that would insure permanent

28 See J.B. Scott, *The Hague Peace Conferences of 1899 and 1907* (Boston/London: Pub. for the International School of Peace, Ginn & Company, 1908).

29 Concluded among the Republics of Costa Rica, Guatemala, Honduras, Nicaragua, and El Salvador, 20 December, 1907.

peace among them and foster their development."[30] The Conference was attended by delegates of the five Central America nations: Costa Rica, Guatemala, Honduras, Nicaragua and El Salvador from 13 to 20 December, 1907. A preliminary conference had been held at the Bureau of American Republics in Washington, D.C. on 16 and 17 September of that year.

This was a well-planned and -run conference, with solid rules of procedure and good vision. It resulted in the conclusion of the following treaties: 1. A general treaty of peace and amity; 2. A convention additional to the general treaty of peace and amity; 3. A convention for the establishment of a Central American Court of Justice; 4. A protocol additional to the convention for the establishment of a Central American Court of Justice; 5. An extradition convention; 6. A convention for the establishment of an International Central American Bureau. 7. A convention for the establishment of a Central American pedagogical institute; 8. A convention concerning future Central American Conferences; 9. A convention concerning railway communications.

As a precedent, and a model, this conference has much to commend it (leaving aside how successful it was in actual practice), and we discuss it in more detail in the chapter on conflict prevention later in this book. It is interesting to note that each Republic undertook not to recognize in another a Government resulting from a coup d'etat (something that Africa was to try to institutionalise towards the end of the twentieth century) nor to intervene in favour of, or against, the existing government of another republic in cases of disorder therein. They also agreed to use their efforts to secure constitutional reforms that would prohibit the election of a President for a second term.[31]

Paris Peace Conference, 1919

Twenty seven countries were invited to participate in the Paris Peace Conference of 1919. The USA was represented by President Woodrow Wilson, and the UK, France, and Italy by their Prime Ministers. A Council of Ten took the key decisions, consisting of the Heads of state and foreign ministers of the four principal allies and Japan. It had been intended to invite Germany to join the discussions once the principal powers had decided on terms for a preliminary settlement, but the latter did not come to agreement easily and, in the end, the

30 Report of Mr William I. Buchanan, Representative of the USA to the Central American Peace Conference Held at Washington, D.C., 1907. Washington, Government Printing Office, 1908, p. 3.

31 Ibid, p. 13.

idea of German formal participation did not materialise. Fifty eight commissions were empanelled during the conference, including a leading one on the establishment of a League of Nations, chaired personally by President Wilson.

Margaret Macmillan has written:

> The Paris Peace Conference is usually remembered for producing the German treaty, signed at Versailles in June 1919, but it was always about much more than that. The other enemies – Bulgaria, Austria and Hungary, now separate countries, and the Ottoman empire – had to have their treaties. New borders had to be drawn in the centre of Europe and the Middle East. Most important of all, the international order had to be recreated, perhaps on a different basis. Was the time now ripe for an International Labour Organization, a League of Nations, agreements on international telegraph cables or international aviation?[32]

She set the conference in historical context:

> The Congress of Vienna…took place when the great upheavals set off by the French Revolution in 1789 had subsided. By 1815 its effects had been absorbed, but in 1919 the Russian Revolution was only two years old, its impact on the rest of the world unclear. Western leaders saw Bolshevism seeping out of Russia, threatening religion, tradition, every tie that held their societies together. In Germany and Austria, soviets of workers and soldiers were already seizing power in the cities and towns. Their own soldiers and sailors mutinied. Paris, Lyon, Brussels, Glasgow, San Francisco, even sleepy Winnipeg on the Canadian prairies had general strikes. Were these isolated outbreaks of flames from a vast underground fire.[33]

She noted that in three months the peacemakers were to achieve much: a peace treaty with Germany and the bases of peace with Austria, Hungary and Bulgaria. "They drew new borders through the middle of Europe and the Middle East. Much of their work, it is true, did not last. People said at the time, as they have ever since, that the peacemakers took too long and that they got it wrong. It has become a commonplace to say that the peace settlements of 1919 were a failure and that they led directly to the Second World War."[34]

---

32 M. Macmillan, Peacemakers. Six Months that Changed the World. London, John Murray, 2001, p. 2.

33 Ibid, p. 3.

34 Ibid, p. 6.

Pact of Paris: The Kellog-Brand Pact, 1928

The gathering that produced the General Treaty for the Renunciation of War (Pact of Paris, or the Kellog-Briand Pact) in 1928 was not convened to settle any particular war but, hopefully, to prevent the recurrence of future wars. It patently failed eleven years later, with the outbreak of the Second World War. Nevertheless, it is worth recalling in a book devoted to international peace conferences.

The background to the meeting, and to the Pact, was the decision of the USA to stay out of the League of Nations. French Foreign Minister Briand and US Secretary of State Kellog sought to promote an agreement that would associate the USA with the scheme of collective security of the League. Under the terms of the Pact, signed to begin with by fifteen countries and eventually by sixty eight, the signatories renounced war as an instrument of national policy and undertook that all disputes should be settled by peaceful means.

According to one commentary, "Although the pact was an attempt to strengthen the League's position on the issue of collective security, its articles were far too general and hedged about with too many reservations for it to have any significant impact on developments in international relations, either between the signatory states themselves or between them and the non-signatories."[35]

The San Francisco Conference, 1945

Unlike after the Thirty Years War (Peace of Westphalia), the Napoleonic Wars (Congress of Vienna), and the First World War (Paris Peace Conference, 1919), the Second World War was not followed by a general peace conference. The lines of the post-war settlement had been worked out in war-time meetings of the principal Allied Leaders, held in the Atlantic Ocean off Canada, Casablanca, Moscow, Yalta,Cairo, Teheran, and Postdam.[36] The Allied leaders had agreed on the establishment of the United Nations Organization and its Charter was drafted at the United Nations Conference on International Organization held in San Francisco in 1945.

The work of the San Francisco conference is the subject of extensive literature and we shall limit ourselves here to noting the nexus between the balance

35 G. Evans and J. Newnham, ... in The Penguin Dictionary of International Relations. London, Penguin Books, 1998, p. 292.

36 See, generally, J. Wheeler-Bennett and A. Nicholls, The Semblance of Peace. The Political Settlement After the Second World War. London, St. Martin's Press, 1972.

of power approaches of Westphalia and Vienna on the collective security approach of the Covenant of the League of Nations and the Charter of the United Nations. Edward Vose Gulick, in his study of Europe's Classical Balance of Power,[37] argued:

> One can see from the larger context that 'collective security', far from being alien to the 'age-old tradition of the balance of power', not only derives out of the latter, but also must be regarded as the logical end point of the balance of power system, the ideal toward which it has been moving, slowly and haltingly, for several hundred years. This contention leads to the hypothesis that the League of Nations and the United Nations, when considered as instruments for maintaining the 'continued co-existence of independent governments in contact with one another', were merely further refinements in balance practice – namely, organizations representing a world-wide state system of sovereign, independent, and armed states, intent on preserving their security and independence and prepared to use an automatic coalition to prevent the dangerous expansion of any member state...At bottom...the collective security of 1919 or 1945 was merely an elaboration and refinement of the coalition equilibrium of 1815, just as the latter was an elaboration and refinement of the alliance balance.[38]

The intellectual disciples of Woodrow Wilson would swallow hard at this assessment. We cite it as one attempt to link the major international peace conferences from the seventeenth to the twentieth century and as pertinent background for the suggestion we shall make at the conclusion of this chapter that consideration be given to the eventual organization of a global international peace conference for the twenty-first century.

Paris Peace Conference 1948

As we mentioned earlier, the lines of the post- World War II settlement had been worked out in war-time meetings of the principal Allied Leaders. In the circumstances prevailing at the end of the Second World War, with the division of Germany, and the arrival of the cold war, no peace treaty was concluded, to this day, with Germany. However, the three major powers had decided on six

37 New York, Norton, 1955.

38 Ibid, p. 308.

phases of peacemaking in respect of the other enemy powers. First, the preliminary terms of peace were to be drawn up by their Council of Ministers. Second these draft terms were to be submitted to a conference called by the USA, Britain, the Soviet Union, France and China. Those states that had fought substantively in the war on the allied side would be invited to the conference. Third, at this conference, to be held in Paris by 1 May, 1946, representatives of the five enemy states, Italy, Rumania, Bulgaria, Hungary and Finland, would be given an opportunity to discuss the terms of their respective draft peace treaties. Fourth, the conference would consider the drafts and formulate its recommendations for the final texts. Fifth, the Council of Ministers, keeping in mind the recommendations of the conference, would prepare the final texts. And, sixth, the final texts would be signed by all the states represented at the peace conference.[39]

The Peace Conference opened later than planned, on 29 July,1946, in Paris and met until 4 November that year. There were major procedural wrangles, especially about the decision-making procedure. Smaller powers such as Australia and New Zealand wanted a greater say in the eventual decisions. The major powers made some courtesy concessions to them but kept the levers of decision-making firmly in their hands. Representatives of the enemy powers were given opportunities to present their views but the drafts as prepared by senior officials of the major powers on behalf of their Foreign Ministers were largely kept as drafted. The Paris conference did not conclude with signature of the treaties. The Council of Ministers continued their deliberations on the work of the Paris Conference at meetings in New York to which they had travelled for the UN General Assembly. The Ministers decided in New York that their senior officials should be given time to finalise the treaties, which would be formally signed on 10 February, 1947. As matters turned out, the five treaties were signed by the USA in Washington, then taken to Moscow, London and Paris for signature.

Wheeler-Bennett and Nicholls commented:

> There was no sense of finality about these peripatetic treaties; no real belief that they ushered in a new world or a new age. Already there hung above Europe a premonitory cloud of conflict and of the denial of the very principles which were supposed to be enshrined within these agreements. Irony and cynicism were more justifiably the transcendent sentiments of the hour, rather than hope and optimism. The treaties were nominally to deny the use of force and to ensure the liberties of man.

39 This summary is based on Wheeler-Bennett et.al, op cit, p. 430 ff.

> Yet, in little more than a year from the time of their signature, one man among those present in the Salle de l'Horloge had been hounded to death by acts of force and the denial of such liberties. Jan Masaryk, Czechoslovakia's Foreign Minister, that most lovable and humane of men, met his death on 10 March, 1948.[40]

Round Table Conference on Indonesia, 1949

As a sequel to the Indonesian war of independence against the Dutch, and in the wake of the condemnation of The Netherlands by the UN Security Council, a Round Table Conference on Indonesia took place in The Hague between 23 August and 2 November, 1949 which laid the basis for peace and for Indonesian independence. This was essentially a bilateral negotiation between the two sides and need not be discussed further here.[41]

Japanese Peace Conference, San Francisco, 1951

Following the defeat of Japan in the Second World War it came under US occupation and administration. General Macarthur functioned as the de facto Viceroy of the country. This coincided with the emergence and intensification of the Cold War. The USA therefore took direct charge of negotiating a peace treaty with Japan and this task was given to then Under-Secretary of State John Foster Dulles (later Secretary of State). He spearheaded the discussion of the treaty with Japanese leaders and after a treaty had been worked out, the US convened a conference of different powers to endorse the treaty.[42] We discuss this peace treaty further in the chapter on peacebuilding below.

Geneva Conference on Indo-China, 1954

The Geneva Conference on Indo-China has been historically controversial and we mention it here for the record. It was held from 26 April to 20 July, 1954 to

40 Op. cit., p. 438.

41 See, generally, G.M. Kahin, Nationalism and Revolution in Indonesia. Ithaca, N.Y., Cornell University Press, 1952 A.M. Taylor, Indonesian Independence and the United Nations. Ithaca, N.Y, Cornell University Press, 1960.

42 See on this, Wheeler-Bennett, et. al, op cit., pp. 487–527.

deal with the aftermath of the Korean conflict and the conflict then underway in Vietnam.[43] It produced little of lasting effect.

London Conferences on Cyprus, 1959

We mention this conference for the record. As Cyprus approached the end of British colonial rule, conflict arose over the governance of the country. An agreement between Greece and Turkey on issues regarding the Greek and Turkish ethnic communities was reached in Zurich on 11 February, 1959. On 19 February at a conference in London, a final agreement was reached by Greece, Turkey, Britain and the two Cypriot groups that led to the drafting of a constitution and Cyprus' independence on 16 August, 1960.[44]

Geneva Conference on Laos, 1962

An international conference on a settlement of the Laotian question was held in Geneva from 16 May to 23 July, 1962.[45] Participating in the conference were representatives of Laos, USSR, the Peoples Republic of China, North and South Vietnam, Poland, the USA, France, Great Britain, India, Burma, Cambodia, Canada, Thailand. Representatives of the three political forces in Laos were invited to the conference on an equal basis. The Co-Chairmen of the conference were the UK and the USSR. In June, 1962, the three Laotian political groupings reached an agreement to create a coalition government in Laos. The Geneva Agreement of 1962 included a Declaration on the Neutrality of Laos.

Paris Talks on Vietnam, 1969–73

The Paris talks on Vietnam, 1969–73 were essentially bilateral negotiations between the USA and the North Vietnamese authorities. We mention it here for the record.[46]

---

43 See, generally, S. Bailey, The Korean Armistice. London, St. Martin's Press, 1992.

44 This is based on a note on the web-site of the Council on Foreign Relations: http://www.cfr.org/cyprus/london-zurich-agreements-1959/p24844.

45 See C.R. Mark, The Geneva Conference on Laos, 1961–62. Published by the Reference Service of the US Library of Congress, 1968.

46 See, generally, H.A. Kissinger, « The Vienna Negotiations », Foreign Affairs, 1969, p. 218.

Geneva Conference on the Middle East, 1973

On 6 October 1973, there was a coordinated Egyptian-Syrian attack to regain territories occupied by Israel during the Six-Day War of 1967 and Egyptian forces crossed the Suez Canal to the east bank. During the night of 24 October, at 11.35 pm, concerned about the possibility of the USSR inserting forces in Egypt and determined to prevent this, the US placed its forces, including its nuclear forces, on high military alert and warned the USSR and Egypt of grave consequences should USSR forces be inserted in Egypt. A most dangerous super-power face-off, with the possibility of resort to nuclear weapons, then took place over the next two days. Fortunately, that face-off was brought to an end.

As part of their efforts to contain and end the conflict, the USA and the USSR arranged for the Geneva Conference on the Middle East. Egypt, Israel, and Jordan attended but not Syria. The conference was a brief affair, the main event being that on 21 December, 1973, UN Secretary-General Kurt Waldheim opened the conference and emphasised that return to the 22 October position called for in Security Council resolution 338 had not been implemented.

Camp David, 1978

The Camp David talks that led to the 1978 Camp David Accords on the Middle East had some of the features of an international peace conference that make them of direct relevance in a study of international peace conferences. In his letter of 3 August, 1978 inviting President Anwar Sadat and Prime Minister Menachem Begin to the talks, US President Jimmy Carter stated:

> I have no strong preference about the location, but Camp David is available. My hope is that the three of us, along with our top advisors, can work together in relative seclusion. Maximum direct contact between you (President Sadat and Prime Minister Begin) is very important. To create the best climate for our meeting, public statements should be constructive and positive, expectations should not be raised too high, and quiet and mutual preparations should lay a foundation for optimum progress. It is important that this proposal be kept completely confidential.[47]

47 See http://www.jewishvirtuallibrary.org/source/Peace/cdinvite.html, consulted 25 June, 2012.

There is extensive literature on the conduct of the Camp David talks and we do not intend to pursue them further here.

International Conferences on Kampuchea, 1981, 1989

In 1981, the United Nations sponsored an International Conference on Kampuchea in which 83 countries participated. The conference called for the withdrawal of all foreign forces and the restoration of Cambodian independence. Another international conference was held in Paris in August, 1989, attended by eighteen governments. The conference broke down over disagreement on power-sharing in the country in the future. Subsequently, peace talks sponsored by ASEAN, with the support of major powers, would lead to the conclusion of a peace treaty, followed by a UN mission that watched over its implementation. The Cambodian conferences need not detain us further here.

Central American Peace Processes, (Contadora and Esquipulas) 1983–1991

Between 1983 and 1991 a remarkable series of meetings, summits, negotiations, observer missions, confidence-building measures, treaties, peace operations and verification missions were organized involving Foreign Ministers of Central American and Latin American nations, Heads of State, support by Canada, and cooperation between the United Nations and the Organization of American States and their Secretaries-General with the aim of bringing conflicts in Central America to an end and laying the foundations for peace on the basis of respect for human rights and fundamental freedoms and of economic and social equity.[48]

What is significant about these peace processes is that regional leaders took the initiative in the face of aggressive involvement in some of the conflicts by a super-power, the USA, and had to steer the process with much nimbleness and caution. They opened the substantive process with an Objectives Document of 9 September, 1982.

The process was a rolling one and at different times different countries took the initiative. There was no conference structure as such, and no secretariat. The organizational lead was taken at different times by different Foreign

48 See J. Child, The Central American Peace Process, 1983–1991. Boulder, Lynne Rienner, 1992. Appendix I contains a good Chronology of the process.

Ministries, with the broad support of the OAS and the United Nations Secretariat. However, the sustained nature of the peace processes over almost a decade, and the multiple activities undertaken, make them largely indistinguishable from a formal peace conference. The efforts of the International Conference on the Former Yugoslavia, for example, involved activities over a four-year period similar to those of the Central American peace process. However, the ICFY had designated leaders and negotiators whereas in the case of the Central American Peace Process different statesmen took the lead at different times.

We discuss the Contadora/Esquipulas peace processes in more detail in later chapters.

European Community Conference on Yugoslavia, 1991

As the cold war was ending and Yugoslavia faced disintegration, the European Community, as it was then, established the EU Conference on Yugoslavia led by Lord Peter Carrington, former UK Foreign and Defence Secretaries and former Secretary-General of NATO, to help work out an agreement on the future of the country. Under the leadership of Lord Carrington there were different working groups, including one on Bosnia and Herzegovina, one on economic issues, and one on confidence-building measures.[49]

Lord Carrington's central concept was that of a comprehensive framework convention providing for a loose confederation among the constituent entities of the then Yugoslavia and the highest levels for the protection of minority rights. Then Serbian President Slobodan Milosevic rejected the provisions on minority rights. The Chairman the Working Group on Bosnia and Herzegovina, Portuguese diplomat and former Secretary-General of the Western European Union, Jose Cutileiro negotiated principles for a constitution of Bosnia and Herzegovina providing for the recognition of three constituent peoples, Bosniacs, Croats, and Serbs. The three Bosnian parties at first accepted these principles but President Alija Izetbegogic repudiated his acceptance afterwards.

Lord Carrington felt that he could achieve an overall agreement but, against his advice, Germany, first, followed after by its EU partners, recognized Croatia and Slovenia as independent states. Lord Carrington considered that recognition had cut the ground from under his feet and he withdrew from the process.

49 See H. Wynaendts, *L'Engrenage: Chroniques yougolaves Juillet 1991-aout 1992*. Paris: Edition Denoel, 1992.

From the point of view of building blocks for peace, the comprehensive framework convention put on the table by Lord Carrington is deserving of note and we shall revert to it later in this work. Also deserving of note is the Arbitration Commission, which gave a number of opinions on the qualifications of constituent republics for recognition as independent states.

Lord Carrington, in his efforts for the formation of a loose confederation among the Yugoslav Republics put on the table draft "Treaty Provisions for the Convention" which would place the new relations between the Republics on comprehensive arrangements, including supervisory mechanisms for the protection human rights and special status for certain groups and States.[50]

Chapter 2 of the draft treaty dealt with human rights. Article 2 envisaged that the Republics would guarantee enumerated human rights grounded in instruments such as the Universal Declaration of Human Rights, the International Covenants on Human Rights, the Final Act of the Helsinki Conference, the European Convention for the Protection of Human Rights and Fundamental Freedoms and other international and European instruments. It also envisaged that the Republics would guarantee human rights as applied to national or ethnic groups as embodied in a number of international and European instruments including the International Convention on the Elimination of Racial Discrimination and the Convention on the Prevention of the Crime of Genocide.

Furthermore, the Republics would undertake to guarantee enumerated rights of persons belonging to a national or ethnic group. These included the principle of non-discrimination, the right to be protected against any activity capable of threatening their existence, and the guarantee that no disadvantage shall arise from a person's choice to belong or not to belong to a national or ethnic group.

Areas in which persons belonging to a national or ethnic group formed a majority would enjoy a special status of autonomy. Such a status would provide for the right to have and show the national emblem of that area; an administrative structure, including a regional police force and a judiciary responsible for matters concerning the area, which reflected the composition of the population of the area. There would also be appropriate provisions for international monitoring.

The Republics would provide for international monitoring of the implementation of the special status of autonomy. To this end, they would conclude agreements that would provide for a permanent international body to monitor the implementation of the special status of autonomy.

50 The text of the draft convention is reproduced in UN doc. S/23169.

The draft convention envisaged the establishment of a Court of Human Rights which would have jurisdiction within the republics to consider appeals from courts in the republics involving questions of human rights. It also envisaged the establishment of Mixed Commissions where such mixed commissions might assist in preventing or dealing with disputes concerning human rights and the rights of ethnic or national groups and areas having special status.

As mentioned earlier, this Conference ended without results following Western recognition of Croatia and Slovenia, later followed by recognition of Bosnia and Herzegovina.

London Conference on the Former Yugoslavia, 1992

With the recognition of Croatia and Slovenia, war broke out in Bosnia and Herzegovina in the spring of 1992 and the conflict worsened after that. Bosnia and Herzegovina also received recognition in the spring of 1992. Faced with an escalating conflict, the United Kingdom, as Chair of the European Union, convened in August, 1992, the London Conference on the Former Yugoslavia. The conference brought together the main Yugoslav leaders, regional leaders, leaders of major powers, and the Secretary-General of the United Nations. The United Nations was formally a co-sponsor of the conference but the British government did all the groundwork for it.[51]

The London Conference adopted a Statement of Principles, other policy declarations, and provided for the establishment of the International Conference on the Former Yugoslavia, co-chaired by the European Union and the United Nations. Lord David Owen, former British Foreign Secretary, was designated EU Co-Chairman and Cyrus Vance, former US Secretary of State was designed the UN Co-Chairman. The London Conference provided that the Co-Chairmen of ICFY would engage in continuous negotiations for peace in the former Yugoslavia.

The London Conference of August 1992 was held for variety of reasons. The newly elected Secretary-General of the United Nations had had a controversial encounter with the Carrington Conference when it had concluded an agreement on the control of heavy weapons and sought to entrust supervision of its implementation to the United Nations. The protests of the Secretary-General were vehement. The European Community, for its part, was in a quandary and wished to pass the Yugoslav dossier to the United Nations. In the end result, Prime Minister John Major in his capacity as President of the Presidency of the

51 See on this, M. Goulding, Peacemonger, London, John Murray, 2002.

European Community and the Secretary-General of the United Nations co-chaired the London Conference held in August, 1992. That Conference was more in the nature of a parliamentary than a negotiating exercise. Pages of do's and dont's were legislated for parties on the ground in the former Yugoslavia to observe – with scant regard for the willingness of the parties to observe them.

From the point of view of peacemaking approaches, the Principles of the London Conference are worth noting. The Principles provided for (1) The guarantee of the highest standards of human rights, including individual rights and fundamental freedoms in a democratic society, as set out in a series of important human rights instruments of the United Nations, the Council of Europe, and the Conference on Security and Cooperation in Europe; (2) Special guarantee of the rights of ethnic and national communities, as well as of minorities; (3) Constitutional and legal structures that can assure democratic governance and the protection of the above-mentioned rights; (4) Respect for international treaties and agreements.

The International Conference on the Former Yugoslavia (ICFY)

The International Conference on the Former Yugoslavia (ICFY) began operations from a base at the United Nations Office in Geneva on 3 September, 1992.[52] Its structure, as determined at the London Conference, comprised a Steering Committee of some thirty leading States, two Co-Chairmen of the Steering Committee, one each from the United Nations (Cyrus Vance, and later Thorvald Stoltenberg) and the European Union (Lord David Owen, and later Carl Bildt), and six Working Groups on: Bosnia and Herzegovina; Confidence-Building Issues; Humanitarian Issues; Ethnic Communities, Nationalities and Minorities; Economic Issues; and Succession Issues.[53]

The Conference functioned from September 1992 until the end of March, 1996. It assembled various building blocks of peace that would be successfully used at the Dayton conference. It could not, by itself, make a peace agreement for Bosnia stick largely because the USA had determined that the Bosniacs (the Muslims) should be aided to continue fighting so that they could recover ground that had been taken from by the Serbs through the use of force. The Humanitarian Issues Working Group, led by the UN High Commissioner for Refugees, Mrs Sadako Ogata, performed heroically in coordinating the provision of relief

52 The author served as Director of ICFY until it formally closed in March, 1996.

53 See, generally, B.G. Ramcharan (Ed.), The International Conference on the Former Yugoslavia. Collected Papers. 2 Vols. The Hague, Martinus Nijhoff, 1997.

assistance to communities throughout the former Yugoslavia. Vance and Owen made a landmark contribution in recommending the successful preventive deployment of UN peacekeepers on the borders between Serbia and Albania. The Working Group on Ethnic Communities, Nationalities and Minorities helped stabilise various situations of potential ethnic conflict, and the Working Group on Succession Issues patiently worked away at agreements for the distribution of assets of the former Yugoslavia among the successor republics.

ICFY provides two important lessons for peacemakers: First, Parties with the means and the will to fight will continue to fight unless superior countervailing force can be brought to bear on them. When the USA finally decided to use its power against the Bosnian Serbs, the conflict ended. Second, when one or more Great Power is/are determined to block a peace agreement, a conflict can only be settled when the Great Power(s) in question decides that it was time to end the conflict. This is what happened when the USA finally decided that the time had come to end the Bosnian conflict and acted to do so. The Dayton Peace Accord was not better than agreements that ICFY had negotiated earlier, and in the meantime, thousands of people had died needlessly. The US was defensive about the Dayton Accord, arguing that it was what could be achieved in the circumstances. But it had earlier been critical of the Vance-Owen peace plan and the Owen-Stoltenberg peace plan. The difference between ICFY and the USA was that the former, representing the UN and the European Union, could only use persuasion, which was not enough, whereas the USA could marshal all the power at its disposal.

The Dayton Conference on the Former Yugoslavia, 1995

The Dayton (Ohio) Conference of November, 1995, brought to an end three and half years of war in Bosnia and Herzegovina and contributed to a settlement of the conflict in Croatia as well.[54] On 21 November, 1995, after three weeks of proximity talks, the Bosnian parties, joined by the Federal Republic of Yugoslavia and the Republic of Croatia, initialled a General Framework Agreement for Peace in Bosnia and Herzegovina, together with twelve Annexes.[55] Following an implementation conference held in London on 6 and 9 December 1995, the General Framework Agreement and its accompanying Annexes were signed in Paris on 14 December 1995 and came into force upon signature.

54 See, generally, R. Holbrooke, To End a War. New York, Random House, 1998.

55 Dayton Agreement, 2 International Peacekeeping 138–167 (1995).

The Dayton accords provided for a Constitution of Bosnia and Herzegovina in which the parties committed themselves to Bosnia and Herzegovina as a democratic state, operating under the rule of law and with free and democratic elections. The Constitution drew inspiration from the Universal Declaration of Human Rights, the International Covenants on Human Rights, and the UN Declaration on the Rights of Persons Belonging to National or Ethnic, Religious and Linguistic Minorities, as well as other human rights instruments. The Constitution recognized Bosniacs, Croats, and Serbs as constituent peoples. It made provisions for the establishment of a Human Rights Commission and specified that, in addition to the European Convention on Human Rights and Fundamental Freedoms and its Protocols, fifteen additional human rights agreements were to be applied by the Commission.

The annexed Agreement on Military Aspects of the Peace Settlement invited the UN Security Council to adopt a resolution authorizing member states or regional organizations to establish a multinational military Implementation Force (IFOR) which would be involved in an enforcement operation. In view of the complexities facing them, the parties requested the designation of a High Representative, to be appointed consistent with relevant UN Security Council resolutions, to facilitate the parties' own efforts and to mobilize and, as appropriate, coordinate the activities of the organizations and agencies involved in the civilian aspects of the peace settlement by carrying out, as entrusted by a UN Security Council resolution, a number of specified tasks, including to monitor implementation of the peace settlement.[56]

Bonn Conferences of 2001, 2011 on Afghanistan

We discuss these two conferences in the chapter on peacebuilding, below.

Quartet Process on the Middle East

The Quartet process on the Middle East was meant to be a framework to facilitate negotiations between Israel and Palestine but the negotiations have stalled as of the time of writing and have so far not seen tangible progress. We mention it briefly here because it could have promoted peace negotiations between the two sides. Even if it has so far not met with much success, it is still

56 For a summary of the Accords, see B.G. Ramcharan, The Bosnian Peace Accord, 9 Leiden Journal of International Law (1996), No. 1, pp. 131–140.

an interesting model that might be kept in mind in a study of international peace conferences.

The 'Quartet', consisting of the United States, Russia, the European Union and the United Nations came into existence in 2002. In June of that year, US President George W. Bush made history by being the first US President to call for a Palestinian State. Following efforts made by former US Senator George Mitchell to facilitate peace talks between Israel and Palestine, the Quartet drew up a 'Road Map' in 2003 suggesting how a future settlement might be approached. It proposed a timetable, putting the establishment of security before a final settlement. It was designed to create confidence, leading to final status talks.

In Phase 1, both sides would issue statements supporting the two-state solution, the Palestinians would end violence, act against 'all those engaged in terror', draw up a constitution, hold elections, and the Israelis would stop settlement activities and act with military restraint. In Phase 2 an international conference would be convened for the establishment of a Palestinian state with 'provisional borders'. Phase 3 would involve talks on a final agreement.[57] The Road Map had called for the final implementation agreement to be reached in 2005 but this did not materialise as the two sides became deadlocked over different issues.

The Quartet has since held a succession of meetings seeking to help restart the negotiations and has issued a number of statements in this regard. For example, the Quartet met in Washington DC on 11 April 2012. Among other things, it reaffirmed its commitment, as expressed in its 23 September 2011 statement, to examine possible mechanisms it could actively support going forward, individually and together, to advance peace efforts and strengthen the Palestinian Authority's ability to meet the full range of civil and security needs of the Palestinian people both now and in a future state. The Quartet encouraged the parties to cooperate to facilitate social and economic development and asked Quartet Representative, former UK Prime Minister Tony Blair, to continue 'his intensive work with the parties toward this end'.

Reminding both parties of their obligations under the roadmap, the Quartet reiterated its call for them to avoid actions that undermine trust and to focus on positive efforts that can strengthen and improve the climate for a resumption of direct negotiations on the basis of the Quartet's statement of September 23 2011. The Quartet expressed concern about unilateral and provocative actions by either party, including continued settlement activity, which cannot

57 See BBC News, 'History of failed peace talks', http://newsvote.bbc.co.uk/mpapps/pagetools/print/news.bbc,co,uk/2/hi/middle_east/6666393.stm, consulted on 25 June, 2012.

prejudge the outcome of negotiations, the only way to a just and durable solution to the conflict. The Quartet underscored its commitment to remain actively engaged in the coming period.[58]

Geneva Conference on Syria, 2012

We discussed the Action Group conference on Syria of 30 June, 2012 earlier in this chapter.

Conclusion

In Peace and War: Conflicts and International Order 1648–1989,[59] to which we referred at the beginning of this chapter, K. Holsti concluded that all the great peace settlements of the past had failed in one important respect: the architects of peace had been backward-looking. They had focused on resolving the issues that had been the source of the previous war and some lesser ones as well. They had attempted to construct international orders that would prevent a recurrence of previous crises, but most were insufficiently far-sighted to note important new issues already appearing on the diplomatic horizon.

Peace settlements, he continued, should anticipate and devise means to cope with issues of the future so that they could help mould reasonably stable and less war-prone international orders. Where they fail to do so, or where their recipes for dealing with the last war are seriously flawed, they help create the conditions for the wars of the future. Peace then becomes the father of war. Victors should create a coalition, including the vanquished, that is committed to the settlement. That coalition should be large enough so that the defection of one great power (or perhaps more, depending upon the total number in the coalition) will not destroy the capacity of the remainder to enforce, by means of arms if necessary, the major terms of the settlement and the norms of the system, or to change them through peaceful processes. Peace agreements should provide procedures for peaceful change: No peace settlement can successfully hope to freeze a moment in history. They should provide for anticipation of future issues: Closely related to the problem of peaceful change is the

58 See U.S. Department of State, Statement of the Middle East Quartet, 11 April, 2012; http://www.state.gov/r/pa/prs/2012/04/187723.htm, consulted on 25 June, 2012.

59 K. Holsti, Peace and War: Conflicts and International Order 1648–1989 Cambridge University Press, 1991,

peace-maker's ability to anticipate the kinds of issues that will generate international conflict in the future.

To what extent might one say that the international peace conferences reviewed in this chapter have sought to anticipate the kinds of issues that will generate international conflict in the future? One could answer that there were some efforts to deal with the protection of minorities and human rights and to promote economic and social justice, which is one of the rationales of the UN Charter. One could also refer to the blueprints for the prevention of conflicts agreed upon at Vienna, Paris, and San Francisco, notably Article 99 of the UN Charter.

Some of the big challenges of our times, such as climate change and nuclear terrorism, could hardly be anticipated, say, in 1945. But the vision and arrangements of the UN Charter were certainly comprehensive and supple enough to grapple with them as they emerged if reasonableness and the political will were present. However, practical cooperation has been affected by political differences and varying perceptions of national interest.

Keeping in mind the experiences of the general international peace conferences we have reviewed in this chapter, bearing in mind the comments of Holsti above, recalling that there was no general peace settlement after the Second World War, noting the contemporary challenges of global governance, and recognizing the numerous problems confronting the United Nations, one might pose the question: has the time come for the convening of a world-wide international peace conference to deliberate on the peace challenges of the present and the future and to recommend an architecture for peace in the twenty-first century? A case could be made for such a conference. However, the idea should first be studied by the academic and research community.

CHAPTER 2

Institutional Architectures

Introduction

Harold Nicholson devoted a chapter of his book on the Congress of Vienna to 'The Problems of Procedure'. He commented that "The first two problems which face any international Conference are 'Who is to issue the invitations?' and 'Who is to be invited'."[1] He continued: "In every Conference the problems of organisation, the actual plan of procedure, acquires a significance which is often underestimated. However much the conveners of a Conference may twist or turn or prevaricate, they cannot prevent this problem from imposing itself at the very outset of their deliberations."[2]

In actual fact the position has varied from conference to conference. The institutional architecture of international peace conferences has differed a great deal historically, depending on the inviting government(s), the participating states or entities, the stage of the conflict and of related peacemaking efforts, the involvement, in the modern era, of international organizations, and the influence of the international media. Some conferences have had rudimentary or no formal rules of procedure while others have had elaborate ones. Some conferences have had traces of open deliberations while others have been heavily steered by the leading power or powers.

In early European practice one or more power might invite the warring parties and other interested states to meet, have in mind possible elements of a solution, and seek to persuade the warring parties to agree. The leading inviting power would have devoted staff working on the conference, possibly putting drafts together, and generally being at the disposal of their principals. The inviting power often made accommodation and other facilities available to the invited powers. The same pattern may be seen in the early European conferences that preceded the Congress of Westphalia.

The Congress of Westphalia involved more bilateral negotiations than did the successor conferences of Vienna 1814, Paris 1919 or Paris 1946. More recent conferences such as those organized to deal with conflicts in Asia, Central America, and the former Yugoslavia involved more bilateral discussions,

1 H. Nicholson, The Congress of Vienna. A Study in Allied Unity 1812–1822. London, Constable, 1946, p. 134.

2 Ibid, p. 135.

 DOI 10.1163/9789004245907_004

sometimes facilitated by third powers or mediators. The San Francisco conference of 1951, where the Japanese peace treaty was concluded after World War II, saw little negotiation itself. The negotiations had been largely conducted beforehand by American diplomats, notably John Foster Dulles, and the San Francisco conference ratified the results of the earlier negotiations.

Ramond Cohen and Stuart Cohen, in a helpful 1974 paper on the formal aspects of peace conferences[3] looked at a number of past international peace conferences and sought to highlight their procedural, as distinct from their substantive, dimensions, examining issues such as the agenda, the chairmanship and the structure of the delegations.[4] They took as their point of departure the following dictum of Henry Kissinger: "…the way negotiations are carried out is almost as important as what is negotiated. The choreography of how one enters negotiations, what is settled first and in what manner, is inseparable from the substance of the issues."[5]

They defined a peace conference as "a forum regulated by agreed rules of procedure at which representatives of sovereign states (or of groups aspiring to that status) meet, ostensibly to settle points of dispute following previous hostility, within the framework of formal negotiations."[6] This was an understandable but somewhat rigid definition. As will have been seen in the previous chapter, international peace conferences, in our view, self-define themselves.

Discussing the Participants at international peace conferences they noted that few peace conferences in the modern period had been attended solely by the recent belligerents. Overlapping involvements, alliances and Great Power rivalries had invariably extended the number of interested parties to the dispute.[7]

On the Agenda of international peace conferences, they noted that many conferences had been preceded by lengthy discussion on the content of the agenda (notably the Paris Peace Conference of 1946). "In its barest outlines, an agenda may be seen as a reflection of the aims which the participants to a conference set out to achieve."[8]

On the Chairmanship of international peace conferences, they noted that since the task of the chairman is to ensure the smooth functioning of the conference, responsibility for settling these problems devolves upon him (or her).

---

3 R. Cohen and S. Cohen, Peace Conferences: The Formal Aspects. Jerusalem Papers on Peace Problems, Jerusalem, The Hebrew University, January, 1974, 28 pp.

4 They wrote the paper having regard to "expectations of the structure of the peace conference on the Middle East now being held in Geneva" – Ibid, p. 5.

5 H.A. Kissinger, « The Vienna Negotiations », Foreign Affairs, 1969, p. 218.

6 Cohen and Cohen, op. cit., p. 5.

7 Ibid, p. 5.

8 Ibid, p. 13.

They have a helpful discussion of the responsibilities of the chairperson, his or her procedural powers, status, and mediating functions in some instances. They noted that on some occasions there had been a rotating chairman and in at least one instance, that of the Paris Peace Talks on Vietnam, even no Chairman at all.[9]

They continued: "Preliminary discussions concerning the participants, agenda, chairmanship and venue of a peace conference are conducted between the home government and other interested parties. Simultaneous with these external contacts, however, home governments also set about the task of selecting and appointing the delegates who are to present their case."[10]

On the Organization of an international peace conference they found that formally speaking, conferences can be organized along two lines (a) all work is conducted in plenary session, or (b) work is delegated from the plenum to committees which then report back.[11] They could have noted also a third possibility from the historical practice, namely, that, as at Vienna in 1815, Paris in 1919 and 1946, major powers basically decided among themselves what outcomes they wanted and secured the acceptance of the powers concerned. It could be argued that the USA basically did this at the Dayton Peace Conference of 1995, which brought an end to the war in Bosnia and Herzegovina. Cohen and Cohen do write in the concluding part of their short paper about "when the influence of the Great Powers at the conference is imperceptible" and recognized that "Even if a small state does possess a Great Power patron, it is likely to discover that major points of procedure, as those of substance, have largely been decided above its head. This is obviously true where the Great Powers have arrived at a significant measure of agreement."[12]

The foregoing summary of this helpful essay provides a useful point of entry for the issues of organization and procedure that we shall discuss in this chapter. In the presentation that follows we shall seek to draw upon the diverse experiences of international peace conferences with a view to highlighting strands of the institutional architecture that might be borne in mind by those considering the convening of international peace conferences in the future.

I Inviting Powers

Any one or more third power or organization that feels that it might be able to contribute to the settlement of a conflict is at liberty to invite for a conference.

9 Ibid, p. 18.
10 Ibid, p. 19.
11 Ibid, p. 24.
12 Ibid, p. 26.

In considering such an initiative they would need to consider their own influence or capacity for leverage, the stage and characteristics of a conflict, the ripeness of a conflict for settlement, whether the combating parties would be willing to attend and to negotiate seriously and in good faith, how they would finance the conference, conference facilities and arrangements, seating issues, and communications strategies. They would also need to have done some discreet initial groundwork on what a possible peace agreement might look like. Without an idea of the possible outcome it could be like going into the process blindfolded. On the other hand, it might be considered that one has to start somewhere and that the peace package could be worked out step by step.

When it comes to international organizations, they would normally take the initiative to sponsor a conference only when there is a broad consensus among the membership to do so. They would need to exercise some care so as not to engage in illusory exercises. The Secretary-General of the United Nations also needs to be prudent in undertaking initiatives. He or she would need to be mindful of the political situation and also of the costs involved. If it is a limited exercise he/she could arrange for the financing from his/her peacemaking budget. Or he/she could arrange for voluntary contributions. An interesting precedent is that of the London Conference on the Former Yugoslavia of August, 1992, which the British Prime Minister and UN Secretary-General Boutros Boutros-Ghali co-sponsored and co-chaired. That conference led to the establishment of the International Conference on the Former Yugoslavia, co-sponsored and co-chaired by the European Union and the United Nations. Secretary-General Boutros-Ghali took the decision on his own to agree to UN co-sponsorship but he could do so because the leading powers of the United Nations were present at the London Conference and adopted the decision to establish the International Conference on the Former Yugoslavia, co-chaired by the European Union and the United Nations.

II Financing

Depending on the number of participants, the duration of the process and the number of peace negotiators, one or more inviting power might be able to defray the costs of the conference. If, however, protracted efforts are called for by multiple actors, the costs could be considerable. One way to cover the costs might be to establish a Voluntary Fund and appeal for contributions from Governments. Some well-meaning governments might, on their own volition, offer contributions in order to help a peace process to get underway.

One precedent that bears mentioning is that of having a Steering Committee of the Conference whose members would contribute to the budget according to an agreed formula. This occurred in the case of the International Conference on the Former Yugoslavia, which had a Steering Committee of invited States that met periodically to discuss the progress of the negotiations and which contributed to the budget of ICFY over the three and a half years of its existence.

III Rules of Procedure

Some international peace conferences of the past have had detailed rules of procedure, which, in some instances, were largely for the record. A lot depended on the structure of the conference and the negotiating strategies of the lead mediators. At the end of the day the key is to negotiate an end to the conflict and to get the agreements negotiated ratified by the parties and the main interested powers.

There has been flexibility going back for a long time. The Congress of Westphalia broke new ground in that it dispensed with an official chair or mediator. There were no plenary sessions. Instead, negotiations proceeded through bilateral talks, often held in parallel with multiple partners. Talks with the Swedes were held in Osnabruck, while those with France took place in Munster. Mediation was restricted to that by Chigi and his able Venetian colleague Alvisi Contarini, who acted as go-between for France with the Hapsburgs who had refused formal direct talks.

At the Congress of Vienna rules of procedure were of secondary relevance. The major powers had decided to work out the key issues among themselves and to indicate their decisions to the other participants. Ideas to have plenary sessions largely came to naught in the end. The Congress did, however, have a number of committees, some of which did useful work.

Margaret Macmillan writes that, from the outset, the Paris Peace Conference of 1919 suffered from confusion over its organization, it's purpose and its procedures. The Big Four powers, Britain, France, Italy and the USA had planned a preliminary conference to agree on the terms to be offered to the defeated powers, after which they intended to hold a full-scale peace conference to negotiate with the enemy. In light of the reactions of other powers to this, however, the Big Four gave way and plenary sessions of the conference 'became ritual occasions'. The real work was done by the Four and Japan in informal meetings "and when those in turn became cumbersome, by the leaders of the Four"[13]

13 M. Macmillan, Peacemakers. Months That Changed the World. London, John Murray, 2001, pp. 4–5.

The Paris Peace Conference of 1946 convened under the aegis of a Council of Foreign Ministers of the UK, USA and the USSR together with those of France and China. The Council had been established by the Potsdam Protocol of 2 August, 1945. According to the Protocol, the immediate task of the Council of Ministers was the preparation and drafting of treaties of peace with Italy and with the four other minor satellites of Germany: Bulgaria, Finland, Hungary, and Romania. The Council was also tasked with the preparation of a peace settlement with Germany "to be accepted by the Government of Germany when a Government adequate for the purpose is established," a task that was overtaken by events.[14]

Following serious wrangling among the leading three powers, the UK, USA, and USSR, they agreed on a six-stage peacemaking process.[15] The Postdam Protocol had provided for the deputies of the Foreign Ministers to work on the text of draft treaties. According to Wheeler-Bennett, "much credit must be given to the great amount of drafting and preparation which had been achieved by the deputies... That the Paris meetings of the Council of the Council achieved anything at all was largely due to their labours."[16]

The representatives of twenty-one states convened in Paris on July 1946. According to Wheeler-Bennett, they were almost immediately plunged into a maelstrom of disagreement on the issue of procedure. The Council of Ministers had recommended, among the rules of procedure that on the various commissions that the Conference might set up, a two-thirds majority would be required for a recommendation but that the minority also would have the right to express its views. The smaller nations argued instead in favour of majority decision. After a week of lively discussions it was agreed that those proposals that received the votes of a simple majority of the members of the conference would be received by the Council. The Conference also agreed to draw up its own rules of procedure as a whole.[17]

IV Conference Structure

The conference structure has depended greatly on the inviting powers, prevailing circumstances, such as whether the inviting powers are victorious powers, and the negotiating strategy of the lead mediators. At the Congress of

14 Wheeler-Bennett, pp. 419–420.

15 Ibid, p. 428.

16 Ibid, p. 430.

17 Ibid, p. 434.

Westphalia, altogether, 235 official envoys and representatives attended, but the total number of participants was far larger, since all were accompanied by additional staff. The proceedings attracted wide public interest, which the delegates deliberately cultivated and manipulated. Westphalia's significance lies not in the number of conflicts it tried to resolve, but in the methods and ideas it applied. The first article of both the IPO and IPM stated they were instruments of a 'Christian, general and permanent peace' intended to establish lasting friendship across the continent. This, in the assessment of Peter Wilson, was more than merely a statement of good intentions. The congress offered a new charter for European relations. The sections on the imperial constitution did refer to the Empire's earlier settlements of 1552 and 1555, but otherwise the documents made no mention of other European treaties, instead offering a new framework for peace. The treaties ending other wars were regarded as extensions to Westphalia, pacifying additional parts of the continent. The Westphalian treaties continued to be invoked in major European settlements up to the Congress of Vienna in 1814–15 that ended the Napoleonic Wars. These later settlements rested on the same understanding of international law as a voluntary contract superior to all existing secular and religious law.[18]

As we saw earlier, the positive interpretation of Westphalia regards it as the birth of the modern international order based on sovereign states interacting (formally) as equals within a common secularized legal framework, regardless of size, power or internal configuration.[19]

The Paris Peace Conference of 1946 established ten commissions including a General Commission, which never met and a Legal and Drafting Commission. These consisted of representatives of the twenty-one nations participating in the conference. In addition there were five Political and Territorial Commissions varying in composition in that they consisted of representatives of the four sponsoring members of the Council of Foreign Ministers, plus those of the states that had been at war with each individual ex-enemy state and also an Economic Commission for Italy and an Economic Commission for the Balkan States and Finland.[20]

The International Conference on the Former Yugoslavia (ICFY) had a structure that might well be kept in mind when considering the organization of

18 Peter H. Wilson, The Thirty Years War. Europe's Tragedy. Cambridge, Mass., The Belknap Press of Harvard University Press, 2009, p. 754.

19 Ibid.

20 J. Wheeler-Bennett and A. Nicholls, The Semblance of Peace. The Political Settlement After the Second World War. London, St. Martin's Press, 1972, p. 433.

future conferences. The Conference was formally co-chaired by the European Union and the United Nations, each of which designated a full-time co-chairman. There was a Steering Committee of more than thirty states, which met periodically to support the efforts of the negotiators, put pressure on the conflicting parties where called for, and which considered, approved, and apportioned the budget of the conference. Under the leadership of the co-chairs, there were six Working Groups: on Confidence-Building and Security, Bosnia, Humanitarian Issues, Economic Issues, Ethnic Communities, Nationalities and Minorities, and on Succession Issues. The co-chairmen served full-time, as did some Chairs of the six working groups. The working group on confidence-building and security met mainly at the beginning of the activities of the conference when there were critical stabilization issues to be dealt with. The working group on humanitarian issues met throughout the existence of the conference under the chairpersonship of the UN High Commissioner for Refugees. The working groups on ethnic communities, nationalities and minorities, and on succession issues were active through most of the conference. The working group on economic issues was active at the beginning but became dormant as the conflict wore on.

V Secretariat

A Secretariat of the conference can be quite helpful to the peace negotiators, the parties, and third parties. Historically, the main sponsoring powers established teams of officials to prepare for, and service, conferences they had initiated.

The experience of the International Conference on the Former Yugoslavia is worth noting. As mentioned earlier, the conference was co-sponsored by the United Nations and the European Union. It had its Secretariat at the United Nations office in Geneva. The United Nations Secretary-General designated its Director and a small core-team of staff (about five). The European Union provided a core team (also about five) for specialised tasks such as assisting the Economic Issues Working Group. The state holding the rotating chairmanship of the EU designated a senior member on the staff of the secretariat. The Secretariat prepared the budget of the conference for the approval of the Steering Committee. The Secretariat also provided the services of political, legal, drafting and press officers, some of whom were deployed on secondment and some of whom were hired on renewable contracts.

VI Communications

A communications strategy is crucial for any peace conference. Parties and their supporters will invariably seek to put out their own spin in order to gain advantage in the negotiations. Well-meaning journalists will have their own approaches and interpretations and will seek to put pressure on the mediators. It is therefore important to arrange from the outset for experienced communicators and to provide them with the staffing and other resources they need to present the approaches and views of the leading negotiators.

At the Congress of Westphalia the two treaties were formally sworn on 24 October accompanied by a seventy-gun salute. Two copies of each were prepared for the ceremonies, followed by further copies over the subsequent days that were witnessed by the envoys to ensure no changes were slipped in. These were dispatched to the relevant courts, while at least another 42,000 copies were printed for an eager public over the coming year.

Conclusion

As could be seen from the foregoing, there is rich practice to be consulted when it comes to considering the institutional architecture of an international peace conference. One may study history for its own sake, as a record of what might have occurred. One might also study it with a view to deriving insights that could be helpful to each generation. We have sought in this chapter to keep both perspectives in mind, offering some glimpses of the architectures of past conferences and at the same time drawing attention to experiences that might be particularly worth bearing in mind in establishing international peace conferences in the future.

The six dimensions discussed in this chapter would all deserve consideration in such an exercise: the initiative to sponsor a conference, its financing, its rules of procedure, its structure, its secretariat, and its communications strategies. At the end of the day, what would be of paramount consideration is the assessment of the sponsoring power(s) or organization as to what peacemaking strategy might work best. This is the decisive element.

At the Dayton Conference on the former Yugoslavia the late Ambassador Richard Holbrook could draw on US power to pursue a peacemaking strategy that emphasized arm-twisting rather than negotiations as such. He had a blueprint of the outcome he sought, a map of Bosnia that partner-countries had little role in shaping, and he organized and structured the Dayton conference in a way that he thought conducive to achieving the result he sought. His European partners had little influence on issues of structure or strategy. At the conference itself their representatives fumed that they were largely kept on the sidelines. Ambassador Holbrook could do this because behind him stood the power of the USA. Organizational structure counted for less than political strategy and power.

At the end of the day, each initiative for an international peace conference would need to be considered in light of the specifics and dynamics of the conflict concerned. Results are what matter. Organizational structure must be put in service of the quest for positive outcomes.

CHAPTER 3

Conflict Prevention

Introduction

This chapter will look at whether, and to what extent, international peace conferences have contributed to efforts for the prevention of conflicts. A distinction should probably be made between general peace conferences such as those of Westphalia, Vienna, Paris, and San Francisco and peace conferences called upon to deal with particular conflicts or situations. As we saw in chapter I above, Holsti found that all the great peace settlements of the past had failed in one important respect: the architects of peace had been backward-looking. They had focused on resolving the issues that had been the source of the previous war and some lesser ones as well. They had attempted to construct international orders that would prevent a recurrence of previous crises, but most were insufficiently far-sighted to note important new issues already appearing on the diplomatic horizon.[1]

Nevertheless, the prevention of conflicts has been a prominent feature of international peace conferences such as the Congress of Vienna, the Versailles peace conference that led to the establishment of the League of Nations, and the San Francisco conference that led to the establishment of the United Nations. Conferences such as the International Conference on the Former Yugoslavia also made important contributions to efforts for prevention including, in this case, the establishment of the first-ever preventive deployment of international peacekeepers. In this chapter we present some of the significant preventive experiences at these conferences.

The Congress of Vienna

In discussing the contribution of the Congress of Vienna to efforts for the prevention of conflicts some care is needed to distinguish between the policies of the major players, particularly the United Kingdom, and the objective results. The Congress did lead to the Quadruple Alliance and its idea of periodic meetings of the allies, but the United Kingdom was downright opposed to the idea of

1 K. Holsti, Peace and War: Conflicts and International Order 1648–1989, Cambridge University Press, 1991.

 | DOI 10.1163/9789004245907_005

discussing 'potential as opposed to actual dangers'.[2] In the words of Castlereah, "...this country cannot, and will not, act upon abstract and speculative Principles of Precaution."[3] As Kissinger noted, "the fixed principle of British foreign policy, whether acknowledged or not, was its role as protector of the balance of power, which in general meant supporting the weaker against the stronger."[4]

Notwithstanding the above, the objective reality is that Article VI of the Treaty of Defensive Alliance of 1815 – the Quadruple Alliance, provided for periodic meetings of the allies to consider measures to maintain the peace of Europe. Article VI provided as follows:

> To facilitate and to secure the execution of the present Treaty, and to consolidate the connections which at the present moment so closely unite the Four Sovereigns for the happiness of the world...the High Contracting Parties have agreed to renew their meeting at fixed periods...for the purpose of consulting upon their common interests, and for the consideration of the measures which at each of these periods shall be considered the most salutary for the repose and prosperity of Nations, and for the maintenance of the peace of Europe.[5]

At the Vienna Congress the Great Powers had been moved by a desire to re-establish the law of nations against the ambitions of a conqueror. Their aim was to re-establish a world where order, not war and revolution, prevailed. They sought to promote peace, security, and order within States as well as between them. The Congress of Vienna led to the birth of the Congress system, which some historians consider an integral part of the Concert system.

The Concert of Europe provided direct antecedents for the idea of preventive diplomacy that would be brought into prominence in the twentieth century. Diplomacy was intended as the principal method of action within the Concert, and preventive diplomacy was precisely the hope. At its core was the idea that, by combining their efforts through diplomatic action, the principal powers of the time, Austria, France, Great Britain, Prussia, and Russia, subsequently joined

2 H. Kissinger, Diplomacy, New York, Simon & Schuster, 1994, p. 88.

3 Ibid. Kissisnger noted that "Britain remained aloof from the Congress system, which its own Foreign Secretary had devised, just as, a century later, the United States would distance itself from the League of Nations, which its president had proposed.", Ibid, p. 90.

4 Ibid, p. 98. In Kissinger's assessment, "The reason the Vienna settlement had worked for fifty years was that the three Eastern powers – Prussia, Russia, and Austria – had seen their unity as the essential barrier to revolutionary chaos and to French dominion of Europe." – Ibid, p. 94.

5 Ibid, 39.

by Turkey, could help avoid another European conflagration in the aftermath of the Napoleonic wars. In some situations the Concert succeeded, such as the Belgian revolt of 1830 and the Eastern Question. In others, such as the Crimean War, it failed.

Like the Congress system, the Concert of Europe continued to emphasize the role of the Great Powers and was based on the concept of a balance of power among them. The principles of the Concert of Europe were great power responsibility for dealing with European problems and for maintenance of the territorial status quo, no unilateral changes in the order of things, and consensus in decision-making among the great powers.[6]

In 1856, the Concert of Europe introduced an historic innovation that could be said to have laid the foundations for what, a century later, would be labelled as preventive diplomacy. The Declaration of Paris of 1856 contained, in Protocol 23, the following provision:

> The Plenipotentiaries do not hesitate to express in the name of their governments the desire that States...should, before appealing to arms, have recourse, so far as circumstances allow, to the good offices of a friendly Power. The Plenipotentiaries hope that governments not represented at the Congress will unite in the sentiment which has inspired the desire recorded in the Protocol.[7]

Gladstone welcomed this declaration as "the first time that...the principal nations of Europe have given an emphatic utterance to sentiments which contain at least a qualified disapproval of the results of war." The *Times of London* hoped that it would make "all Europe one court of appeal." Hinsley commented: "It was certainly the first clause of its kind to be included in a multilateral treaty."[8]

The Concert broke down after 1870, not being able to avoid wars between Prussia and Denmark, Prussia and Austria, and then Prussia and France. This breakdown would leave the major European Powers without a framework of cooperation that could help prevent the slide to generalised war in the first half of the twentieth century. Notwithstanding its eventual failure, the Concert would pass on a set of ideas and methods directly related to the practice of preventive diplomacy in our times.[9]

6 F. Hinsley, Power and the Pursuit of Peace. Cambridge, Cambridge University Press, 1967, 225.

7 Ibid, 233.

8 Ibid, 233.

9 See J. Lowe, *The Concert of Europe: International Relations 1814–1870*, London: Hodder and Stoughton, 1994.

The Hague Peace Conferences

The idea of the prevention of war through resort to good offices or mediation, expressed for the first time in Protocol 23 of the Declaration of Paris, would be picked up explicitly at The Hague Peace Conferences of 1899 and 1907. The two Peace Conferences had as their fundamental aim to contribute to the avoidance of war through the development of international law, the promotion of peaceful methods for the settlement of disputes, the advancement of international arbitration, and the lessening of human suffering in war by codifying and developing the rules of warfare.[10] Out of the Hague Peace Conferences came the Permanent Court of Arbitration and the Hague provisions on the laws of war.

In Article 2 of The Hague Convention on the Pacific Settlement of International Disputes, of 18 October, 1907, the contracting powers agreed, in the event of a dispute, to have recourse to the good offices or mediation of one or more friendly powers before resorting to arms. Article 3 gave the right to powers not involved in the dispute to offer good offices, even in the course of hostilities. The exercise of this right was not to be considered an unfriendly act.

The ideas for the peaceful settlement of disputes and, thereby, the prevention of war, elaborated upon at the Hague Peace Conferences would be picked up after the devastation wrought by the First World War and inserted into the Covenant of the League of Nations.

Central American Peace Conference, Held at Washington, D.C., 1907

The Central American Peace Conference of 1907 was, as we mentioned in Chapter I earlier, an interesting model of efforts to prevent conflicts and to engage in confidence and peace-building. The seven treaties concluded at the conference all had these ends in view. The Treaty of Peace and Amity declared that any disposition or measure tending to alter the constitutional organization of any of the Republics shall be deemed a menace to the peace of all. The Treaty made the territory of Honduras neutral in conflicts that might arise between the other four Republics, so long as Honduras remained neutral. The report of the US representative on the conference noted: "It will be seen by a reference to the map of Central America that the position of Honduras is such

10 See J.B. Scott, *The Hague Peace Conferences of 1899 and 1907*, Boston/London: Pub. for the International School of Peace, Ginn & Company, 1908.

that if this neutrality of Honduranean territory is carried out, war between the signatory republics is practically made impossible."[11]

Articles XVI and XVII of the treaty had distinctly preventive aims:

> Article XVI: Desiring to prevent one of the most frequent causes of disturbances in the Republics, the contracting Governments shall not permit the leaders or principal chiefs of political refugees, nor their agents, to reside in the departments bordering on the countries whose peace they might disturb. Those who may have established their permanent residence in a frontier department may remain in the place of their residence under the immediate surveillance of the Government affording them an asylum, but from the moment when they become a menace to public order they shall be included in the rule above.
>
> **Article XVII.** Every person, no matter what his nationality, who, within the territory of one of the contracting Parties, shall initiate or foster revolutionary movements against any of the others, shall be immediately brought to the capital of the Republic, where he shall be submitted to trial according to law.[12]

In Articles I and II of the convention additional to the Treaty of Peace and Amity each Republic committed itself not to recognize in another a Government resulting from a coup d'etat nor to intervene in favour of or against the existing government of another Republic in cases of disorder in that Republic.

The Convention creating a Central American Court of Justice gave the court three forms of jurisdiction: the obligatory submission to the court of all questions arising between the Central American Republics which could not be adjusted by their respective foreign offices; the power to determine cases involving alleged violations of treaties or conventions where denial of justice was alleged by a citizen of one Republic against the Government of another; and the power to determine any question mutually submitted by two of the signatories. The decision of the court, which had to be a majority decision, would be final and must be in writing.

The Convention concerning future conferences had for its object the preparation of the people of Central America for ultimate political union in some

11 Report of Mr William I. Buchanan, Representative of the USA to the Central American Peace Conference Held at Washington, D.C., 1907. Washington, Government Printing Office, 1908, p. 12.

12 The texts of all seven treaties are reproduced in the Report of Mr Buchanan cited in the preceding footnote.

form.[13] The subsequent history of the Central American Republics would not be as peaceful as envisaged in the agreements of 1907 but the conference of 1907 as such, and the agreements it concluded, provide a good model of preventive and peacebuilding measures that any region or sub-region could usefully consider.

The League of Nations

The prevention of war was the central idea of the Covenant of the League of Nations. In Article 8, the Members of the League recognized that the maintenance of peace required the reduction of national armaments to the lowest point consistent with national safety and the enforcement by common action of international obligations. In Article 10 the Members undertook to respect and preserve as against external aggression the territorial integrity and existing political independence of all members.

Any war or threat of war, whether immediately affecting any of the Members of the League or not, was declared by Article 11 to be a matter of concern to the whole League. The Article also declared it the friendly right of each Member of the League to bring to the attention of the Assembly or of the Council any circumstance whatever affecting international relations which threatened to disturb international peace or the good understanding between nations upon which peace depended. Under Article 11 of the Covenant, the Council or the Assembly was competent to intervene or mediate in any circumstances affecting the peaceful relations of members of the League.

Article 12 provided for resort to arbitration or judicial settlement or to enquiry by the Council and Members agreed in no case to resort to war until three months after the award by the arbitrators or the judicial decision, or the report by the Council. By Article 13 the Members further agreed that whenever any dispute arose between them which they recognized to be suitable for submission to arbitration or judicial settlement, and which could not be satisfactorily settled by diplomacy, they would submit the whole subject-matter to arbitration or judicial settlement. Taking forward the ideas developed at the Hague Peace Conferences, Article 14 of the Covenant provided for the establishment of a Permanent Court of International Justice.

13 Report of Mr William I. Buchanan, Representative of the USA to the Central American Peace Conference Held at Washington, D.C., 1907. Washington, Government Printing Office, 1908, p. 17.

In the event that a Member did not choose to go to arbitration or judicial settlement, the dispute, under Article 15 was to be submitted to the Council of the League of Nations. Any party to the dispute could make such a submission by giving notice of the existence of the dispute to the Secretary-General, who would make arrangements for a full investigation and consideration of the matter. The Council would then endeavour to effect a settlement. The Council could refer a dispute to the Assembly.

Should any Member of the League resort to war in disregard of the provisions of Articles 12, 13, or 15 of the Covenant, it would *ipso facto* be deemed to have committed an act of war against all other Members of the League, who were then authorized to institute sanctions against the aggressor. It was made the duty of the Council in such a case to recommend to the Governments concerned what effective military, naval or air force the Members of the League should contribute to the armed forces to be used to uphold the provisions of the League Covenant.

The Council of the League developed procedures for dealing with potential hostilities, which included immediate intervention by the President, who could issue a warning to the disputants and call for a ceasefire; immediate convening of the Council, to which representatives of the disputants were summoned for the purpose of ending hostilities; the appointment of a commission of officers to supervise, on the spot, the cessation of hostilities, secure the maintenance of the *status quo*, or execute some other provisional arrangement, pending a settlement of the dispute; the establishment of a commission to examine the facts and make a report with recommendations for a solution to the dispute.

Wainhouse, in *International Peace Observation* provided an extensive survey of the efforts of the League of Nations to prevent or contain war. In the Aaland Islands case, the Council, on the initiative of Great Britain, took up the matter before hostilities could begin.[14] Sir Eric Drummond, the Secretary-General of the League of the Nations, took the lead in the efforts to avoid the dispute escalating into war between Finland and Sweden. He advanced ideas, which were followed and implemented, and which led to defusing and settling the conflict. Drummond suggested that the Council of the League should establish a commission of inquiry which would endeavour to settle the matter by mediation and to secure agreement between the parties. This course of action was adopted and proved successful.

As Rovine observed, "the pattern for the Drummond model was determined from the start – he would work quietly and his diplomatic activity would take the form of recommendation and suggestion, even on consequential procedural

14 See D.W. Wainhouse, *International Peace Observation*, Baltimore: Johns Hopkins Press, 1968, p. 8.

or political matters."[15] In February, 1921, Drummond took the initiative of bringing to the attention of the Council of the League a border dispute between Panama and Costa Rica that had resulted in fighting. Drummond did so even without any request from either party or a Member of the League as required by the Covenant.[16]

In the Greek-Bulgarian case, Drummond and the President of the Council took action within a matter of hours after hostilities had begun.[17] Rovine's assessment of Drummond's efforts in this case was as follows:

> Drummond, as always working quietly, attempted to exert some authority in matters of vital concern to the League and world politics, and in so doing, he maintained the reality of a political function for the Secretary-General as mediator and aide in shaping the terms of settlement, and as a leading channel for communications between the parties to the conflict and the international community.[18]

Unfortunately, the League, too, would eventually suffer the fate of the Concert of Europe and the Hague Peace Conferences, and would be unable to avoid the recurrence of another global conflagration, and it would be the turn of the United Nations to take forward the torch of conflict prevention.

A *The United Nations*

The first purpose of the United Nations, stated in the opening article of the Charter, is to maintain international peace and security and, to that end, to take effective collective measures for the prevention and removal of threats to peace, as well as to bring about by peaceful means and in accordance with the principles of justice and international law, adjustment or settlement of international disputes or situations which may lead to a breach of the peace.

The Security Council is mandated to determine the existence of any threat to the peace, breach of the peace, or act of aggression and to make recommendations, or decide what measures shall be taken to maintain or restore international peace and security. The Security Council, in order to prevent an aggravation of the situation, may call upon the parties concerned to comply with such provisional measures as it deems necessary or desirable. The Security

15 A.W. Rovine, *The First Fifty Years: The Secretary-General in World Politics 1920–1970*, Leyden: Sijthoff, 1970, 59.

16 Ibid, 65.

17 See Wainhouse, et. al, *International Peace Observation*, 48.

18 Ibid, 72.

Council may also decide what measures not involving the use of armed force are to be employed to give effect to its decisions.

The Charter thus places primary responsibility for prompt and effective action on the Security Council. Next, the Secretary-General has been given a responsibility for bringing matters to the attention of the Security Council. Article 99 of the Charter states that the Secretary-General may bring to the attention of the Security Council any matter which, in his opinion may threaten the maintenance of international peace and security.

Third, the General Assembly may discuss any question relating to the maintenance of international peace and security brought before it by any Member of the United Nations, or by the Security Council, or by a state which is not a Member of the United Nations. Fourth, the General Assembly, under paragraph 3 of Article 11, may call the attention of the Security Council to situations which are likely to endanger international peace and security.

Fifth, there is room for the indication of provisional measures by the Security Council. Sixth, the possibility also exists for the International Court of Justice to indicate interim measures in cases where it is vested with jurisdiction.

Article 99 of the Charter, and the Secretary-General's status as a principal organ of the UN, are the principal legal bases, and the inspiration, for the Secretary-Generals' development of the concept of preventive diplomacy at the United Nations – even if, at times, diplomatic actions have also been pursued on the basis of specific requests from the Security Council and the General Assembly.

When Article 99 was discussed at the San Francisco Conference there were different views whether the exercise of the competence should be made obligatory or optional. The majority agreed that the right should be exercised at the discretion of the Secretary-General and should not be made a duty.[19] The Preparatory Commission considered that the responsibility Article 99 conferred upon the Secretary-General would require the exercise of the highest qualities of political judgment, tact and integrity.[20]

In one of the early studies on the Office of the Secretary-General, Dr Stephen Schwebel, who later served as a Judge, and President, of the International Court of Justice, identified "seven interlocking powers" flowing from Article 99 of the Charter including, among others, the Secretary-General's right to make such inquiries and investigations as he or she may think necessary in order to

19 L.M. Goodrich, E. Hambro, and A.P. Simons, *Charter of the United Nations. Commentary and Documents*. Third Revised Edition. New York, Columbia University Press, 1969, 589.

20 Ibid, 589. Report of the Preparatory Commission, 87.

determine whether or not to invoke the powers under Article 99; and the Secretary-General's right to choose the most appropriate means of implementing the article. He also thought that Article 99 supplied the Secretary-General with a Security Council springboard for a dramatic appeal to world public opinion fully comparable to that provided in the case of the General Assembly by the annual report provision of Article 98.[21]

If the Secretary-General is to be able to act pursuant to Article 99 of the Charter, he must be provided with up-to-date information, analysis, and risk assessment inside the United Nations Secretariat. Historically, all three of these have been in short supply. However, the regional political divisions of the Department of Political Affairs have been endeavouring to gather and analyse such information as they are able to obtain from public sources, and to submit risk assessments for the consideration of the Secretary-General.

ICFY and the Establishment of the first ever Preventive Deployment of Peacekeepers

We discuss this ground-breaking development in prevention in the chapter on peacekeeping below.

Conclusion

In this chapter we have seen a thick thread of prevention running through major international peace conferences from Vienna to Paris in 1919 and we have also seen the core preventive rationales of the League of Nations and the United Nations. We presented the work of the Central American peace conference of 1907 as an interesting model of regional efforts to head off future conflicts, something that could also be said of the Contadora and Esquipulas peace processes. We would end by recalling, here also, the advice of Kalevi Holsti, which we cited in Chapter One that peace settlements should anticipate and devise means to cope with issues of the future so that they could help mould reasonably stable and less war-prone international orders. Peace settlements should provide for anticipation of future issues: the kinds of issues that will generate international conflict in the future. Every planner of an international peace conference should have this advice prominently in view.

21 S. Schwebel, *The Secretary-General of the United Nations: His Political Powers and Practice*. Cambridge: Harvard University Press, 1952, 23–26.

CHAPTER 4

Peacemaking

Introduction

The experiences of international peace conferences suggest the following: first, after major wars victorious powers have convened conferences at which they have essentially laid down the terms of peace, which were then formalized in treaties concluded at the conference. This took place at Vienna in 1814, Paris in 1919, Paris in 1946, and San Francisco in 1951. Second, after major wars and the parties were exhausted, some international peace conferences have provided a framework for bilateral negotiations leading to the conclusion of peace treaties. This occurred at Westphalia in 1748. Third, international peace conferences have been used to express the sense of the international community and to provide a framework of principles or goals for negotiations. This took place at the London Conference on the Former Yugoslavia in August of 1992, which put down a Statement of Principles for future negotiations. Fourth, international peace conferences have been used by mediators as fora or frameworks for stitching together the elements of a peace agreement or of building up such elements over time. One could say that this took place within the framework or the Contadora process on Central America. Fifth, some international peace conferences have provided an umbrella or a framework for bilateral negotiations by parties towards a settlement. The ASEAN-led negotiations on Cambodia is an example of such a process a work. Sixth, an international peace conference might be used as a forum to ratify the results of prior negotiations. The San Francisco conference of 1951, where the peace treaty with Japan was concluded, is an example of such a process at work.

At the end of the day, it is the peacemaking strategy that is of importance, having regard to the prevailing political circumstances. For the most part, the international peace conference is called in aid of the lead negotiators. It might well be the case, however, that, in some instances the core strategy emerges out of a conference framework. This chapter will seek to present some snapshots of peacemaking strategies from past international peace conferences. The presentation will be thematic rather than chronological. This is inevitable if one wants to derive insights from past conferences that might be helpful in future situations.

 | DOI 10.1163/9789004245907_006

I Some General Issues Regarding Peacemaking Strategies for International Peace Conferences

Someone contemplating the convening of an international peace conference would need to reflect on peacemaking issues such as the following: First, a statement of objectives. Without getting too detailed, or tying up oneself in knots, it is a good idea to give a general indication of the peacemaking objectives of the conference.

Second, whether it might be desirable to indicate policy parameters. Whether one does so or not would depend on the nature of the conflict and the intensity, or not, of moral issues that might be involved. In the contemporary world, with modern communications strategies, one can expect engaged commentators to be searching in their examination of what is taking place during peace negotiations. A general umbrella statement of policy might be the Principles of the United Nations Charter.

Third, should one consider indicating principles of peacemaking? We discuss this issue specifically later in this chapter. Our inclination is to advise against the indication of such principles because we think that, for the most part, the peacemaker will need to pursue pragmatic strategies rather than pursuing a strategy of fleshing out a statement of principles. The Oslo accords on Palestine had been hailed initially as a success because it got the parties to agree on a short statement of what the parties would work towards. In the end it turned out that it papered over too many serious issues to allow for meaningful negotiations to follow.

A fourth issue that might be reflected upon is whether one would put down, early on, a draft peace agreement or whether one would allow time for initial discussions with the parties before beginning to trace the outlines of a peace agreement. The latter approach is probably preferable, unless, as in the case of the peace treaty with Japan in 1951, detailed negotiations precede the actual convening of a peace conference.

A fifth issue in the actual negotiations is whether one might start by getting the parties to agree to short statements of negotiating objectives or whether one pieces together the parts of an eventual peace agreement as the talks go along. There are precedents for both approaches in the past practice. In the negotiations for what eventually became the Erdut Agreement on Eastern Slavonia (1995), in Croatia, the negotiators, Thorvald Stoltenberg and Peter Galbraith, pursued the first approach successfully. In the negotiations on Afghanistan mediated by Diego Cordovez during the period of Soviet occupation of that country, he pursued the latter approach to good effect.

A sixth issue that would be well worth considering is whether, before launching an international peace conference, or actual negotiations, one should discreetly seek expert advice and papers on the underlying strategic issues that must be understood if one is to be able to craft appropriate peacemaking approaches. One should not go into negotiations blind on the underlying issues. This point is of particular importance when one is dealing with historic grievances or long-standing ethnic rivalries. This author has participated in peace negotiations on complex historical and ethnic issues and considered that at the outset and for most of the negotiations the principal actors understood very little of what was actually moving the parties. One cannot go into peacemaking blindfolded.

A seventh issue that must be considered rather carefully has to do with the power balances between or among the protagonists, and the attitudes of major powers. Unless one understands this one could be condemned to a futile exercise. In the case of the International Conference on the Former Yugoslavia, the Clinton administration in the USA and the German government played their hands quietly in supporting the Bosniacs in the case of the USA and the Croats in the case of Germany and, however hard the negotiators tried, they could not overcome the influence of these major powers. It was only when the USA was ready for a peace agreement that one could be concluded at Dayton in 1995. It is probably the case that an inadequate assessment of the attitudes of major powers towards the contemporary Syrian conflict has contributed to its prolongation so far.

The power dimensions and their impact on an international peace process are of such fundamental importance that we consider it further historically, especially as regards balance of power and collective security approaches.

II International Peace Conferences, Balance of Power, and Collective Security

In a discussion of the peacemaking strategies of international peace conferences it is helpful to consider as a group the great peace conferences of Westphalia, Vienna, Paris, and the war-time peace blueprints of the allied leaders. Westphalia, and Vienna were largely concerned with the balance of power. The idea of the balance of power would also be present among the British and French delegation at Paris in 1919 but would be overtaken by the idea of collective security, even if Kissinger has argued that the idea of collective security was very much on the mind of Metternich at Vienna.[1] The idea of collective

1 Kissinger writes: "Ironic as it may seem Metternich presaged Wilson, in the sense that he believed that a shared concept of justice was a prerequisite for international order, however

security would be retained in the United Nations Charter but in the actual peace that followed the Second World War, the practice of spheres of influence implied the practice of the balance of power.

Henry Kissinger in his book, Diplomacy,[2] provides some of the best interpretations of the peace conferences at Vienna and Paris, and of the approaches to peace of Roosevelt, Stalin, and Churchill during World War II. By the time the Napoleonic Wars were ending, Kissinger writes, "Europe was ready to design – for the only time in its history, an international order based on the principles of the balance of power."[3] By the time the First World War was upon it, however, Great Britain, which had hitherto identified its security with the balance of power which it protected by supporting the weaker side against the stronger was changing its position. By 1914, Great Britain, "felt less and less comfortable in this role. Sensing that Germany had become stronger than all the rest of the Continent combined, Great Britain felt it could no longer play its traditional role of trying to remain above the fray in Europe"[4] and began to become interested in the idea of collective security. France still looked to the balance of power and "needed an ally in the East that could force Germany to fight a two-front war,"[5] something that the Versailles settlement made impossible by interposing Poland between Russia and Germany. France was unsuccessful in obtaining a pledge from the USA to guarantee its security. America, for its part, "disdained the concept of the balance of power and considered the practice of *Realpolitik* immoral. America's criteria for international order were democracy, collective security and self-determination..."[6] Collective security was the leitmotif of the League of Nations.

Kissinger is devastating in his assessment of the Treaty of Versailles:

> The debacle of the Treaty of Versailles was structural. The century of peace produced by the Congress of Vienna had been buttressed by three pillars, each of which was indispensable: a peace of conciliation with France: a balance of power; and a shared sense of legitimacy. The relatively conciliatory peace with France would not in itself have prevented

---

diametrically opposed his idea of justice was to what Wilson sought to institutionalize in the twentieth century." Diplomacy, p. 79.

2 H. Kissinger, Diplomacy, New York, Simon & Schuster, 1994.

3 Ibid, p. 77.

4 Ibid, p. 220.

5 Ibid, p. 243.

6 Ibid, p. 221. "European leaders," Kissinger commented, "had no categories of thought to encompass such views" – Ibid, p. 222.

> French revisionism. But France knew that the Quadruple and Holy Alliances could always assemble superior power, making French expansionism far too risky. At the same time, periodic European congresses gave France an opportunity to participate in the Concert of Europe as an equal. Above all, the major countries had shared common values so that existing grievances did not coalesce into an attempt to overthrow the international order.
>
> The Treaty of Versailles fulfilled none of these conditions...
>
> Paradoxically, France's vulnerability and Germany's strategic advantage were both magnified by the Treaty of Versailles despite its punitive provisions.[7]

When it came to the approaches of the three allied leaders during World War II, Kissinger noted that Churchill wanted to reconstruct the traditional balance of power in Europe, Roosevelt envisioned a postwar order in which the three victors, along with China, would act as a board of directors of the world, enforcing the peace against any potential miscreant, while Stalin's approach reflected both his communist ideology and traditional Russian foreign policy: "He strove to cash in on his country's victory by extending Russian influence into Central Europe. And he intended to turn the countries conquered by Soviet armies into buffer zones to protect Russia against any future aggression."[8]

In the end, as we know, there was no comprehensive peace conference after World War II and the security of the world, nominally with the United Nations, would pass to international military alliances such as NATO and the Warsaw Pact. As Kissinger summed it up, "...the war ended with a geopolitical vacuum. The balance of power had been destroyed, and a comprehensive peace treaty remained elusive. The world was now divided into ideological camps. The postwar period would turn into an extended and painful struggle to achieve the settlement which had eluded the leaders before the war ended."[9]

This discussion of what we may term the power and political dimensions was needed to inject a dose of realism when considering the peacemaking strategies of international peace conferences. We would see this also when considering efforts to negotiate on the basis of prior principles, which we discuss next.

---

7 Ibid, p. 242.

8 Ibid, p. 395.

9 Ibid, p. 422.

III Negotiation on the Basis of Principles (Paris, 1919, and ICFY, 1992–1995)

The issue that arises for reflection here is whether pre-existing principles of international peace conferences can be sustained in the actual negotiations. We select two instances in which this experiment was tried, with negative results: Paris, 1919, and ICFY, 1992–96.

Harold Nicholson has been scathing in his assessment of the actual results of the effort to negotiate at Paris on the basis of President Wilson's prior principles, fourteen to begin with, twenty-three in the end. It will be recalled that ten days before the Conference, President Wilson presented to the US Congress his Fourteen Points as the basis for negotiations in Paris. The fourteen points, in summary, were as follows: 1. Open covenants of peace, that is to say no secret or separate ones; 2. Freedom of navigation upon the seas outside territorial waters. 3. Free trade on equal terms for parties to the peace: 4. The reduction of national armaments consistent with domestic safety; 5. Adjustment of imperial claims with equal weight given to colonist and colonized; 6. Evacuation of and assistance to Russia and its self-determination; 7. Likewise with Belgium; 8. Restoration of Alsace-Lorraine to France; 9. Readjustment of Italy's borders along recognizable lines of nationality; 10. Autonomous development for the peoples of Austro-Hungary. 11. Economic independence, territorial integrity and old alliances for Balkan States; 12. Autonomous development for former Ottoman peoples and open Dardanelles; 13. An independent Polish state inhabited by indisputably Polish populations; 14. A general association of nations to guarantee political independence and territorial integrity to great and small states alike.[10]

Harold Nicholson, in his book on the Paris Peace Conference made the following comment, which we reproduce in full because of its devastating assessment:

> ...Let me contrast the principles enunciated by the Fourteen points with the extent to which those principles were embodied in the eventual Treaties of Peace.
>
> Our covenants of Peace were not openly arrived at: seldom has such secrecy been maintained in any diplomatic gathering. The Freedom of the seas was not secured. So far from Free Trade being established in

10 We have taken this summary from A. Adolf, Peace. A World History. Cambridge, Polity, 2008, pp. 188–189.

> Europe, a set of tariff-walls were erected, higher and more numerous than any known before. National armaments were not reduced. The German Colonies were distributed among the victors in a manner which was neither free, nor open-minded, nor impartial. The wishes, to say nothing of the interests, of the populations were (as in the Saar, Shantung and Syria) flagrantly disregarded. Russia was not welcomed into the Society of Nations, nor was she accorded unhampered freedom to develop her own institutions. The frontiers of Italy were not adjusted along the lines of nationality. The Turkish portions of the Ottoman Empire were not assured a secure sovereignty. The territories of Poland include many people who are indisputably not Polish. The League of Nations has not, in practice, been able to assure political independence to Great and Small Nations alike. Provinces and peoples were, in fact, treated as pawns and chattels in a game. The territorial settlements, in almost every case, were based on mere adjustments and compromises between the claims of rival States. Elements of discord and antagonism were in fact perpetuated. Even the old system of Secret Treaties was not entirely and universally destroyed.
>
> Of President Wilson's twenty-three conditions, only four can, with any accuracy be said to have been incorporated in the Treaties of Peace.[11]

We might also recall President Wilson's accent on the principle of self-determination which played practically no part in the negotiations in Paris.

Turning to ICFY, its parent conference, the London Conference on Yugoslavia, in August 1992, had adopted a Statement of Principles which we summarise as follows: (1) The imperative principle that all parties should cease fighting; (2) Non-recognition of all advantages gained by force or *fait accompli* or of any legal consequences thereof; (3) The need for all parties to engage actively in negotiations on the basis of these principles; (4) Respect for the highest standards of individual rights and fundamental freedoms in a democratic society; (5) Implementation of constitutional guarantees of the human rights and fundamental freedoms of persons belonging to ethnic and national communities and minorities; (6) Total condemnation of forcible expulsions, illegal detentions and attempts to change the ethnic composition of populations; (7) Compliance by all persons with their obligations under international humanitarian law; (8) The fundamental obligation to respect the independence, sovereignty and territorial integrity of all states in the region; and to

11 H. Nicholson, Peacemaking 1919, New York, Grosset and Dunlap, 1965, pp. 43–44.

respect the inviolability of all frontiers; Rejection of all efforts to acquire territory and change borders by force. (9) A final settlement of all questions of succession to the former Yugoslavia; (10) *Full compliance with all UN Security Council resolutions* (!). (11) The vital need for humanitarian aid to be provided; (12) The obligation on all parties to cooperate wholeheartedly in the international monitoring, peacekeeping and arms control operations; (13) The need to provide international guarantees to ensure the full implementation of all agreements reached within the framework of ICFY.[12]

It would be fair to say that while these principles were in the minds of the negotiators, what predominated was the pragmatic pursuit of peace. Vance and Owen arrived in Geneva on 3 September, 1992, and set about their tasks with determination – with a meeting of the Steering Committee of the Conference that very day. In less than two weeks they were on a mission in the Former Yugoslavia and by the end September, they had assembled the Bosnian parties for continuous talks in Geneva. On 30 September they brought together the Presidents of Croatia and of the Federal Republic of Yugoslavia for talks. The two leaders issued a joint communique providing for the resolution of outstanding disputes and laying down steps for future cooperation between them. A further meeting was held between these leaders in October. During that month also, a meeting was held between the Presidents of Bosnia and Herzegovina and the Federal Republic of Yugoslavia. They too issued a joint statement. Missions to Macedonia, Albania, Slovenia, Croatia, Bosnia and Heregovina and the Federal Republic of Yugoslavia sought to develop the outlines of blueprints for peace.

On the Bosnian question, Vance and Owen, assisted by Martti Ahtisaari, later the President of Finland, sought to write on a clean slate. Ahtisaari first invited the Bosnian parties to offer their views on the framework for a settlement. The Croats and the Serbs argued for a return to the Cutileiro Statement of Principles which had been the basis of negotiations in the Carrington Conference. The Muslims argued for a unified, integral, multi-ethnic Bosnia and Herzegovina. Ahtisaari asked them to submit maps indicating majority areas of the main population groups. Numerous meetings were held with the three delegations individually between the end of September and the middle of December, 1992 to discuss a constitutional framework and maps. Joint meetings could not be held because the Muslims took the position that they would not meet with the Serbs led by Radovan Karadzic.

In the last week of December, 1992 a joint meeting of Croat and Muslim leaders was held in Geneva on the eve of all-party talks scheduled to open in

12 The London Conference. Statement of Principles. Approved by the Conference on 26 August, 1992. LC/C2 (FINAL).

Geneva on 2 January, 1993. A constitutional framework was discussed providing for the establishment of ten largely-autonomous provinces within a unified Bosnia and Herzegovina, and maps were discussed. What was at work, in effect, was the development of an alliance strategy on the eve of all-party talks: an alliance of Croats and Muslims supported by the Co-Chairmen. The mediators were acting politically. In the light of experience one can pose the question whether political mediation against one of the parties could be successful mediation. Earlier in December, the Co-Chairmen, Vance and Owen had publicly invited the electorate in the Federal Republic of Yugoslavia to vote against Slobodan Milosevic and for Milan Panic in Serbia's Presidential elections. It was a high-risk strategy.

Fortunately for the duo, Cyrus Vance had developed relations of confidence with Milosevic when Vance had mediated an end to the conflict in Croatia the previous year. So when the Bosnian parties assembled in Geneva on 2 January, 1993, in the presence of the Presidents of Croatia, the Federal Republic of Yugoslavia, Montenegro and Serbia, Vance got Milosevic to bring immense pressure to bear upon Radovan Karadzic to get him to accept a constitutional framework for Bosnia and Herzegovina providing for ten largely autonomous provinces within a unified country. This brought the Vance-Owen process to a new stage: from consultations to alliance, to politicking to pressure. Radovan Karadzic, acting under severe pressure from Milosevic, joined the Croat leader Mate Boban, and the Bosniac leader Alija Izetbegovic, in signing the constitutional framework in January, 1993. It was only a framework; the map depicting ten provinces had to be agreed upon; arrangements for implementing a cessation of hostilities had to be negotiated.

Vance and Owen put down a map which was signed by the Croat leader Mate Boban. Karadzic and Izetbegovic wanted changes. Vance and Owen decided to move the negotiations to New York where they could be nearer to the Security Council. The thinking was that the members of the Security Council could be marshalled to bring pressure to bear upon the Muslim and Serb leadership to settle the map and to proceed with implementation of the plan. To the Vance-Owen methods of negotiation could now be added attempts to marshall pressure upon recalcitrant parties. It would appear to work after some time but then fail, thus inviting the question: If pressure tactics are overused are they doomed to failure?

After President Clinton was elected Vance, a respected former Democratic Secretary-of-State, under whom Secretary-of-State Christopher served as Deputy, personally briefed senior members of the Clinton transition team on the nature of the Bosnian problematique and on the lines being pursued in the search for a settlement. After President Clinton was inaugurated Vance personally sent to Secretary Christopher copies of plans and maps under discussion with the Bosnian parties. Before long the Clinton Administration, Secretary Christopher included, began to snipe at the Vance-Owen plan and to take swipes at Vance himself. Vance, a dignified, honourable, disciplined person, kept his cool and refrained from replying in public.

Vance and Owen had done their utmost to devise a peace plan for Bosnia and Herzegovina that would maintain the integrity of the country and would reverse ethnic cleansing by the Bosnian Serbs. This author was present in many conversations with them in which they both expressed their determination to help reverse ethnic cleansing and to make sure that the Serbs returned territories they had taken by force.

However, the Clinton Administration's special envoy for the Bosnian talks, Ambassador Reginald Bartholomew began to play the role of advocate for the Bosniac side, and to press for more territory to be allocated to the Muslims in the allocation of territory among the ten provinces. It was precisely on this issue that Vance and Owen were endeavouring to persuade Radovan Karadzic to come on board the map they had put down – as Izetbegovic engaged in a stand-off to see what more Bartholomew could obtain for him. When Bartholomew did succeed in getting the map changed to allocate more territory to the Muslims, Izetbegovic signed in March, 1993. But the reasons for Izetbegovic's signature were the very reasons why Radovan Karadzic stayed further away from the map. Pressure from the United States in favour of one side, however well-intentioned, pushed another side away from the peace table.

In the end, Principles, though present, did not drive the negotiations. What was decisive was the need to stop the fighting. Going down to the Dayton peace conference, pragmatic approaches would prevail.

IV Assembling the Building Blocks of Peace (Contadora/Esquipulas)

The Contadora/Esquipulas processes were initiated by Latin American leaders as conflicts raged in Central America in the midst of cold war great-power rivalry and the direct military involvement of the USA. Their great achievement was to spearhead the search for peace in the face of American scepticism and even opposition, to develop objectives and principles for peacemaking, to launch ideas for peacekeeping and peace observation, and, over time, to integrate these ideas into peace agreements that helped stop the conflicts and set the sub-region on new courses towards peace, development and reconciliation that are still at work to our day.

The Contadora/Esquipulas processes involved a series of meetings in the decade of the 1980s that, step by step, put down the building blocks for peace. Jack Child considers that the key to their success was the use of confidence-building and peacekeeping measures.[13] The initiatives, at different times, came from different national leaders or groups of leaders. National ministries of foreign affairs performed organizational and related tasks and there was no conference secretariat as such.

The Contadora and Esquipulas processes consisted of a number of meetings of Foreign Ministers and of which Heads of State that had the characteristics of international peace conferences, literally put together, block by block, a framework for peace in Central America. The First Meeting held by the Foreign Ministers of Colombia, Mexico, Panama, and Venezuela (the Contadora Group) on 8 and 9 January, 1983, agreed that there was a need to increase communication among Latin American nations as an effective means of facing the political, economic and social problems which compromised the peace, democracy, stability and development of these nations. They examined the 'complex panorama existing in Central America' and advised that it was highly desirable to classify the conflicts in the context of East–west confrontation, and they agreed upon the need to eliminate the external factors that made them worse. They reiterated the need to continue the economic strengthening of Central America.[14]

The Ministers of Foreign Affairs of Colombia, Mexico, Panama, and Venezuela (the Contadora nations) made joint visits to Costa Rica, Nicarague, El Salvador, Honduras and Guatemala on 12 and 13 April, 1983 and met all together in Panama City on 21 April, 1983. According to the Information Bulletin issued on the latter meeting, the Contadora Ministers agreed that among the matters that required the most attention were: the arms race, arms control and reduction, the transfer of armaments, the presence of military advisers and other forms of outside military assistance, actions aimed at

13 See J. Child (Ed.), Conflict in Central America. Approaches to Peace and Security. London C. Hurst and Company, London, published for the International Peace Academy, 1986. J. Child, The Central American Peace Process, 1993–1991. Boulder: Lynne Rienner, 1992, J. Child (Ed.), Regional Cooperation for Development and the Peaceful Settlement of Disputes in Latin America. New York, International Peace Academy/ Dordrecht, Martinus Nijhoff Publishers, 1987,

14 Information bulletin issued in Contadora Island, Panama on January 9, 1983. Reproduced in B. Bagley, et. al, Contadora and the Central American Peace Process. Selected Documents. School oif Advanced International Studies, Johns Hopkins University (SAIS Papers No. 9). Boulder and London, Westview Press, 1985, pp. 164–165.

destabilizing the internal order of other countries, threats and verbal aggression, warlike incidents and frontier tensions, the violation of human rights and individual and social guarantees, and the grave economic and social problems that were at the heart of the region's prevailing crisis.[15]

The Ministers of Foreign Affairs of the Contadora nations reiterated their deep conviction that the conflicts prevailing in the area could be successfully dealt with through formulas for a peaceful solution and a genuine spirit of negotiation and considered that the consultation process already established should be maintained, 'since it had already demonstrated its usefulness, effectiveness, and timeliness'.[16]

The Contadora Foreign Ministers met again with their Central America counterparts ain Panama City on 28–30 May and issued an Information Bulletin on 30 May according to which they had identified four major areas: a conceptual framework; political and security problems; economic and social objectives and machinery for the implementation and monitoring of the agreements reached. They had decided on specific discussion topics under each of these headings.[17] An Observer Commission had visited Costa Rica and Nicaragua the previous week and reported to the Ministers of the Contadora Group. Members of the Commission 'reported on the outcome of their interviews and contacts with the authorities of both countries and on their fact-finding visit to the Costa Rica-Nicaragua frontier region'.[18]

It will be noticed that thus far the Contadora process had used communications, visits, consultations, policy frameworks, observation, and fact-finding. They proceeded to put down further elements of a peacemaking machinery. In the course of this meeting the Central American Foreign Ministers 'presented various proposals for the establishment of formal conditions for regional co-existence'. The Foreign Ministers of the Contadora Group decided to set up a technical group consisting of representatives of the nine countries which would, within a reasonable period, hear the various views on the agreed items, gather whatever information was relevant in each case and propose the most appropriate procedures for dealing effectively with the problems identified.[19] The technical group would meet in Panama beginning on 14 June and would report to the Third Meeting of Foreign Ministers to be convened in due course by the Contadora Group.

15 Ibid, p. 167.
16 Ibid, p. 168.
17 Ibid, p. 169.
18 Ibid, p. 169.
19 Ibid, p. 170.

In view of a request that had been made by the UN Security Council in resolution 530 of 19 May, 1983, the countries of the Contadora Group agreed they would, through their Permanent Missions to the United Nations, keep the Secretary-General of the United Nations informed of any developments in their efforts.[20] The UN Secretary-General thus entered the process and would later come to make decisive contributions to the search for peace in the area.

In view of the worsening of the conflicts in Central America, the Heads of State of the four Contadora nations met in Cancun, Mexico, on 17 July, 1983, and issued the Contadora Declaration on Peace in Central America. They considered that peace in Central America could become a reality only in so far as respect was shown for the basic principles of coexistence among nations: non-intervention; self-determination; sovereign equality of States; cooperation for economic and social development; peaceful settlement of disputes; and free and authentic expression of the popular will.[21]

The Presidents of the Contadora Group assessed that the efforts of the Contadora Group had thus far led to 'the initiation of a dialogue involving all the Governments of Central America, the establishment of machinery for consultation and the drawing up, by unanimous agreement, of an agenda covering the salient aspects of the problems of the region'.[22] The Presidents of the Contadora Group agreed on 'the general lines of a programme to be proposed to the countries of Central America which requires, in addition to strict compliance with the essential principles governing international relations, the conclusion of agreements and political commitments that will lead, region-wide, to effective control of the arms race; the elimination of foreign advisers; the creation of demilitarized zones; the prohibition of the use of the territory of other States; the eradication of transit of and traffic in arms; and the prohibition of other forms of aggression or interference in the internal affairs of any country in the area'.[23]

The Presidents of the Contadora nations went on to put down detailed elements of a framework for peace. They considered that in order implement the foregoing general programme, it would be necessary to conclude agreements embodying political commitments designed to ensure peace in the region. Those agreements could include: Commitment to put an end to all prevailing situations of belligerency; Commitment to freeze offensive weapons at their current level; Commitment to begin negotiations on agreements for the

---

20 Ibid, p. 170.
21 Ibid, p. 171.
22 Ibid, p. 171.
23 Ibid, p. 172.

control and reduction of current stocks of weapons, with the establishment of appropriate supervisory machinery; Commitment to prohibit the existence in national territory of military installations belonging to other countries; Commitment to give prior notice of troop movements near frontiers, when the contingents exceed the limits set in the agreement; Commitment to organize, as appropriate, a joint boundary frontier of international supervision of frontiers by groups of observers chosen by common agreement of the parties concerned; Commitment to establish mixed security commissions, with a view to preventing and, where appropriate, resolving frontier incidents; Commitment to establish internal control machinery to prevent the transit of weapons from the territory of any country in the region to the territory of another; Commitment to promote a climate of detente and confidence in the area by avoiding statements and other actions that jeopardize the essential climate of political confidence required; and Commitment to coordinate systems of direct communication between Governments with a view to preventing armed conflicts and generating an atmosphere of mutual political confidence.[24]

The Presidents of the Contadora Nations went on to urge that, simultaneously with the implementation of the general programme summarised above, the task of resolving specific differences between countries should be tackled intially be the signing of memoranda of understanding and the establishment of mixed commissions that would enable the parties to undertake joint action and guarantee the effective control of their territories, especially in frontier areas. These measures, aimed at eliminating the factors that disturbed the peace of the region, should be accompanied by a major internal effort to strengthen democratic institutions and guarantee respect for human rights. To this end, it was necessary to improve methods of consulting the people, ensure that the various currents of opinion have free access to the electoral process and promote the full participation of citizens in the political life of their country.

The strengthening of democratic political institutions, the Presidents continued, was closely linked to evolution and progress in the field of economic development and social justice. Those were two aspects of a single process whose ultimate goal was the implementation of the fundamental values of mankind. The economic backwardness that lay at the root of the instability in the region and was the immediate cause of many of its conflicts, should be approached from this standpoint.[25]

---

24 Ibid, pp. 172–173.

25 Ibid, p. 173.

The Presidents appealed to all members of the international community, and to the Secretary-General of the United Nations and the Chairman of the Permanent Council of the OAS, to contribute, with their experience and diplomatic capability, to the search for peaceful solutions to the problems of Central America. The Contadora Declaration was a remarkable blueprint for peace.

In the aftermath of the Presidential meeting the Foreign Ministers of the Contadora Group met with their counterparts from Central America on 28, 29, and 30 July, 1983 and stressed the necessity of laying the foundations for the agreements essential for achieving peace.[26] The Foreign Ministers of the four Contadora nations met again from 3–9 September, 1983, and adopted a document containing 21 objectives and laying down some principles for future peacemaking. The Document began with a statement of principles of international law governing the actions of States, including the self-determination of peoples; non-intervention; the sovereign equality of States; the peaceful settlement of disputes; refraining from the threat or use of force; respect for the territorial integrity of States; pluralism in its various manifestations; full support for democratic institutions; the promotion of social justice; international cooperation for development; respect for and promotion of human rights; the prohibition of terrorism and subversion; the desire to reconstruct the Central American homeland through progressive integration of its economic, legal and social institutions; the need for economic cooperation among the States of Central America so as to make a fundamental contribution to the development of their peoples and the strengthening of their independence; the undertaking to establish, promote or revitalize representative, democratic systems in all the countries of the region; the unjust economic, social and political structure which exacerbate the conflicts in Central America; the urgent need to put an end to the tensions and lay the foundations for understanding and solidarity among the countries of the area; the arms race and the growing arms traffic in Central America, which aggravated political relations in the region and diverted economic resources that could be used for development; the presence of foreign advisers and other forms of foreign military interference in the zone.[27] The principal objectives were to promote detente and to put an end to situations of conflict in the area.

On 9 June, 1984, the Foreign Ministers of the Contadora Group transmitted to the Heads of State of the Central American Nations, a draft 'Contadora Act for Peace and Cooperation in Central America'. On 7 September, 1984, they revised and issued it in a Communication of 7 September, 1984. The document,

26 Ibid, p. 175.

27 Ibid, pp. 176–180.

in addition to a preamble, consisted of Chapter I on General Commitments, Chapter II, Commitments on Poltical Affairs, Chapter III, Commitments on Security Affairs, Chapter IV Commitments on Economic and Social Affairs.[28] This Contadora Act would not, in the final outcome, be adopted as drafted due largely to the influence of the USA, but its intellectual and policy influences was beyond question and certainly influenced the final outcome for peace in Central America.

Between 1984 and 1986 further meetings were held resulting in various Contadora statements and Acts. These Acts produced rolling, incremental ideas, including ideas for verification and confidence-building. Building on the Contadora ideas, in 1987 the Esquipulas process took over with the prominent involvement of Costa Rican President Oscar Arias. The Esquipulas (or Arias) peace Plan was launched in 1987. The Esquipulas process would continue the process of consultations and confidence-building and lead to efforts under the aegis of the United Nations Secretary-General for eventual ending of the different conflicts. We discuss the results of some of these efforts in later chapters on peacekeeping and peacebuilding.

In June, 1991, plans were announced for the establishment of a hot line among the Presidents of the five Central American nations plus Panama. In June, 1991, the OAS General Assembly, meeting in Santiago, Chile, decided on the adoption of a Working Group on Cooperation for Hemispheric Security. In July 1991, at a Presidential Summit held in San Salvador, Honduras proposed the adoption of a Central American Security Treaty.

The peace processes begun by Contadora and continued by Esquipulas would see their eventual fruition through negotiations conducted by the United Nations Secretary-General, Javier Perez de Cuellar and, on his behalf, by his Special Representative, Alvaro de Soto.

V Various Forms of Peace Facilitation

As we saw in Chapter I above, international peace conferences have contributed to peacemaking strategies in diverse ways, including through providing a framework for bilateral negotiations (Westphalia); Great Powers determining the content of the peace (Vienna, Paris, and Dayton); Great powers providing an opportunity for the vanquished powers to state their views but determining the content of peace (Paris, 1946); and negotiating the peace beforehand and

28 Ibid, pp. 190–217.

ratifying them after at a conference (Japanese peace treaty, 1951). Power thus played a decisive role in many instances.

Conclusion

This chapter has shown the essentially pragmatic nature of the peacemaking process at international peace conferences, depending on the circumstances of particular conflicts. Attempts to lay down prior principles have had to be finessed in the end. One saw this at Versailles in 1919 and at Dayton in 1995. Nevertheless, the Contadora-Esquipulas processes built peacemaking strategies on the foundations of concepts such as democracy and respect for human rights. Some of this also took place at Dayton. We saw the fusion of regional and United Nations efforts that helped bring the Contadora-Esquipulas processes to fruition. We also saw the weight of the Great Powers in more than one instance, including at Dayton in 1995.

Any attempt to draw broader lessons from the peacemaking experiences of international peace conferences would not travel far. Peacemaking strategies emerge from the circumstances of particular conflicts and from the power configurations attending them. We must approach each situation on a case-by-case basis.

A key question that arises for reflection is whether and to what extent international peace conferences can contribute to the resolution of conflicts. The answer to this question is that, depending on the conflict and the circumstances, they may or may not do so. A negotiated end to a conflict might be worked out if the parties are ready to negotiate in good faith or can be squeezed by powerful members of the international community to do so. Parties with the will, and the means, to fight will fight on, unless countervailing power can be marshaled against one, some, or all of them.

This is what took place when the Bosnian conflict was raging in 1995. The Dayton peace conference almost failed but could be salvaged at the last moment on account of the power of the USA, supported by Germany. The parties had already fought for some three and a half years. The International Conference on the Former Yugoslavia (ICFY) had facilitated negotiations on Bosnia for three and a half years between 1992 and 1995 but could not succeed in getting a lasting peace because the parties were armed and supported on different sides internationally and the conference lacked countervailing power that it could marshal against recalcitrant parties. Richard Holbrook had access to such power – and used it.

By contrast, in 2012, as the conflict in Syria raged on, none of the parties paid much attention to the six-point peace plan of Kofi Annan, Envoy of the United Nations and the Arab League. When an international conference was called in June 2012 to help marshal international support for the plan it made little difference, because Russia and China would not support a policy that called for President Assad to step down and the parties continued to fight even as the conference was held. As July ended, Annan resigned, criticizing the parties, divisions among the powers, and the Security Council. The conflict raged on.

CHAPTER 5

Peacekeeping

Introduction

The term peacekeeping is of relatively recent origin and the concept is generally considered to have been developed within the United Nations – even if the practice of 'international peace observation' was well known to the League of Nations.[1] From the perspectives of international peace conferences, such practice as might be found would date from the second half of the twentieth century and the years of the current century to date. One would need to distinguish between deployments of peacekeepers, understood in the broad sense as including observers, for humanitarian, stabilisation, and peacemaking purposes generally, and peacekeeping with a direct link to international peace conferences. In the recent conflict in Syria, for example, the six-point plan put forward by former Special Envoy Kofi Annan called for, and achieved, the deployment of United Nations observers who had a precarious existence on the ground and were eventually withdrawn. In comparison with this, there have been instances where international peace processes such as the Contadora process, or a conference such as ICFY, arranged for the deployment of observers (in the latter case on the border between Serbia and Bosnia along the Drina river with a view to containing the conflict and helping in the search for peace). In this chapter we shall seek to highlight instances in which international peace conferences drew upon peacekeepers to help contain conflicts, to stabilise situations, to provide humanitarian relief, to aid the peacemaking process, and to keep the peace in the aftermath of a peace agreement.

I ONUCA

In a rolling process of peacemaking and peacekeeping efforts, and with a fusion of efforts by regional leaders, the OAS, and the United Nations, the United Nations became directly involved in peacemaking and peacekeeping efforts in Central America in 1989, when the Governments of Costa Rica, El Salvador, Guatemala, Honduras and Nicaragua requested its assistance in the implementation of their collective agreement, the Procedure for the

1 See, Wainhouse, International Peace Observation. (Baltimore: Johns Hopkins Press, 1968)

 | DOI 10.1163/9789004245907_007

Establishment of a Firm and Lasting Peace in Central America, known both as the Esquipulas II Agreement and the Guatemala Procedure.[2] The Esquipulas II Agreement dealt with issues of national reconciliation, an end to hostilities, democratisation, free elections, termination of aid to irregular forces and insurrectionist movements, non-use of the territory of one State to attack other States, negotiations on security verification and the control and limitation of weapons, refugees, and displaced persons, cooperation, democracy and freedom for peace and development, international verification and follow-up and a timetable for the fulfilment of commitments.

"A complex and difficult process of negotiations,"[3] beginning in 1983, reversed the cycle of turmoil that had engulfed Central America for many years. At its various stages, the process involved countries from inside and outside the region, as well as the opposing parties within several of the Central American countries. These initiatives were actively supported and facilitated by the United Nations. As a result of the negotiations and the agreements reached, the United Nations was requested to establish a number of mechanisms for observing and verifying commitments. These included the United Nations Observer Group in Central America (ONUCA), the United Nations Observer Mission to verify the electoral process in Nicaragua (ONUVEN), the International Support and Verification Commission (CIAV), the United Nations Observer Mission in El Salvador (ONUSAL), the United Nations Mission in El Salvador (MINUSAL) and the United Nations Mission for the Verification of Human Rights in Guatelala (MINUGUA).[4]

ONUCA was established by Security Council resolution 644 (1989), of 7 November 1989, with a mandate to conduct on-site verification of compliance by the Governments of Costa Rica, El Salvador, Guatemala, Honduras and Nicaragua with their security undertakings contained in the Esquipulas II Agreement, namely (a) the cessation of aid to irregular forces and insurrection movements; and (b) the non-use of the territory of one State for attacks on other States. The latter undertaking was to include preventing the establishment or use of facilities for radio or television transmissions for the specific purpose of directing or assisting the military operations of irregular forces or insurrectionist movements in any of the five countries.

On 27 March, 1990, the Security Council, by its resolution 650 (1990), authorized on a contingency basis an enlargement of the mandate of ONUCA and

2 This summary is taken from http://www.un.org/Depts/DPKO/Missions/onucabacgr.html, consulted on 12 September, 2012.

3 Ibid.

4 Ibid.

the addition of armed personnel to its strength in order to enable it to play a part in the voluntary demobilization of the Nicaraguan Resistance.

On 20 April 1990, following the signing by the Nicaraguan parties of a set of agreements relating to the voluntary demobilization of the members of the Nicaraguan Resistance in Nicaragua, the Security Council, by its resolution 653 (1990), decided to expand ONUCA's mandate to include additional tasks of monitoring the ceasefire and separation of forces, and the demobilization process. After the completion of the demobilization process in June/July 1990, ONUCA continued to implement its original tasks and to contribute to the peace efforts in the region. The mandate of the Mission was terminated in January, 1992.[5]

II ONUSAL

Again in a rolling process of peacemaking and peacekeeping, and with a fusion of efforts by regional leaders, the OAS, and the United Nations, the United Nations Observer Mission in El Salvador (ONUSAL) was established under Security Council resolution 693 of 20 May 1991. It had Human Rights, Military and Police Divisions. An Electoral Division was created in September 1993, pursuant to Security Council resolution 832 (1993) and was dissolved on 30 April 1994 upon the culmination of the electoral process.[6]

The establishment of ONUSAL in 1991 came about as a result of a complex negotiating process, initiated by the Governments of El Salvador and the Frente Farabundo Marti parta la Liberacion Nacional (FMLN) in September, 1989 and conducted by the parties under the auspices of the United Nations Secretary-General. The objective of the negotiations was to achieve a series of political agreements aimed at resolving the prolonged armed conflict in El Salvador by political means as speedily as possible, promoting democratisation in the country, guaranteeing unrestricted respect for human rights and reunifying Salvadorean society. It was envisaged that implementation of all agreements that might be signed between the two parties would be subject to verification by the United nations.

The first substantive agreement was achieved on 26 July, 1990,when the Government of El Salvador and FMLN signed, at San Jose, Costa Rica, the

5 This summary is taken from http://www.un.org/Depts/DPKO/Missions/onucamandate.html, consulted on 12 September, 2012.

6 This summary is taken from http://www.un.org/Depts/DPKO/Missions/onucamandate.html, consulted on 12 September, 2012.

Agreement on Human Rights. The Agreement provided for the establishment of a United Nations verification mission to monitor nationwide respect for and the guarantee of human rights and fundamental freedoms in El Salvador. According to the Agreement, the Mission was to take up its duties as of the cessation of the armed conflict. However, shortly after signing the Agreement, the two parties independently requested that the Mission be set up even before a cease-fire, leading the UN Secretary General, Javier Perez de Cuellar, to send a preliminary mission in March 1991 to help him determine the feasibility of acceding to this request.

On 20 May, 1991, following the Secretary-General's recommendation, the Security Council, by its resolution 693 (1991), decided to establish the United Nations Observer Mission in El Salvador (ONUSAL), as an integrated peacekeeping operation, to monitor all agreements concluded between the Governments of El Salvador and FMLN. The Mission's initial mandate was to verify the compliance by the parties with the San Jose Agreement on Human Rights. At one stage, the tasks of the Mission included actively monitoring the human rights situation in El Salvador, investigating specific cases of alleged human rights violations; promoting human rights in the country; making recommendations for the elimination of violations; and reporting on these matters to the Secretary-General and, through him, to the United Nations General Assembly and Security Council.[7]

III Containing Conflict (Preventive Deployment in FYROM)

The preventive deployment of UN peacekeepers in the former Yugoslav republic of Macedonia, the first of its kind, and a great success, owed its establishment to the International Conference on the Former Yugoslavia. The initiative for a preventive deployment first came from the Co-chairman of the International Conference Vance and Owen. They had discussed this idea with President Kiro Gligorov who, in turn, wrote to the Secretary-General of the United Nations on 11 November 1992 asking for such a preventive deployment. In a letter of 18 November 1992, to the United Nations Secretary-General, Co-chairmen, former US Secretary of State Cyrus Vance and former British Foreign Minister Lord David Owen, told him there was growing need to take preventive measures to avoid the outbreak of violence in Macedonia and Kosovo. They recalled that they had warned the Security Council a few days

7 This summary is taken from http://www.un.org/Depts/DPKO/Missions/onusal_b.htm, consulted on 12 September, 2012.

earlier, on 13 November 1992, that a tragedy of dreadful proportions could occur if conflict were to break out in Macedonia and Kosovo, engulfing the neighbouring countries.

Elaborating upon their idea, the Co-chairmen stated that in terms of preventive diplomacy it would be desirable to put United Nations personnel, under the aegis of UNPROFOR, into Macedonia so as to provide a calming influence for all sides and give a sense of stability. They suggested to the Secretary-General the deployment of a contingent of UNPROFOR personnel within Macedonia, who could have their headquarters in Skopje and be distributed in the main population centres, as well as on the Macedonian borders with Serbia (including Kosovo) and Albania. Their efforts would be complemented by those of the CSCE, which already had a small 'spill-over mission' in Skopje.

The Co-chairmen further suggested that, as a start, about a dozen United Nations military and police officers, with supporting political staff, be sent. They could be stationed in Skopje and could travel to the border areas. In the light of their experience and recommendations, the United Nations presence could be built up as needed. The Co-chairmen were conscious of the scarcity of United Nations resources and they were seeking to indicate a way to implement their recommendation even in the face of that scarcity.

Upon receipt of the Co-chairmen's recommendation, Secretary-General Boutros Boutros-Ghali advised the Security Council that he would be sending an exploratory mission to the FYR of Macedonia to look into the possibility of establishing a preventive deployment of United Nations peace-keepers in the country. Following its visit, the exploratory mission made the following recommendations:

> that a small UNPROFOR presence be established on the Macedonian side of the Republic's borders with Albania and the Federal Republic of Yugoslavia (Serbia and Montenegro) with an essentially preventive mandate of monitoring and reporting any developments in the border areas which could undermine confidence and stability in Macedonia or threaten its territory.
>
> that a small group of United Nations civilian police be deployed in the border areas to monitor the Macedonian border police.

The rationale for the latter deployment was that incidents arising from illegal attempts to cross the border had led to increased tension on the Macedonian side. The Mission believed that the presence of a small United Nations civilian police detachment would have a calming effect.

In December 1992, the Secretary-General reported to the Security Council on the findings of the exploratory mission, together with his recommendations.[8] On 11 December 1992, the Security Council authorized the Secretary-General to establish a presence of the United Nations Protection Force (UNPROFOR) in the FYR of Macedonia. The Council requested that the Secretary-General deploy immediately the military, civil affairs, and administrative personnel he had recommended in his report, as well as police monitors.

In mid-December 1992 a United Nations team discussed practical arrangements with the Government in Skopje. The first UNCIVPOL monitors arrived on 27 December 1992. They were eventually deployed along the northern and western borders. On 28 December, a reconnaissance team went to the country to make arrangements for the interim deployment of a Canadian company. On 7 January 1993, a Canadian company arrived in the country pending the arrival of a joint battalion from Finland, Norway and Sweden. On 25 January, Brigadier-General Finn Saermark-Thomsen of Denmark, who had been designated Commander of the Macedonia Command of UNPROFOR, arrived in Skopje. On 18 February, the Nordic battalion took over the operation from a Canadian company.

The Nordic battalion was 434 strong, composed of three rifle companies. It was deployed on the western border from Debar northward and on the northern border up to the border with Bulgaria. At the beginning there were 19 United Nations Military Observers (UNMOs) in the area of operations. The western border south of Debar was covered solely by UNMOs.

From early January 1993, the northern border and the western border north of Debar were constantly monitored from observation posts and by regular patrols, with a view to reporting any activities that might increase tension or threaten peace and stability. The UNMOs conducted regular patrols in their area of operations to monitor the situation. They also carried out a programme of visits to border villages aimed at gaining the confidence of their inhabitants and assisting in defusing possible inter-ethnic tensions.

While carrying out their border visiting programme, the UNMOs were approached by representatives of different ethnic groups who lodged various complaints about alleged discriminatory practices by the authorities. In those cases where the complaints were relevant to the mandate of the mission, they were brought to the attention of the appropriate authorities. Some were also brought to the attention of the competent international bodies, such as the International Conference of the Former Yugoslavia.

8 S/24923.

UNCIVPOL also conducted regular patrols to specific crossings and the border areas in general on a daily basis. In the course of doing so, it received through local mayors a number of complaints concerning the local border police. In those cases where there appeared *prima facie* to be a basis for the complaint, UNCIVPOL took up the matter with the relevant police authorities.

The Civil Affairs component of the mission established, from the outset, an information programme to explain the role of UNPROFOR in the country. UNPROFOR maintained close coordination with the CSCE mission in the country.

By the middle of 1993, UNPROFOR's assessment was that it had been successful in its preventive mandate in the country. It was concerned, however, about the internal situation and the possibility of instability should there be an increase in the inter-ethnic tensions, a possibility which, it reported, was repeatedly mentioned by local and international sources. A related concern of UNPROFOR was about the deterioration of the economic situation stemming from the implementation of sanctions which, it was felt, could contribute to heightened inter-ethnic tensions.

By September 1993, the Secretary-General reported to the Security Council that the FYROM Command of UNPROFOR consisted of 1,190 military and civilian, including UNCIVPOL personnel. A Nordic battalion was based at Kjojila, east of Skopje, and a United States contingent of 315 troops had arrived in Skopje in early July, deploying to the FYROM side of the border with the Federal Republic of Yugoslavia on 20 August 1993. United Nations Military Observers, UNCIVPOL and Civil Affairs officers were also continuing their activities. UNPROFOR reported: "This first venture in the field of preventive peacekeeping on the part of UNPROFOR continues to be successful, and to enjoy an excellent cooperative relationship with the FYROM Government, and to be fully supported by the people of the country."

The leadership of the preventive deployment would come to conclude that "the increasing internal instability in the FYROM could prove to be more detrimental to the stability of the country than outside threats." UNPROFOR would therefore need "to consider what its role should be, if any, in the event that internal instability results in some form of civil conflict."[9]

Thus it was that the deployment developed the second of its three pillars, as presented by Sokalski, good offices and political action, alongside troop

9 Background paper submitted by the FYROM Command to Brainstorming Exercise on the future of UNPROFOR, Zagreb-Mokrice, 15–17 February 1994. Paper in the possession of the author, who participated in the exercise.

deployment and the human dimension. As Sokalski has written, the mission developed and maintained active contacts with political forces and ethnic groups in the country as a means of promoting domestic stability. Efforts were made to reduce the level of mistrust among the country's political and ethnic actors and UNPREDEP set in place a dialogue on questions regarding the rights of ethnic communities and national minorities. Sokalski has written:

> UNPREDEP was recognized as a significant instrument for facilitating dialogue, restraint and practical compromise between the different segments of Macedonian society. UN troop patrols along the northern and western borders of the country effectively complemented such activities; this outreach had a calming and stabilizing effect throughout the area. The contingent of UN military observers and the team of civilian police monitors rendered equally invaluable services.[10]

The preventive deployment in the FYR of Macedonia worked effectively – externally as well as internally. The model of United Nations observers patrolling sensitive areas where ethnic tensions were high, receiving complaints, transmitting them to the authorities, and serving as an intermediary and confidence builder is one that clearly has great relevance to situations of ethnic and religious tension, in situations where there are minority populations or in other situations where internal strife or conflict could result in gross violations of human rights. The establishment of a UN rapid reaction force would certainly help facilitate the dispatch of preventive deployment of UN peacekeepers in situations of urgent need.

IV Aiding Peacemaking (ICFY Mission)

ICFY's International Monitoring Mission on the Drina can be considered a successful preventive operation. The background was that the Bosnian Serb leadership had peeled itself off from the leadership in Belgrade when it came to the negotiation of a settlement of the conflict in Bosnia and Herzegovina. In the process the Bosnian Serb military was behaving more and more in a criminal manner leading countries of the NATO alliance to threaten Belgrade with bombing raids unless it brought the Bosnian Serb leadership to book.

---

10 H. Sokalski, *An Ounce of Prevention: Macedonia and the UN Experience in Preventive Diplomacy*, Washington, D.C.: United States Institute for Peace, 2003, 108. See also, A. Williams, *Preventing War: The UN and Macedonia* Lanham, MD: Rowman & Littlefield, 2000.

Under pressure from NATO countries, President Slobodan Milosevic, then President of the Federal Republic of Yugoslavia, instituted economic sanctions against the Bosnian Serbs: fuel and goods would no longer be permitted to move from Serbia across the Drina River to Bosnian Serb territory. This did not satisfy the NATO leadership. They called for international monitoring of the sanctions. President Milosevic, and probably the Serbian people, were not prepared to countenance the idea of international monitors on Serbian territory.

Thorvald Stoltenberg and Lord Owen met President Milosevic frequently to explore the options for peace and to help defuse dangerous situations. The year was 1993 and the international community was still in quest of peaceful solutions to the conflicts in the Former Yugoslavia. During a meeting with Thorvald Stoltenberg and Lord Owen, at which this author was present, President Milosevic intimated that he would look favourably upon the deployment of humanitarian personnel, by humanitarian organizations, to witness the implementation of sanctions against the Bosnian Serbs across the Drina River.

This was a faint opening. That very evening, Thorvald Stoltenberg, a former Foreign Minister of Norway, called his friends, the Foreign Ministers of Denmark, Finland, Norway and Sweden, with a request: would they consider providing, each, ten humanitarian personnel from humanitarian organizations and give a start up contribution of one hundred thousand dollars each for a humanitarian operation to witness the sanctions on the Drina? They all replied positively, either on the spot, or within twenty-four hours.

As Director of the International Conference on the Former Yugoslavia this author worked personally on the establishment of this mission and watched over its operations substantively and managerially during its existence. It was an extraordinary effort on the part of all involved and it shows what can be achieved with a sense of daring and innovation: Two Norwegian humanitarian operatives came from Oslo with one hundred thousand Deutschemarks in a suitcase and proceeded to Belgrade. There they secured office-space in a hotel, began to acquire a fleet of vehicles, purchased fuel on the black-market in Belgrade, and laid the ground-work for an operation that would last three years and at one stage would have dozens of international monitors on the ground and hundreds of locals supporting them.

Stoltenberg and Owen designated Brigadier-General Bo Pellnas as Head of the Mission and he was later succeeded by a Finnish General, Tauno Nieminen. Both served the international community with great distinction. ICFY financed the Mission through contributions from a coalition of countries participating in the International Conference on the Former Yugoslavia. Stoltenberg and Owen insisted from the outset on flexibility for the Mission. The UN Director of

Administration in Geneva was dead set against this and it fell to this author to set up a system, audited by Price Waterhouse, at it then was, outside of the UN framework. This author had Price Waterhouse audit the Mission regularly to ensure that it was above board in all respects. Price Waterhouse issued several audit reports certifying the financial soundness of the Mission's administration.

The task of the Mission, in this instance, was to monitor the application of sanctions imposed by Belgrade against Pale and it did this professionally. The precedent, however, is one that could be used, as needed, on specifically human rights tasks where required. The ICFY Mission showed that the mediators, on their own authority, could establish and operate for a period of three years a Mission of hundreds of personnel, operating in a framework of accountability outside of the United Nations administrative rigidity, and render credible reports to the negotiators and the international community. The precedent is one that offers much to peace negotiators wishing to establish or use *ad hoc* international human rights field missions in situations of concern.

V The High Representative for Bosnia and Herzegovina

A noteworthy peace implementation concept that came out of the Dayton peace conference on Bosnia and Herzegovina was the establishment of the position of High Representative for the Implementation of the Peace Agreement on Bosnia and Herzegovina, who was given a mandate to mobilize and coordinate all civilian activities and to be the final authority regarding civilian implementation of the peace agreement. On 15 December, 1995, the Security Council, by its resolution 1031 (1995), endorsed the establishment of a High Representative to "mobilize and, as appropriate, give guidance to and coordinate the activities of the civilian organizations and agencies" involved with the civilian aspects of the Peace Agreement.

Article II of the Dayton Peace Agreement directed the High Representative to Monitor the implementation of the peace settlement; maintain close contact with the parties to the Agreement, to promote their full compliance with all civilian aspects of the Agreement; Co-ordinate the activities of the civilian organizations and agencies in Bosnia and Herzegovina to ensure the efficient implementation of the civilian aspects of the peace settlement. The High Representative was to: respect their autonomy within their spheres of operation while, as necessary, giving general guidance to them about the impact of their activities on the implementation of the peace agreement; facilitate, as the High Representative judged necessary, the resolution of any difficulties arising in connection with civilian implementation; participate in meetings of donor organizations; report periodically on progress to the United Nations, European Union, United States, Russian Federation and other interested governments, parties and organisations; and provide guidance to the United Nations International Police Task Force (IPTF).

One might mention here three peacekeeping operations that back-stopped the implementation of the Dayton accords and the efforts of the High Representative: the deployment of NATO forces, (IFOR and SFOR) and the deployment of a United Nations policing operation, (UNMIBH).

Conclusion

The aim of this chapter has been to present the peacekeeping blueprints that have emerged from some peace conferences with a view to noting how peacemaking and peacekeeping were interwoven in situations like Central America and the former Yugoslavia and also with a view to showing how peacekeeping was used to facilitate peacemaking. Perhaps the most inventive experience was that of Contadora-Esquipulas, but ICFY's experiment in preventive deployment and in border-monitoring on the Drina were also quite innovative. Dayton's resort to the concept of the High Representative could be useful in the future – but with one caveat: the power must be there to make it work. In Bosnia, the High Representative had the power of NATO and Western nations behind him. Without this kind of power a High Representative would soon become unrepresentative!

CHAPTER 6

Peacebuilding

Introduction

Peacebuilding as a specialised term came into usage after the publication of Secretary-General Boutros Boutros-Ghali's Agenda for Peace of 1992. It has come, in contemporary parlance, to signify mainly post-conflict peacebuilding. However, it has a generic meaning, embracing activities designed to promote and reinforce peace. The first draft of Agenda for Peace used the term in this sense but the final version narrowed it down to its post-conflict dimensions.

This chapter will discuss peacebuilding in its post-conflict sense when discussing the role of international peace conferences. It deserves to be mentioned, however, that from the outset, international peace conferences have contributed to generic peacebuilding in a variety of ways. In the practice of the Italian city states, they contributed to stabilisation regimes intended to shore up the peace. The same may be said of the early conferences held within the broader European practice. The Congress of Westphalia established a public order of Europe that laid down the ground rules for relations among European states and these ground rules were subsequently extended world-wide. The Congress of Vienna, by establishing a Concert of the leading powers, was meant to head off disputes that could lead to broader conflict. This preserved order until the breakdown of the First World War.

President Wilson's championship of the League of Nations, which the Paris Peace Conference of 1919 endorsed, had as its fundamental rationale the preservation of peace. This was continued at the San Francisco conference that established the United Nations. All of these were essentially peacebuilding ideas in the broader sense of the term. So was the idea of the peaceful settlement of disputes through arbitration which the Hague Peace Conferences promoted.

In the narrower sense of post-conflict peacebuilding, specifically efforts to help nations coming out of conflict to repair damage and tackle root causes of conflict, one does not find much in the practice of international peace conferences up to the Paris Peace Conference of 1946, where treaties were concluded with defeated German allies after the Second World War. The peace treaty with Japan concluded at the San Francisco conference in 1951 had some elements of post-conflict peacebuilding. But it is in more recent practice that one finds distinct traces of post-conflict peacebuilding efforts at international peace

 | DOI 10.1163/9789004245907_008

conferences. The Contadora process on Central America was probably the most notable.

The International Conference on the Former Yugoslavia sought to make a contribution through its Working Group on Confidence-Building and Security Measures, its Working Group on Economic Issues, its Working Group on Ethnic Communities, Nationalities and Minorities, and its Working Group on Succession Issues. However, its efforts could only come to fruition after the Dayton Peace Conference that ended the conflict in Bosnia and helped end the conflict in Croatia. The Dayton Peace Conference had significant post-conflict peacebuilding blueprints. The Bonn conference on Afghanistan also had notable peacebuilding ideas. In this chapter we shall discuss these five conferences: San Francisco on Japan, Contadora, ICFY, Dayton and the Bonn conference on Afghanistan

I The Japanese Peace Treaty, 1951

The Japanese peace treaty of 1951 was concluded after the Cold War had descended on the world and Western powers, notably the USA, were keen on making Japan a power friendly to the western alliance. This undoubtedly influenced the content of the Japanese peace treaty. The peace treaty with Japan was signed on the same day, 8 September, 1951, as the United States-Japanese Security Treaty. In Article I of this treaty Japan granted the USA the right to dispose United States land , air and sea forces in and about Japan. Such forces might be utilized to contribute to the maintenance of international peace and security in the Far East and to the security of Japan against armed attack from without, including assistance given at the express request of the Japanese Government to put down large-scale internal riots and disturbances in Japan, caused through instigation or intervention by an outside power or powers.

In the second preambular paragraph of the Treaty of Peace with Japan, Japan declared its intention to apply for membership in the United Nations and, in all circumstances to conform to the principles of the Charter of the United Nations; to strive to realize the objectives of the Universal Declaration of Human Rights; to seek to create within Japan conditions of stability and well-being as defined in Articles 55 and 56 of the Charter of the United Nations and already initiated by post-surrender Japanese legislation; and in public and private trade and commerce to conform to internationally accepted fair practices. The operative parts of the treaty dealt with Peace, Territory, Security, Political and Economic Clauses, Claims and property, Settlement of Disputes, and Final Clauses.

Between 1945 and 1951 American administration of Japan had already laid down the foundations for what is today's modern Japan, including its constitution and its commitment to constitutionalism, the rule of law and respect for human rights, all core peacebuilding ideas. Under Article 5 of the Peace Treaty, dealing with security, Japan accepted the obligations set forth in Article 2 of the Charter of the United Nations, and in particular the following obligations: (i) to settle its international disputes by peaceful means in such a manner that international peace and security, and justice, are not endangered; (ii) to refrain in its international relations from the threat or use of force against the territorial integrity or political independence of any State or in any other manner inconsistent with the Purposes of the United Nations; (iii) to give the United Nations every assistance in any action it takes in accordance with the United Nations Charter and to refrain from giving assistance to any State against which the United Nations may take preventive or enforcement action. The Allied Powers for their part confirmed that they would be guided by the principles of the Article 2 of the Charter of the United Nations in their relations with Japan.

Japan emerged from the Second World War as one of the most successful economic powers whose stability has continued ever since. While the efforts of the Japanese people were primarily responsible for this, the foundations laid by General Mac Arthur and American administration helped lay the foundations for this. The San Francisco conference of 1951 at which the Japanese peace treaty was concluded took place in the context of US administration and of Allied efforts to turn Japan into a friendly power, a policy that concluded remarkably. The post-conflict peacebuilding efforts towards Japan were already well underway when the Japanese peace treaty was concluded. However, as seen above, the treaty did contain important structural provisions designed to anchor Japan in the post-war peace.

II Contadora/Esquipulas Processes

The Contadora/Esquipulas process on Central America are more apposite when it comes to discussing the peacebuilding contributions of international peace conferences. The Contadora/Esquipulas processes are remarkable from three perspectives: first, they contributed to building up a framework of principles and policies which could be used to help bring the conflicts to an end. Second, those policies and principles were anchored in the peace agreements eventually concluded; and third, those policies and principles have subsequently become part of the Central American public order that guides the aspirations of Central American nations. All three of these were solid peacebuilding contributions.

By way of background it needs to be borne in mind that the Central American countries, in the backyard of the USA, had been basically 'Banana Republics' in which privileged rich landowners lorded it over the poor, the overwhelming majorities of their countries. In the context of the cold war, the USA was content with this situation. The prevailing attitude towards unscrupulous rulers such as Somosa of Nicaragua was 'He may be a son of a bitch but he is our son of a bitch'! The conflicts in Central America were, at base, conflicts for economic and social justice. Viewing it through the lens of the global struggle with communism, the USA was keen to support the prevailing order with financing, arms and ammunitions.

It was in these circumstances that the Foreign Ministers and Heads of State of the Contadora processes launched their initiatives to take charge of the peace processes, a story we related in an earlier chapter on peacemaking. The Contadora leaders put down principles and objectives that were rolled along and further developed and eventually included in peace agreements. They emphasised the role of democracy, the rule of law, economic and social justice, peaceful settlement of disputes, the verification of agreements, peacekeeping and observer operations. The principles, objectives, and approaches of Contadora were taken forward by the Esquipulas process and together they helped shape the new public order of Central America.

Even though the wars have ended, the countries are still striving to consolidate their democracies, reinforce the rule of law, entrench human rights, and pursue economic and social justice. Historical inquiries have been launched into, for example, the patterns of gross violations of human rights in Guatemala. A new ethos has been superimposed on the political culture of Central America, and this is the greatest peacebuilding contribution of the Contadora/Esquipulas processes, a truly remarkable achievement.

III ICFY

The International Conference on the Former Yugoslavia, had a Confidence Building Working Group[1] and an Economic Issues Working Group.[2] The former, led by Vicente Berasategui, a senior official from the UN disarmament

1 See B.G. Ramcharan (Ed.), Collected Papers of the International Conference on the Former Yugoslavia. 2 Vols. The Hague, Martinus Nijhoffs, 1996.

2 Ibid.

secretariat concentrated, while it lasted, on the regulation and control of weapons and never had occasion to address broader confidence-building measures that would come under the heading of today's concept of peacebuilding measures. The Economic Issues Working Group, led by a senior economist from the secretariat of the European Community, Jean Durieux, sought to plan for the economic future of the area but, in the end, was overtaken by fighting on the ground. A Succession Issues Working Group[3] of the ICFY did groundwork for the eventual negotiations among the successor republics on the division of assets and liabilities. It thus contributed to peacebuilding in the long term.

ICFYs Working Group on Ethnic and National Communities and Minorities was one of the unheralded peacebuilding mechanisms of ICFY during its efforts for peace with justice in the former Yugoslavia. In line with the arrangements established at the London Conference in August, 1992, the Working Group started its extensive work with a plenary meeting in Geneva on 15 September, 1992 with the participation of delegations from Slovenia, Croatia, Bosnia and Herzegovina, and Macedonia. The framework for the discussions was Chapter II of the Treaty Provisions for a Convention that the Carrington Conference had been working on. All those present reconfirmed their commitment to the principles of the Convention. The delegations from Serbia, Montenegro and the Croatian Serbs were not able to travel to the meeting.

During the same week there were talks in Geneva with Albanians from Kosovo, Albania, and Macedonia, Muslims from Serbia, Muslims and Albanians from Montenegro, Hungarians from Vojvodina, Croats from Vojvodina, and Serbs from Croatia. A note on these meetings reported:

> These talks showed, probably with the exception of Macedonia, pictures of continuous and at places dangerous ethnic conflicts that were to be taken up urgently with the Governments concerned. There will be another Working Group Plenum on 2 November in Geneva.[4]

For the next three and a half years, this Working Group, under its able chairman, German Ambassador Geert Ahrens, would patiently and persistently foster discussions on all of these situations, keeping parties talking, and endeavouring to work out negotiated solutions to perceived problems.

In order to discuss complaints and to hear the opinion of the Belgrade Government on matters falling within the province of the Working Group, a

3 Ibid.

4 Note dated 27 October, 1992 by Geert Ahrens, Chairman of the Working Group. Text in the possession of the author.

delegation travelled to Belgrade in the following week, 22–24 September. It reported that talks with Federal Ministers showed a general readiness to address critical issues, but also hesitation to accept ICFY mediation on some issues. "Moreover, there has so far not been a clear commitment of the Belgrade Governments, the Federal or the Serbian, to all of Chapter Two of the Treaty Provisions for the Convention."[5]

The Sub-Group on Macedonia held two meetings between Government representatives and Albanians in Geneva on 17 September, and in Skopje on 15 October. Ambassador Ahrens reported that although progress had been achieved, the overall situation of the Republic (economic blockade in the eyes of the Government), non-recognition, an upsurge of nationalism, made it increasingly difficult for the moderate Government to compromise on ethnic questions. He advised: "In my opinion, everything has to be done to uphold the so far positive internal development in Macedonia which is in real danger."[6]

The Sub-Group on Vojvodina and on the Sandzak was due to meet soon to start trilateral talks but there had been some hesitation in Belgrade. However, meetings had been held in Geneva, Belgrade and Subotica with Hungarians and Croats. Ambassador Ahrens reported that the situation in the Sandzak, "which is related to the Bosnian war, is alarming. Large numbers of Muslims have already left. Hopefully, the presence of CSCE observers there will help to defuse the tense situation on the ground which is a serious obstacle to meaningful dialogue."[7]

On the Serbs in Croatia, the Working Group held talks with Mr Goran Hadzic "President of the Republic of Krajina" and several meetings with Croatian representative. Mr Hadzic said that he was quite prepared for talks on human rights, economic and communication issues, but not on any form of Serbian autonomy inside Croatia. "The Krajina would rather resort to renewed warfare than become a part of Croatia again. It was not possible so far to convince Mr Hadzic or any other Knin representative that a solution has to be found on the basis of the London Principles."[8] Ambassador Ahrens would – and didcontinue his efforts.

Ambassador Ahrens reported that the most intensive work had been done in the Special Group on Kosovo. The basic approach agreed to by both sides was to try a pragmatic breakthrough in one important sector in order to

5 Ibid.

6 Ibid. It bears mentioning that thanks in part to the efforts of ICFY, Macedonia never descended into conflict.

7 Ibid.

8 Ibid.

improve the political atmosphere for talks on more fundamental issues where positions were still irreconcilable. The Albanians had chosen education. Ambassador Ahrens reported that after difficult and tedious preparations, in which the release from prison of the Chairman of the Albanian Teachers Federation was achieved, the first ICFY-sponsored talks between the Federal and the Serbian Governments from Belgrade, on one side, and Albanian representatives from Kosovo on the other, had taken place. On 14 October, all the parties had agreed on a statement which read as follows:

> 1. Representatives of the Government of the FRY and Serbia led by the Federal Minister of Education, Mr Ivic, and representatives of the Albanians met in Pristina on 13/14 October with the participation of the Geneva Conference Special Group on Kosovo, under the Chairmanship of Ambassador Ahrens. A representative of the CSCE mission was also present.
> 2. After detailed discussion of the problems of education in the Albanian language, the participants agreed that the present situation must be changed. They further agreed on the urgent desirability of the return to normal working conditions for schools and other educational institutions.
> 3. It was agreed that, to achieve this, it would be necessary to adopt a pragmatic approach requiring urgent resolution, without prejudice to the positions of the parties on broader political issues.
> 4. The Albanian representatives agreed to provide a list of schools and other educational institutions to be covered by the measures mentioned in (2); as well as a list of teaching plans and programmes.
>
> The Group agreed to meet again in Belgrade on 22 October. At that meeting discussions will be held on all the issues mentioned above and on the equal working status of teaching and educations personnel with the aim of reaching the necessary decisions for immediate action.[9]

Further talks were indeed continued on 22 October in Belgrade with meetings held with President D. Cosic, President of the FRY and with Mr I. Rugova, the Kosovar Albanian leader. They had both reaffirmed their commitment to the necessity of changing the then prevailing situation in the field of education, and to the urgent need for a return to normal conditions in schools and other educational institutions in Kosovo as set out in the statement of 14 October.

9 Ibid.

Ambassador Ahrens and his Working Group would patiently and persistently continue working on the foregoing and similar issues for the next four years and would help nurture agreements on practical issues of human and minority rights on the ground.

IV Dayton

The 1995 Dayton accord on Bosnia provided for some of the most extensive peacebuilding efforts in the history of international peace conferences. In the preceding chapter we discussed the establishment of the Office of High Representative which had many dimensions, one of them distinctly being peacebuilding efforts. The post of High Representative endured for over a decade and a half and continues as of the time of writing.

Another distinctly peacebuilding contribution was the establishment of the Human Rights Chamber for Bosnia and Herzegovina, basically a dedicated human rights court whose composition provided for a majority of international judges. The Chamber adjudicated numerous landmark cases, including a claim for compensation for the victims of the Srebrenica massacres.

Peacebuilding contributions were also provided by several international organizations, including the UN, OSCE, the EU, and NATO. They all accompanied the process of peace-consolidation and nation-building in Bosnia and Herzegovina, a process that remains fragile even at the time of writing, a decade and a half after the Dayton conference. But for these peacebuilding efforts one does not know what the future of Bosnia might have been.

V Bonn Conferences on Afghanistan

In Afghanistan, following Soviet invasion and defeat, Taliban control, Al Quaeda terrorism against the USA, the US-led international coalition's invasion of the country and dislodging of the Taliban, the country was in need of peacebuilding from ground level, block by block. At the time of writing its future is still precarious. Two international conferences, held in Bonn in 2001 and 2011 contributed the foundation blocks for peacebuilding.[10]

10 See, generally, M. Field and R. Ahmed, A Review of the 2001 Bonn Conference and Application to the Road in Afghanistan. Centre for Strategic Research, Institute for National Strategic Studies, National Defense University, Washington, D.C., November 2011.

The 2001 conference produced the Agreement on Provisional Arrangements in Afghanistan Pending the Re-Establishment of Permanent Government Institutions. The Agreement provided for the establishment of an Interim Authority, interim legal framework and judicial system, interim administration, and a special independent commission for the convening of the Emergency Loya Jirga (parliament). Annexes to the Agreement provided for an international security force, the role of the United Nation s during the interim period, and made some specific requests to the United Nations.

The Agreement provided that the judicial power shall be independent and shall be vested in a Supreme Court of Afghanistan, and such other courts as may be established by the Interim Administration. The Interim Administration "shall establish, with the assistance of the United Nations, a Judicial Commission, to rebuild the domestic judicial system in accordance with Islamic principles, international standards, the rule of law and Afghan legal traditions." The Interim Administration shall also, with the assistance of the United Nations, establish an independent Human Rights Commission, whose responsibilities would include human rights monitoring, investigation of violations of human rights, and development of domestic human rights mechanisms. The Interim Administration might, with the assistance of the United Nations, also establish any other commissions to review matters not covered in the Agreement. Under the aegis of the Bonn Agreement a Constitution was drafted for Afghanistan and a Commission on Human Rights established.

In December, 2011 another International Conference on Afghanistan was held, again in Bonn. It had been preceded the previous month by a conference in Istanbul called to discuss Afghan security, recruitment, training and equipment of Afghan security forces, as well as the reconciliation process. The Istanbul conference also focused on regional economic needs. The Bonn 2011 International Conference on Afghanistan adopted Conference Conclusions recalled that ten years ago Afghanistan had charter a new path towards a sovereign, peaceful, prosperous and democratic future and that the International Community had accepted the responsibility to help Afghanistan along that path. "Together we have achieved substantial progress over these ten years, more than in any other period in Afghanistan's history. Never before have the Afghan people, and especially Afghan women, enjoyed comparable access to services, including education and health, or seen greater development of infrastructure across the country. Al Quaeda has been disrupted, and Afghanistan's national security institutions are increasingly able to assume responsibility for a secure and independent Afghanistan."[11]

11 Para. 3.

The Conference recognized that "our work is not yet done" and stressed the need for a political solution in order to achieve peace and security in Afghanistan. To ensure enduring stability, in addition to building Afghanistan's capacity to defend itself, a political process was necessary, of which negotiation and reconciliation were essential elements. In addition, the process of reintegration would pave the way for postconflict rehabilitation of Afghan society through improvement of security, community development and local governance.

No one knows what the future of Afghanistan will be like. But one could see here evidence of two international conferences contributing to the peacebuilding process in the country. We must await the judgment of history to see how successful they were.

Conclusion

It is not clear whether any general lessons can be learned from the peacebuilding experiences of the international peace conferences discussed in this chapter. Each situation shaped the peacebuilding approaches attempted. Contadora-Esquiplulas, in this chapter also, is worthy of particular note because they sought to build foundations for the future grounded in democracy, human rights, social justice, and equitable problem-solving.

The 1951 peace treaty with Japan laid the foundations for modern Japan, a nation anchored in democracy, the rule of law and liberal governance subscribing to international human rights norms. The Dayton peace accord has held Bosnia and Herzegovina together and sought to steer it on a course towards tolerance, democracy, and liberal governance.

Afghanistan is a work in process, and the challenges remain daunting. It proves the point that each case must be approached on its own specificities, with a generous dose of hope!

CHAPTER 7

Human Rights

Introduction

A significant involvement with human rights issues at international peace conferences goes back to the Congresses of Westphalia and Vienna. The latter saw accords on the abolition of slavery and the protection of minorities. Human Rights were prominently discussed at the Versailles and San Francisco conferences. In the twentieth century, the Central American peace conferences and conferences on the former Yugoslavia built peace packages on strong human rights foundations.

Westphalia, 1648

The Treaty of Osnabruck, which came out of the Westphalian process and was signed in 1648 at the end of the Thirty Years War, provided for a degree of toleration for Protestants in Catholic States and for Catholics in States which had established a Reformed Church. But "it did not go so far as to provide for freedom of thought, conscience and religion for all individuals and groups. Later, under the Treaty of Berlin of 1878, the great European Powers compelled the newly recognized independent and autonomous States of Bulgaria, Montenegro, Romania and Serbia, as well as the Ottoman Empire, to assure religious freedom to all their nationals."[1]

The Congress of Vienna

The Congress of Vienna was mainly about power and politics. But it did register historic agreements on the curtailment of slavery and for the protection of particular minorities. The building blocks laid at Vienna on minority protection would be considerably expanded at the Paris Peace Conference a century later.

David King, in his book, Vienna, 1814, writes that in December, 1814, Talleyrand had proposed that the Great Powers establish a committee to look into the question of the slave trade more closely but this had been blocked by

1 T. Stahnke and J.P. Martin, Religion and Basic Human Rights: Basic Documents. New York, Centre for the Study of Human Rights, Columbia University, 1998, p. 11.

 DOI 10.1163/9789004245907_009

the protests of Spain and Portugal. In the middle of January, 1815.[2] Castlereah renewed the call for a committee, and this time one was appointed by the Committee of Eight of the Vienna Congress. Castlereah, according to King, was particularly anxious to address "…the terrible practice of African slavery. To the horror of an increasing number of reformers, there was an entire industry built on the buying, selling, and trading of human beings."[3]

Abolitionists and special interests were both present at the meetings of the Slavery Commission. Immediately, the commission encountered the problem of implementation that still bedevils the human rights regime in the twenty-first century: "Specifically, one immediate problem that this Slavery Commission encountered was enforcement. If the Vienna Congress banned the slave trade, how would they make sure that this policy was obeyed?"[4] Castlereah thought that naval officers would take it upon themselves to board vessels and search for transgressors.[5] Opponents of a restriction of the slave trade objected that Britain was already well stocked with slaves in its colonies and that a ban would give it permanent advantages.[6]

Castlereah engaged in some hard bargaining and diplomacy and, on February 8, 1815, the Great Powers issued a joint declaration condemning the practice as "repugnant to the principles of humanity and universal morality." They also agreed on the importance of putting an end to slavery. The slave trade should be abolished as soon as possible. France promised to do so in five years, Spain and Portugal in eight years. David King comments: "Admittedly, this was slow and tentative, an abolition of neither slavery nor even of the trade itself. Yet it was a start, and human rights, for the first time, had been made a subject of a peace conference."[7]

Harold Nicholson noted that in the course of the negotiations on the curtailment of slavery two new diplomatic devices were invented:

> It was suggested at one stage that the produce of those countries or colonies which refused to abolish the Slave Trade should be excluded from European markets…This is the first appearance in diplomatic practice of the peace-time imposition of economic sanctions. A second device which was applied in connection with the Abolition of the Slave Trade

2 David King, Vienna, 1814. New York, Harmony Books, 2008, p. 215.

3 Ibid, p. 214.

4 Ibid, p. 215.

5 Ibid, p. 215.

6 Ibid, pp. 215–216.

7 Ibid, p. 217.

> was the institution in London, sitting at the Foreign Office under Castlereah's chairmanship, of a Conference of Ambassadors charged with the duty of watching the execution of the several agreements come to....(T)he constitution of such a 'watching committee' on the part of the Great Powers was at the time a startling innovation and provided a useful precedent for the future.[8]

Harold Nicholson also recorded that the Jewish Community in Germany had succeeded in having the question of their rights inserted on the agenda of the German Committee. "Such rights as they had already obtained in the several German States were formally confirmed together with a somewhat vague recommendation that these rights should be extended."[9]

Harold Nicholson further pointed out that Vienna produced the first recorded agreement for the protection of a minority. It was agreed that the Act of Union between The Netherlands and Belgium "should contain clauses guaranteeing to the Belgian populations complete religious toleration and commercial equality; and these stipulations, incidentally, represent the first 'Minority Treaties' to figure in diplomatic practice."[10]

The Paris Peace Conference

The Versailles negotiations in 1918–1919 and related bilateral negotiations would expand considerably arrangements for the protection of minorities in new states created in pursuance of US President Woodrow Wilson's principle of self-determination. This story has been admirably told by Julius Stone in his classic work on The League of Nations and the Protection of Minorities[11] and we do not need to discuss it further here. Suffice it to say that the experience of the League of Nations in supervising the guarantees of minority rights would contribute to a stock of experience for the protection of human rights that would be invaluable for the successor of the League of Nations, the United Nations.

However, the Paris Peace Conference and President Wilson would not cover themselves in glory because of the way that they scotched a Japanese proposal

---

8 H. Nicholson, The Congress of Vienna. A Study in Allied Unity: 1812–1822. London, Constable, 1946, pp. 215–216.

9 Ibid.

10 H. Nicholson, The Congress of Vienna. A Study in Allied Unity: 1812–1822. London, Constable, 1946, p. 208.

11 London, Stevens, 1932.

for the Covenant of the League to include a clause on racial equality and non discrimination. Margaret Macmillan tells the story in her book, The Peacemakers. Six Months that Changed the World.[12] Japan was a rising power and its emigrants in countries such as the USA and Australia were encountering increasing prejudice. So were its diplomats and citizens travelling abroad.

The Japanese delegation at the Paris Peace Conference therefore came from Tokyo with specific instructions to propose the inclusion in the Covenant of the League of Nations of a provision against racial discrimination. The Japanese delegation lobbied the leading powers behind the scenes and received little support from anyone. Britain, France, the USA, Australia, and New Zealand were distinctly uncomfortable and some, such as Australia and the USA, downright opposed.

On 13 February, 1919, within the framework of the Commission on the League of Nations, Japan made a proposal that the clause in the draft Covenant providing for religious liberty include a provision to the effect that all the members of the League would agree to treat each other's citizens equally without any discrimination. The Japanese proposal met with benign neglect and the draft covenant went forward with no provision on racial or religious equality.

The Japanese delegation pursued the matter still but "The loudest opposition to the racial equality clause came from the British Empire delegation, in particular from Hughes of Australia."[13] On 10 April 1919, at a meeting of the Commission on the League of Nations the Japanese delegation indicated their intention to move a formal amendment and did so the following day, on 11 April when they proposed that a reference to racial equality be included in the preamble to the covenant.

President Wilson was presiding over the Commission. Some delegations supported the Japanese proposal but during the meeting, as delegations were speaking. President Wilson's confidant, Col. House, passed Wilson a note: "The trouble is that if this Commission should pass it, it would surely raise the race issue throughout the world."[14] Wilson urged the Japanese to withdraw their amendment. "When a majority voted for the amendment, Wilson, with the dexterity he had no doubt learned as a university president, announced that because there were strong objections to the amendment it could not carry."[15] If ever there were an infamous act, it was this. As Macmillan wrote, "...Wilson

12 London, John Murray, 2001, Chapter 23, Japan and racial equality.

13 Ibid, p. 328.

14 Ibid, p. 329.

15 Ibid, p. 329.

himself was not especially liberal when it came to race. He was a southerner, after all, and although he had appealed for black votes in his first campaign for the presidency, he had done little for blacks once he was in office."[16]

The Japanese delegation chose not to challenge this 'dubious ruling' and so the racial equality clause did not become part of the covenant.[17] As we shall see in the next section, the atrocities against Jews before and during the Second World War would make the principle of equality a corner-stone of the United Nations Charter drafted at the San Francisco conference.

The San Francisco Conference

There was no comprehensive international peace conference after the Second World War. Rather, the post war peace was constructed at war-time allied conferences in a variety of locations, at the San Francisco conference in 1945 which drafted the United Nations Charter, in some treaties concluded at Paris in 1951, and in the Japanese Peace Treaty concluded at a conference in San Francisco in 1951. We are concerned here with the San Francisco conference of 1945.

We saw earlier in this chapter that the Congress of Vienna had committed the major powers to the abolition of slavery and had provided for guarantees of minority rights. The Paris Peace Conference had declined to include in the Covenant of the League of Nations a provision against racial discrimination proposed by Japan but did provide for minority guarantees in various treaties and established a system of supervision within the League of Nations. The International Labour Organization established after the Paris Peace Conference also pioneered the development of a code of treaties and recommendations on international labour rights and a system of supervision of those rights in the ILO.

But the atrocities committed in Germany on the eve of the Second World War and by it during the war led allied leaders, spurred on by civil society, to commit to a post-war world in which the peace would be grounded in respect for individual human rights and in economic and social progress and equity. This commitment was formalised in the United Nations Charter and, thus, the San Francisco conference and the Charter it produced must take their place as a watershed in world history.

16 Ibid, p. 328.

17 Ibid, p. 329. See, further, N. Shimazu, *Japan, Race and Equality. The Racial Equality Proposal of 1919*. Oxon, Routledge, 1998.

The human rights contribution of the United Nations Conference on International Organization, held in San Francisco in 1945, has been told in detail elsewhere and here we need only focus on those parts of the story relevant from the perspective of international peace conferences. The first thing to note about San Francisco is that like all major international peace conferences before, political interests were predominant throughout. By the time the San Francisco conference was convened, the Cold War was already descending on the world and the major powers, including the USA and UK, had less interest in human rights issues than while the war was being fought. When smaller countries such as Australia proposed that the United Nations should be given the competence not only to promote international cooperation for the universal realisation of human rights but also to protect those rights, the major powers would not accept the mandate of protection, which did not find its place in the Charter. This was an epoch of colonies held by the UK and France, of gulags in the USSR, and of segregation in the USA.

The second thing to note is the influence of NGOs and civil society organizations which were present at San Francisco in good numbers, unlike previous international peace conferences. It was the lobbying of NGOs that brought about the six major human rights provisions of the Charter.

The third thing to note is that at San Francisco some countries proposed the inclusion in the Charter of the United Nations of an International Bill of Human Rights. Shortage of time did not allow the elaboration of such a Charter at San Francisco, but the conference entrusted the drafting of such a Bill to the Commission on Human Rights whose establishment it mandated under Article 68 of the Charter. The Commission on Human Rights, when it set about its work, envisaged the International Bill of Human Rights as consisting of three parts: a declaration, one or more conventions, and measures of implementation. The Commission worked out the Universal Declaration of Human Rights, the two International Covenants, and some measures of implementation. The work of the Commission has subsequently been the foundation for a veritable international code of human rights and various arrangements and machineries that seek to promote and protect human rights. One could say that San Francisco laid the basis for today's universal culture of human rights.

The fourth thing to note about San Francisco is its commitment to the principles of equality and non-discrimination, which are prominent in the Charter and also in the Universal Declaration and in subsequent human rights treaties.

The work begun at San Francisco is still underway and there are major problems still in realising the universal realisation of human rights. But San Francisco started a new era with human rights at the centre of international affairs for the first time in human history.

The Central American Peace Processes

As we saw in an earlier chapter, leaders of the Contadora process put down principles and objectives that were rolled along and further developed and eventually included in peace agreements. They emphasised the role of democracy, the rule of law, economic and social justice, peaceful settlement of disputes, the verification of agreements, peacekeeping and observer operations. The principles, objectives, and approaches of Contadora were taken forward by the Esquipulas process and together they helped shape the new public order of Central America.

The Human Rights Division of ONUSAL

We discussed the United Nations operations in El Salvador in the chapter on peacekeeping earlier. Here, we look further at the operations of its Human Rights Division, which was responsible for verifying the implementation of the Human Rights Agreement. The Division comprised some 30 human rights observers and legal advisers. Its Regional Coordinators also dealt with all the human rights aspects of ONUSAL's mandate and reported to the Director of the Human Rights Division. The active verification carried out by the Division was directed not only at an objective recording of facts, but also at the exercise of good offices aimed at assisting efforts by Salvadoreans to find a remedy to violations. The Division also cooperated with Salvadorean institutions to strengthen their ability to work in promoting human rights. Of particular importance in this regard was the Division's activities with human rights non-governmental organizations, with a view to contributing to the training of their personnel and enhancing their leadership capacity.[18] During the course of the Mission, the Director of the Human Rights Division prepared a number of periodic reports on the situation of human rights in the country. These reports were submitted by the UN Secretary-General to the General Assembly and the Security Council.

MINUGUA

The peacemaking and peacekeeping efforts relating to Guatemala were a continuation of the rolling Contadora-Esquipulas processes that then fused with

18 This summary is taken from http://www.un.org/Depts/DPKO/Missions/onusal_b.htm, consulted on 12 September, 2012.

the efforts of the United Nations Secretary-General and interested governments outside of the Central American region. In 1994, the Government of Guatemala and the Unidad Revolunionaria Nacional Guatemalteca (URNG) agreed to resume negotiations to end the longest conflict then running in Latin America. In September, 1994, the UN General Assembly decided t establish a Human Rights Verification Mission in Guatemala, acting on a recommendation by the UN Secretary-General that such a mission could make a contribution to mitigating a persisting pattern of human rights abuses. From November, 1994, MINUGUA carried out verification activities and institution-building throughout the country. More than 250 human rights monitors, legal experts, indigenous specialists and police were posted throughout Guatemala, including in its remotest areas. Their presence and verification activities focused public attention on human rights and the related problem of impunity, reinforcing the declining trend in political violence.[19]

The UN Verification Mission in Guatemala (MINUGUA) officially ended in December 2004 after a decade of verifying human rights and helping the country implement its peace accords. In all, 430 UN Volunteers performed key tasks such as assessing human rights violations, facilitating the process of rights verification at the community level, and keeping the public informed about progress made. Working closely with counterparts in government, civil society organizations and human rights institutions, UN Volunteers played a vital role in ensuring that acquired knowledge, including the value of volunteerism in protecting and protecting human rights, was retained and continued to serve the cause of human rights in Guatemala.[20]

The Human Rights Approach of the EC Conference

Lord Carrington, in his efforts for the formation of a loose confederation among the Yugoslav Republics put on the table draft "Treaty Provisions for the Convention" which would place the new relations between the Republics on comprehensive arrangements, including supervisory mechanisms for the protection human rights and special status for certain groups and States.[21] Chapter II of the draft treaty dealt with human rights.

---

19 This account is taken from http://www.un.org/Depts/DPKO/Missions/minugua.htm, consulted on 12 September, 2012.

20 This account is taken from http://www.unv.org/en/what-we-do/thematic-areas/human-rights/doc/unv-and-human..., consulted on 12 September, 2012.

21 The text of the draft convention is reproduced in UN doc. S/23169.

Article 2 envisaged that the Republics would guarantee enumerated human rights grounded in instruments such as the Universal Declaration of Human Rights, the International Covenants, the Final Act of the Helsinki Conference, the European Convention for the Protection of Human Rights and Fundamental Freedoms and other international and European instruments. It also envisaged that the Republics would guarantee human rights as applied to national or ethnic groups as embodied in a number of international and European instruments including the International Convention on the Elimination of Racial Discrimination and the Convention on the Prevention of the Crime of Genocide.

Furthermore, the Republics would undertake to guarantee enumerated rights of persons belonging to a national or ethnic group. These included the principle of non-discrimination, the right to be protected against any activity capable of threatening their existence, and the guarantee that no disadvantage shall arise from a person's choice to belong or not to belong to a national or ethnic group.

Areas in which persons belonging to a national or ethnic group formed a majority would enjoy a special status of autonomy. Such a status would provide for the right to have and show the national emblem of that area; an administrative structure, including a regional police force and a judiciary responsible for matters concerning the area, which reflected the composition of the population of the area. There would also be appropriate provisions for international monitoring.

The Republics would provide for international monitoring of the implementation of the special status of autonomy. To this end, they would conclude agreements that would provide for a permanent international body to monitor the implementation of the special status of autonomy.

The draft convention envisaged the establishment of a Court of Human Rights which would have jurisdiction within the republics to consider appeals from courts in the republics involving questions of human rights. It also envisaged the establishment of Mixed Commissions where such mixed commissions might assist in avoiding or dealing with disputes concerning human rights and the rights of ethnic or national groups and areas having special status.

The Principles of the London Conference

At the start of the negotiations with the Bosnian parties, the lead negotiator on Bosnia and Herzegovina, Martti Ahtisaari, gave them the following "Checklist of London Principles Relating to the future constitution of BH":

(1) The guarantee of the highest standards of human rights, including individual rights and fundamental freedoms in a democratic society, as set out in a series of important human rights instruments of the United Nations, the Council of Europe, and the Conference on Security and Cooperation in Europe;
(2) The special guarantee of the rights of ethnic and national communities, as well as of minorities;
(3) Constitutional and legal structures that can assure democratic governance and the protection of the above-mentioned rights;
(4) Respect for international treaties and agreements.[22]

ICFY Negotiations on the Foundations of International and European Human Rights Norms

From the very outset of the work of ICFY, as the Bosnian delegations advanced claims in the respect of the rights of the constituent peoples of Bosnia and Herzegovina, ICFY personnel raised fundamental issues of principle regarding the human rights foundations of a future peace agreement. Thus, on 21 September, 1991, the late Paul Szasz, Legal Adviser of ICFY, wrote a memorandum titled "Problems in Basing Political Institutions on National or Ethnic Status."[23] Szasz wrote:

> This note will discuss some of the technical difficulties that might be anticipated in including any provisions relating to ethnic or national or similar groupings in the institutional provisions of the proposed BiH constitution (as distinguished from those relating to human rights – though even there, general principles on minority rights would be much easier than any that refer to specific groupings). These considerations are aside from any related anomaly of introducing such provisions into an internationally brokered instrument in the last decade of the 20th century, against the entire trend of international human rights developments of the past several decades (e.g., in particular, the firm rejection of apartheid).
>
> If any institutional political rights are to be based on any group (national, ethnic or other) identification (i.e. in BiH: Muslim, Serb,

22 Document given by Martti Ahtisaari to the Bosnian delegations on 18 September, 1992. Document in the possession of the author.

23 Memorandum in the possession of the author.

> Croat), for example, if one of the houses of the legislature is to be composed of a particular number of members of each group and/or if the executive is to have a multi-group composition, it will be necessary to define in some way how the group representatives in the legislature/executive are to be chosen, i.e. how they are to be elected. For this, there would seem to be two possible approaches:...(a) geographic – based on the assumption that identifiable regions have a pure enough group composition that representatives elected from those regions are, in effect, representatives of that group; (b) personal – which would require classifying citizens to determine which of them may vote for which group representatives.

In discussing these two possible approaches Szasz cautioned that one or both could be the pretext for resorting to, or allowing the continuation, and acceptance the results of "ethnic cleansing." He clearly favoured an approach that based itself on international human rights norms.

1 *Guiding the Delegations on International Human Rights Law*

When discussions began with the three Bosnian parties in Geneva in the second half of September, 1992, Martti Ahtisaari, in addition to giving them a document recaputaling the key principles of the London Conference on human rights, invited each delegation to submit in writing its views on the future constitutional structure of Bosnia and Herzegovina, gave them checklists of issues for discussion based on the provisions of international and European human rights instruments, and requested Paul Szasz and this writer to brief each delegation, step by step, on the provisions of key international and European human rights instruments. Paul Szasz took each delegation separately through the main human rights instruments, explaining them, and answering questions from members of the delegations. This author took detailed notes on these briefings which are in the archives of the ICFY at the United Nations Office in Geneva and copies of which are also in the possession of the author.

The checklists provided to the delegations included the following:

- Checklist of principles related to the future Constitution, 18 September, 1992.
- Checklist of International Human Rights Instruments Relevant to a Constitution for Bosnia and Herzegovina, 22 September, 1992, revised on 25 September.
- List of human rights that might be considered for inclusion in, or other protection under the BiH Constitution, 25 September, 1992.

- Preliminary thoughts for discussion on implementation, enforcement and guarantees of human rights provisions of BiH Constitution, 25 September, 1992.
- Distribution of Governmental Responsibilities between Central Government and other Constituent Instruments (Request for indication of preferences), 29 September, 1992.

We provide below some excerpts from the Notes written by this author on the guidance sessions with each delegation. Mr Szasz first met with the Bosnian (Muslim) delegation on 25 September, 1992, Dr Haris Siladzic, Foreign Minister, Mr Pejanovic, Mr Ljubic, Mr Brkic, Mr Filipovic and Mr Lazovic. Mr Szasz began by introducing the checklists enumerated above. Foreign Minister Silajdzic said that his delegation's human rights expert had had to go back to Zagreb. The delegation would ask him to study the human rights documents provided. The note on the meeting reads:

> Foreign Minister Silajdzic stated that, while his delegation appreciated the work that had gone into preparing the documents, it was very difficult to discuss detailed questions on the human rights contents of the future constitution while aggression was continuing on the ground in Bosnia and Herzegovina. He stressed the urgency of implementing the agreements concluded in London.[24]

On Monday 28 September, 1992, Mr Szasz and this author met again with Mr Pejanovic, Mr Ljubic, Mr Filipovic, and Mr Lazovic of the Bosnian (Muslim) delegation. The note on the meeting reads:

> Mr Ljubic commented on one of the papers that the delegation had received…containing Preliminary thoughts for discussion on implementation, enforcement and guarantees of human rights in a future constitution of Bosnia and Herzegovina…He stated that he and his colleagues had studied these materials and would like to see the wholly domestic and partially international arrangements all incorporated into the future constitutions. If implemented faithfully they would provide full guarantee of human rights. He added that this paper had been well prepared. The proposals were good proposals and he and his colleagues would like all the parties to accept them.
>
> …

24 ICFY/BH/MTG. 11.

> Professor Pejanovic...fully agreed with Mr Ljubic about the importance of accepting international instruments as well as international supervision. He added that gross violations of human rights had appeared in Bosnia and Herzegovina only after the appearance on the scene of authorities beyond the control of the Government....[25]

On Monday, 28 November, Mr Szasz and this author met with Dr Koljevic and Mr Buha of the Bosnian Serb delegation. Mr Szasz began by introducing the checklists enumerated above. The note on the meeting reads:

> Dr Koljevic asked whether the idea was that the international human rights instruments being discussed would be listed in the future constitution, would be quoted from, or whether their essence would be included. Mr Szasz replied that perhaps the best method would be to list the rights, define them concisely, and provide that legislation would spell them out. It could also be provided that the rights included should be interpreted in accordance with, or in the spirit of, the international instruments...
>
> ...
>
> Dr Koljevic agreed with Mr Szasz that there was sense in starting the constitutional negotiations with the human rights provisions, as the parties appeared to be in general agreement as to those and because satisfactory provisions might ease the negotiations on other points.
>
> Mr Buha stated that his delegation needed some clarification on the issue of collective rights. In particular, he wished to know who would determine whether the three nations that make up Bosnia and Herzegovina could each have their own sovereign States, which appeared necessary to him, or whether the Serbs would remain in colonial domination by the other nations. He added that one should keep in mind the rights of peoples to self determination and not to be dominated. What would be the point of departure in dealing with such issues. Mr Szasz replied that answers to the nature of the future State would have to come out of the negotiations among the parties at the Conference.[26]

A guidance meeting was also held with the Bosnian Croat delegation. It was facilitated by a declaration by its leader, Mr Mate Boban, in a meeting with Vance, Owen, Ahtissari, with the participation of Szasz and this author, on 21 September, 1992. Mr Mate Boban had expressed his position on the human

25 ICFY/BH/MTG. 12.

26 ICFY/BH/MTG. 13.

rights foundations of the future constitution of Bosnia and Herzegovina as follows:

> With regard to human rights issues, Mr Boban stated that all three sides had signed the document of 31 March, 1992 which embraced all relevant international documents on human rights. It was on the basis of those principles that Bosnia and Herzegovina was recognized as a State. His side would sign and abide by any list of human rights instruments that Mr Ahtisaari came up with.[27]

2 *Principles and Realities*

On can see from the above, how earnest the ICFY negotiators were in striving to build their negotiating package on Bosnia and Herzegovina on the foundations of human rights. Unfortunately, even as the ICFY negotiators were attempting to take the delegations on the ground of principle, the violence and ethnic cleansing on the ground made these efforts seem unreal.

In a meeting with Mr Ahtisaari, in the presence of Szasz and this author, on 6 October, 1992, when Ahtisaari asked him for his position on human rights in the new constitution, the Bosnian Serb leader Dr Radovan Karadzic replied:

> ...All of the Constituent States would have to incorporate human rights guarantees in their constitutions. There could be coordination at the confederal level, with possible participation of the European Community, and human rights would also be written into the agreement between the three Constituent States. He agreed with Mr Ahtisaari that all the Republics of the FormerYugoslavia should have the same human rights standards.[28]

Two days later, on 8 October, Vance and Owen would have to dress him down as follows in a meeting when they confronted him about the continuing practice of ethnic cleansing:

> Mr Vance: First of all, ethnic cleansing is getting worse.
> Dr Karadzic: Need details.
> Mr Vance: We know that yesterday there had been a meeting of the BH Serb Parliament in Banja Luka at which the local administration had come under heavy attack because ethnic cleansing was not going fast

27 ICFY/BH/MTG. 8.
28 ICFY/BH/MTG. 19.

> enough; that was a totally unacceptable reaction to the Co-Chairmen's visit the previous week. Furthermore, the Muslim leaders who had talked to the Co-Chairmen during that visit had been called to the Serbian party headquarters for questioning; that too was entirely unacceptable. Finally, reports had reached us that in Kator Varos the entire Muslim population had been arrested.
>
> Dr Karadzic: The radicals, i.e. the extreme rightists, in Parliament were not representative of the whole; it was they who had conducted the attack. My party was more moderate.
> Mr Vance: Did the moderates speak up?
> Dr Karadzic: The majority in Parliament is opposed to the extreme rightists; however, the radicals are getting more and more influential. I guarantee that the Muslim leaders would be protected. In any event, what is happening to the Serbs in Sarajevo is much worse than anything in Banja Luka. The Muslims had just announced that they had just killed some 250 Serbs.
> Mr Vance: This cannot justify what is happening in Banja Luka. It was not acceptable to harass those who had spoken to the Co-Chairmen.
> Dr Karadzic: Mr Vance is right. If something like that should happen again, Dr Karadzic would replace the local party leader. But his moderates were losing influence to the radicals.
> Mr Vance: It wasn't apparent that Mr Karadzic was losing influence.
> Dr Karadzic: Showed pictures from a local magazine of foreign Muslims holding heads of slain Serbs.
> ...
> Lord Owen: Majority of EEC Foreign Ministers are for a War Crimes Tribunal. What about the reported arrest of Muslims in Kator Varos.
> Dr Karadzic: There is fighting going on around there.
> Mr Vance/Lord Owen: The horror there is unacceptable to the world community.

The UN peace operations in the former Yugoslavia saw courageous efforts for human rights monitoring on the part of the peacemakers, the peacekeepers, the UN Special Rapporteur, the Office of UN High Commissioner for Refugees, and the Office of the UN High Commissioner for Human Rights.

The Co-Chairmen of ICFY, Cyrus Vance and Lord Owen, convened on Thursday 11 March 1993 an informal meeting on future human rights monitoring in Bosnia and Herzegovina. The purpose of the meeting was to bring together representatives of NGOs working on human rights issues with UN human rights officials and ICFY representatives in order to explore and develop new ideas to make human rights monitoring as effective as possible in Bosnia and Herzegovina. The participants included representatives of Amnesty International, Helsinki Watch, Human Rights Watch, the International Human Rights Law Group, Lawyers Committee for Human Rights, UNA/USA, the World Council of Churches, the UN Centre for Human Rights, the UN Department of Humanitarian Affairs, the UN Department of Political Affairs, the UN Department of Peacekeeping Operations, the UN Office of Legal Affairs, and UNHCR, and officials from ICFY. Martti Ahtisaari, Ambassador Okun and this author co-chaired the meeting.[29]

On the need for human rights monitoring in Bosnia and Herzegovina, participants identified the following needs to be borne in mind in the establishment of a future human rights monitoring mission: to observe and report on the human rights situation in all parts of the country immediately; to provide access for existing monitors, including NGOs; to provide protection for current and future human rights monitors; to obtain the agreement of the parties to the conflict for human rights monitoring; to support local human rights groups; to support and reinforce the functioning of the local judicial establishment; to be more victim-oriented; to monitor the treatment of refugees, including those who wished to return; to deal with human rights violations, war crimes and crimes against humanity; and to address the issues of accountability for human rights violations, war crimes and crimes against humanity.

On the possible functions to be performed by an International Human Rights Monitoring Mission, participants thought that it could: collect the information and get it out to the international community; contribute to effective prosecution of those guilty of international crimes; to monitor the entire country; to address medical and public health aspects (Physician for Human Rights provided a detailed paper on this); to draw upon the United Nations experience in El Salvador, Cambodia, Haiti, and South Africa; to address the question of impunity.

On the organization of a future International Human Rights Monitoring Mission, participants advised to: keep it as an independent entity and safeguard its independence; include women in its leadership and its monitors; plan for a large number of human rights monitors (300 to 1,000); coordinate efforts with the Special Rapporteur of the UN Commission on Human Rights; coordinate with NGOs; pay particular attention to publicity and the

29 See ICFY document, Highlights of an Informal Meeting on Human Rights Monitoring in Bosnia and Herzegovina, 11 March, 1993. Text in the possession of the author.

broadcasting of news; to have a publicity arm; to deploy field officers throughout the country; and to designate as the head someone with great prestige world-wide.[30]

On the timing of the establishment of an International Human Rights Monitoring Mission, there were two schools of thought: One, led by Aryeh Neier, argued forcefully that the Security Council should act immediately, before a peaceful settlement had been achieved, and that an international human rights monitoring mission should be deployed immediately. The second school of thought, with Michael Posner being a prominent adherent to this line thinking, held that without the cooperation of the parties, a monitoring mission could not function. Hence, one should look to the deployment of a human rights monitoring mission *after* a peace agreement had been signed.

In the light of these two schools of thought it was suggested that the most fruitful way to proceed would be to send a small (3–5 persons) team of independent human rights experts to Bosnia and Herzegovina to assess the feasibility of a human rights monitoring mission (a) before a peace settlement was concluded and (b) as part of an overall peace settlement. The team could also provide concrete proposals on the mandate, structure and operations of any mission to be established.

As it happened, the ICFY negotiators decided to proceed with the establishment of an International Human Rights Monitoring Mission. In a report submitted to the Security Council, through the UN Secretary-General, the negotiators reported that it had been agreed with the Bosnian parties that there should be an International Human Rights Monitoring Mission, to be established by the Secretary-General and to be headed by an Interim Human Rights Commissioner for Bosnia and Herzegovina, who would be based in Sarajevo. Deputy Commissioners would be based in various parts of the country.

The Commissioner would be supported by international human rights monitors, deployed throughout the country and particularly in areas affected by 'ethnic cleansing'. They would observe the situation of human rights throughout Bosnia and Herzegovina, would intercede with the interim Presidency, with provincial authorities and with UNPROFOR to provide protection in urgent cases, would refer issues to the ombudsmen and to other human rights agencies as needed, and would work closely with the Office of the United Nations High Commissioner for Refugees (UNHCR), the International

30 The person ICFY approached to perform this role was Professor Thomas Buergenthal, then Judge on the Inter-American Court of Human Rights and later Judge on the International Court of Justice. He was supportive but had to decline on personal grounds.

Committee of the Red Cross and other humanitarian agencies. The Commissioner would submit regular reports to the Secretary-General who would, in turn, report periodically to the Security Council and to other international bodies, including the United Nations Commission on Human Rights and its Special Rapporteur.[31]

The central and other authorities would be required to give the fullest access, in respect of all relevant persons and places, to the Interim Human Rights Commissioner, the Deputy Commissioners and the human rights monitors, as well as to UNHCR, ICRC and other international humanitarian organizations.[32]

The peace plan also envisaged that as part of the UNPROFOR deployment in Bosnia and Herzegovina there should be a sufficiently large United Nations Civilian Police (UNCIVPOL) element whose task would be to see that the police in all parts of the country had an appropriately balanced ethnic composition; did not oppress members of minority ethnic groups; contribute positively to the reversal of ethnic cleansing by protecting persons returning after having been forced to flee; carry out judgments of courts, in particular the Human Right Court; and assist the Interim Human Rights Commissioner, the deputy Commissioners and the human rights monitors.[33]

The Dayton Human Rights Blueprint

The human rights provisions of the peace accords concluded in Dayton, Ohio, on 21 November, 1995, and later signed again at a ceremony in Paris in December, 1995, built on work first done within ICFY. In November, 1992, following the election of President William J. Clinton, this author drafted a letter that Cyrus Vance, ICFY Co-Chairman sent to Warren Christopher, Head of the Transition Team of the incoming President, and later appointed Secretary of State by President Clinton. The letter explained the thinking behind the Vance-Owen peace plan, and sent a full set of the documentation, including the detailed provisions on human rights.

Later, on the eve of the Dayton peace conference, this author, as Director of the International Conference on the Former Yugoslavia, wrote to the US State Department transmitting a full set of the human rights provisions that the ICFY negotiators had developed. This author was present at the Dayton peace

31 S/25403, para. 11.

32 Ibid, para. 12.

33 Ibid, para. 18.

conference and has in his possession the texts on human rights presented to the Bosnian parties. They built largely on the ICFY drafts but were even more expansive initially. However, the Bosnian parties eventually whittled them down and in the end, though important, they were not as extensive as the human rights proposals of ICFY.

In particular, ICFY's idea for the establishment of an international human rights monitoring mission was replaced by more vague provisions in Article XIII of Annex VI to the Dayton accords titled 'Organizations Concerned with Human Rights'. Under Article XIII the Parties joined in inviting the United Nations Commission on Human Rights, the OSCE, the United Nations High Commissioner for Human Rights, and other intergovernmental or regional human rights missions or organizations to monitor closely the human rights situation in Bosnia and Herzegovina, including through the establishment of local offices and the assignment of observers, rapporteurs or other relevant persons on a permanent or mission-by-mission basis and to provide them with full and effective facilitation, assistance and access.

Article XIII acknowledged ICFY's idea of establishing an international human rights monitoring mission with a vague provision whereby all competent authorities in Bosnia and Herzegovina were expected to cooperate with and provide unrestricted access to 'any international human rights monitoring mechanism established for Bosnia and Herzegovina'. In the end result, such a mission, as proposed by ICFY, was never established.

The Agreement on Human Rights concluded at Dayton did, as had been proposed by ICFY, contain a statement of fundamental rights and freedoms. It also provided for the establishment of what was strangely termed a Commission on Human Rights consisting of two parts, the Office of Ombudsman and the Human Rights Chamber. The Agreement provided that allegations of violations of human rights received by the Commission would generally be directed to the Office of the Ombudsman, except where an applicant specified the chamber. The Ombudsman was given the competence to investigate, either on his or her own initiative or in response to an allegation by any Party or person, NGO, or group of individuals claiming to be the victim of a violation by any Party or acting on behalf of alleged victims who were deceased or missing, alleged or apparent violations of human rights.

The Human Rights Chamber was composed of fourteen members. The Chamber was given the competence to receive by referral from the Ombudsman on behalf of an applicant, or directly from any Party or person, NGO, or group of individuals claiming to be the victim of a violation by any Party or acting on behalf of alleged victims who were deceased or missing, for resolution or decision applications concerning alleged or apparent violations of human rights.

At the outset of a case or at any stage during the proceedings, the Chamber might attempt to facilitate an amicable resolution of the matter on the basis of respect for the rights and freedoms referred to in the Agreement.

Article XI provided that following the conclusion of proceedings before the Chamber it would promptly issue a decision addressing whether the facts found indicated a breach by the Party concerned of its obligations under the Agreement; and what steps shall be taken by the Party to remedy such breach, including orders to cease and desist, monetary relief (including pecuniary and non-pecuniary injuries), and provisional measures.

The Human Rights Chamber functioned until 2004 and handed down an impressive body of jurisprudence on human rights issues.[34] Unfortunately, the Governments concerned concluded that the Chamber would end its existence in 2004. This writer, as the person then performing the functions of UN High Commissioner for Human Rights, wrote to the High Representative for Bosnia and Herzegovina, Lord Ashdown, urging that the decision be reconsidered and that the Chamber be continued. This was to no avail and a very useful human rights body first envisaged by ICFY and agreed upon at Dayton, passed from the scene.

Conclusion

This chapter has shown that foundation contributions to international efforts for the promotion and protection of human rights were made by the Congresses of Westphalia and Vienna and by the Paris Peace Conference of 1919 and the San Francisco Conference of 1945. The chapter has also brought forth evidence of the use of human rights considerations in peacemaking and peacekeeping strategies in Central America and in the former Yugoslavia. It would probably be fair advice to anyone contemplating an international peace conference in the future to keep well in mind how peacemaking might be built on human rights foundations and how peace strategies must necessarily take proper account of human rights considerations in the 'age of rights'.[35]

---

34 See, Human Rights Chamber of Bosnia and Herzegovina. Digest. Decisions on Admissibility and Merits, 1996–2002. With an Introduction by Manfred Nowak. Kehl/Strasbourg, Engel Publisher, 2003.

35 The Age of Rights is a felicitous term used by the late Louis Henkin in his book with this title: New York, Columbia University Press, 1996.

CHAPTER 8

Justice

Introduction

The issue of justice has intermittently engaged the attention of participants in international peace conferences since the Vienna Congress of 1814–15 but we cannot say that international peace conferences as such have had much success. The issue came up at Vienna in 1815, at the Paris Peace Conference in 1919, and during the meetings of the allied war leaders during the second world war. The Nuremberg and Tokyo Tribunals have left a strong historical legacy but they were the outcome of decisions by allied war leaders taken at conferences among them.

The quest for justice in Vienna, Leipzig, Paris, Constantinople, Nuremberg, and the Hague has been admirably discussed by Gary Bass in his book, Stay the Hand of Vengeance.[1] More recently, former leaders in Liberia, the former Yugoslavia, and Rwanda have appeared before international criminal tribunals and an indictment has been issued by the Prosecutor of the International Criminal Court against the President of Sudan, Omar El Bashir. In addition, there have been international criminal tribunals for Cambodia, Sierra Leone, and Lebanon.

The question that arises for reflection in this study of international peace conferences is whether any general lessons on the issue of justice may be drawn from the conferences of the past. We think that their practice would justify the following conclusions: first, the issue has been dealt with on a case by case basis; second, victors in war make political assessments in deciding whether or not to pursue trials; third, where the leading powers are dealing with crimes committed in conflicts involving lesser powers, it is easier for them to decide on the prosecution of those who are accused of international crimes; fourth, in our times the Security Council may choose to refer a case to the Prosecutor of the International Criminal Court if the leading powers on the Council are so disposed; and fifth, international peace conferences as such, as already mentioned, have not had much success on this issue.

1 G.J. Bass, Stay the Hand of Vengeance. The Politics of War Crimes Tribunals. Princeton, Princeton University Press, 2000.

 | DOI 10.1163/9789004245907_010

In this chapter we refer briefly to the issue of possibly trying Napoleon after his defeat, the Nuremberg and Tokyo tribunals, and two instances in which international peace conferences did consciously deliberate on the establishment of tribunals to try those accused of crimes against humanity and war crimes: Paris, 1919, and the London and International Conferences on the Former Yugoslavia, 1992–1996.

I Vienna, 1815, Nuremberg, and Tokyo 1939–45

The issue of the possible trial of Napoleon never came before the principal powers as a group at the Congress of Vienna. According to Gary Bass, Germany had been pressing for his trial, but the UK was already mindful of its future relations with France in the face of growing German power. Also, the Duke of Wellington, who had defeated Napoleon in battle, was firmly against his being tried. In the end, the UK acted unilaterally in exiling Napoleon to St. Helena.[2]

We jump the historical sequence and mention next the Nuremberg and Tokyo Tribunals, which established important precedents. From the point of view of this book, they do not need detailed discussions here because the decisions to establish them were essentially taken at meetings of the three principal allied powers, the UK, USA, and USSR.[3] However, the issue of trying alleged axis war criminals in the First World War was actively discussed not only in contacts among the victorious powers, but at the Paris Peace Conference itself. We turn to this next.

II Paris, 1919

Gary Bass has discussed the issue of justice after the First World War at length in his book.[4] Basing ourselves on his discussion, we take up only the part of the story concerning the Paris Peace Conference itself, which did deliberate on the issues, but whose deliberations led to little practical results.

The first item on the agenda of the Paris Peace Conference, Bass notes, was the punishment of war criminals. In January, 1919 the preliminary peace conference established an Allied and American commission to look into creating a

2 Ibid, Chapter 2, St. Helena.

3 Ibid, Chapter 5, Nuremberg.

4 Ibid, Chapter 4, Leipzig.

war crimes tribunal.[5] In its report, the commission envisaged the establishment of a special tribunal, with judges mostly from the victorious powers.[6] In the end result, no such tribunal was ever established.

However, in the Treaty of Versailles that German eventually signed, there were four articles on German war crimes envisaging trials, including of Kaiser Wilhelm II. He, however, had taken refugee in The Netherlands, which refused to cooperate or hand him over. Besides the Kaiser, the allies had drawn up lists of suspects to be put to trial in Germany, but, as Bass has commented, "As expected, the Allied lists were met with shock in Germany."[7]

Pursuant to the Treaty of Versailles a limited amount of trials were held in Leipzig with mixed results. In the end, it turned into a "debacle."[8] Bass writes:

> Allied demands had seemed unimpeachable when they were formed, and German resistance had been seen as yet another sign of the incorrigibly wrong-headed nature of Germany. But as the issue curdled, the Allied pursuit of German war criminals invited disaster: it made the Allies look vindictive and weak,; it divided America and Britain and France from each other; it showed that Germany could get away with failing to comply to the treaty of Versailles; it kept wartime passions from cooling; and worst of all, it galvanized the German right and thus helped to undermine democracy in the Weimar Republic. For many thoughtful leaders, most notably Churchill, Leipzig was proof of the folly of entrusting a political problem to legal methods.[9]

Versailles thus left us with little historical legacy on the establishment of institutions to try persons accused of crimes against humanity and war crimes. It was in relation to Yugoslavia and Rwanda in the 1990s that historic breakthroughs would eventually be made with the establishment, first, of the International Criminal Tribunal for the Former Yugoslavia (ICTY), which would then double as an International Criminal Tribunal for Rwanda (ICTR).

The London Conference on Yugoslavia, 1992, and the International Conference on the Former Yugoslavia, 1992–1996, contributed directly to the

5 Ibid, p. 75. FO 371/4271/62362, Commission on the Responsibility of the Authors of the War and on the Enforcement of Penalties (CRAWEP), report to preliminary peace conference, 29 March, 1919.

6 Ibid, p. 70.

7 Ibid, p. 79.

8 Ibid, p. 104.

9 Ibid, pp. 104–105.

establishment of precursor commissions by the UN Security Council, and eventually to the Council's establishment of the two *ad hoc* tribunals. We discuss next, the roles of the London Conference and ICFY in contributing to the establishment of these tribunals, especially the first, ICTY.

III The London and International Conferences on the Former Yugoslavia, 1992–1996

The London Conference on Yugoslavia, held at the end of August 1992, which established the International Conference on the Former Yugoslavia, had given the latter a mandate to engage in continuous negotiations for the settlement of the Bosnian conflict, laid down principles calling for respect of the highest standards of human rights, and asked ICFY to "carry forward a study of the creation of an international criminal court."[10] But the London Conference had said nothing concrete about bringing the perpetrators of war crimes and crimes against humanity to justice other than requesting the Co-Chairmen of the Steering Committee of ICFY to advise on the establishment of an International Criminal Court. The peace negotiators would have to tread their way carefully on this issue of bringing the perpetrators to justice.

In the end, the Co-Chairmen of ICFY, Cyrus Vance and Lord Owen would take a stance of principle in favour of bringing the perpetrators to justice. This was consistent with the position they took from the outset to place the spotlight on human rights issues in bodies such as the Human Rights Committee and the Council of Europe.

On 17 September, 1992, barely two weeks after Vance and Owen had arrived in Geneva, to begin the process of continuous negotiations for a settlement, the Government of the Netherlands circulated a telegram to its European partners recalling that during the past months the importance of accurate and systematic data gathering on war crimes and gross violations of human rights in the former Yugoslavia had been emphasized in several international fora on different occasions. It expressed the view that the call for international fact-finding and possible persecution of the severe crimes that had taken place could not go unheeded.

The Government of the Netherlands therefore submitted to its partners a proposal for the establishment of *ad hoc* machinery for the investigation and possible prosecution of war crimes and serious human rights violations in the former Yugoslavia. It recalled the example of the War Crimes Commission

10 Specific Decisions of the London Conference (LC/C7 (FINAL)), para. 8.

established in London in 1943 and proposed the establishment of such a commission (WCC) for the former Yugoslavia. In its view, the Commission could catalogue and analyse information received on war crimes as well as serious human rights violations.

Lord Owen, as the EU designated Co-Chairman of ICFY, circulated the Dutch telegram within ICFY and sought the views of different officials, including this author. Lord Owen expressed very tentative views that he could see advantage in public pressure being brought to bear, given that atrocities were still being committed and others very likely would be committed. He favoured an International Court of universal application instead of a Yugoslav-specific body. He added:

> I see merit in an international fact-finding body which may or may not have to prosecute, as proposed by the Dutch, namely an *ad hoc* UN War Crimes Commission.
>
> I believe such a Commission would buttress any investigation undertaken by the Human Rights Committee…[11]

One of the addressees of Lord Owen's memorandum replied that the Dutch proposal sought to respond, as a matter of urgency, to what was considered an issue of principle, namely, that persons guilty of war crimes or serious violations of human rights should not go unpunished. He considered that while this was a commendable objective, neither the procedure suggested, nor the timing, seemed appropriate. In the midst of a war, laden with propaganda on all sides, charges flew in all directions. The Commission on Human Rights had appointed a Special Rapporteur who had already prepared an interim report. He was expected to prepare a follow-up report to the General Assembly that was just beginning, and to the Commission on Human Rights later that year.

It would, the official continued, seem to be the proper course of action to allow the Special Rapporteur to examine the situation and the available evidence and to come up with recommendations on the possible prosecution of persons accused of international crimes. In short, the appropriate course of action seemed to be to let the Rapporteur get on with his job but to invite him to pay particular attention and to include a chapter in his report, if he considered this necessary, on this issue.

11 Memo from Lord Owen to C. Vance, P. Hall, H. Okun, P. Szasz, and B. Ramcharan, 18 September, 1992. Text in the possession of the author.

The official added:

> From the point of view of timing, to launch the initiatives proposed by the Dutch when the Co-Chairmen are exploring avenues for making peace in the area would not seem the wisest course of action. The activities of the Co-Chairmen could even be complicated by setting up an elaborate mechanism which could take on a life and momentum of its own. This would seem to be all the more reason to follow the course of action of letting the Special Rapporteur of the Commission examine the issues calmly and dispassionately.[12]

The late Paul Szasz, a legal adviser of ICFY, submitted his views in a Memorandum dated 29 September, 1992. He noted that the Dutch proposal would have the Statute of the proposed tribunal, be established, by an *ad hoc* UN War Crimes Commission for the Former Yugoslavia (WCC). That would, in effect, remove this task from the ICFY Co-Chairmen. If the Co-Chairmen were content to have the WCC undertake this task they might request to be consulted in due course. If, however, the Co-Chairmen considered that the work should be done under their auspices, as apparently foreseen by the London Conference, it could be done within ICFY. In that case it might be useful to engage the assistance of Professor Cherif Bassiouni, a leading expert in this field, as a consultant.[13]

In the end, the Co-Chairmen took a principled position from the outset on dealing with war crimes in the former Yugoslavia, while maintaining a distinction between the role of peacemakers and those of investigators/prosecutors. Immediately after commencing their activities in Geneva, the Co-Chairmen, Vance and Owen, began internal discussions on the possible establishment of an international criminal court. They maintained contacts on this subject with the European Community, the Council of Europe, and Governments particularly interested, such as those of the Netherlands and the USA. They commissioned papers on the subject from their Legal Adviser, the late Paul Szasz, who provided options to the Co-Chairmen on this topic.

Throughout, the Co-Chairmen maintained an active discussion on this subject with the President of ICFY's Arbitration Commission, Mr Robert Badinter. Several meetings were held to discuss this subject. On 14 October, 1992,

12 Note to Lord Owen dated 21 September, 1992. Text in the possession of the author. Name of the author withheld for the sake of discretion.

13 Text in the possession of the author.

Mr Badinter advised the Co-Chairmen that it was important that the perpetrators of crimes against humanity should not go unpunished. Even if amnesties were declared at the national level eventually, the perpetrators of international crimes should know that they were vulnerable to arrest and prosecution abroad. He encouraged efforts to establish an international criminal court to try the perpetrators of crimes against humanity. With the concurrence and support of the Co-Chairmen, Mr Badinter discreetly contacted concerned Governments seeking to promote the establishment of an international criminal court.

The Co-Chairmen also maintained contacts on this subject with the Secretary-General of the United Nations who went on record as being in favour of the establishment of a tribunal to deal with the perpetrators of war crimes and crimes against humanity in the former Yugoslavia. On 30 December, Secretary-General Boutros-Boutros Ghali told a news conference in Geneva that he was in favour of the establishment of a three-person tribunal on war crimes to examine violations of human rights committed by all three sides in the Yugoslav conflict. Noting that a five-member Commission previously established by the Security council was examining reports on human rights violations and grave breaches of the international human rights conventions, the Secretary-General said that the work of the tribunal and the Commission would be coordinated.

The Co-Chairmen of ICFY continued to use their influence discreetly and publicly in order to promote the establishment of an international criminal court. In a statement to the Steering Committee of the ICFY on 16 December, 1992, they stated:

> We have...taken action on allegations of war crimes and other breaches of international humanitarian law. We have sought to help the Commission of Experts bring about a forensic examination of the mass grave site at Ovcara near Vukovar... (We) believe that atrocities committed in the former Yugoslavia are unacceptable, and persons guilty of war crimes should be brought to justice. We therefore recommend the establishment of an international criminal court.[14]

Also in December, 1992, Lord Owen wrote the following to partners:

> 1. Vance and I have concluded that given the continued existence of ethnic cleansing an *ad hoc* tribunal should now be introduced urgently.

14 See ICFY Aide Memoire: Policy of the Co-Chairmen on War Crimes in the Former Yugoslavia Text in the ICFY archives and in the possession of the author.

> We understand the Security Council could establish a War Crimes Tribunal for Yugoslavia by vetoable decision under Chapter VII of the Charter. Pursuant to Charter Articles 25 and 48(1), such a War Crimes Tribunal could be given the power to demand cooperation from all states, e.g. on extradition of accused persons, the production of witnesses and the punishment of those convicted as well as of uncooperative and perjured witnesses.
> 2. The alternative we preferred some months ago of the General Assembly establishing an International Criminal Court, with general jurisdiction, i.e. not only in respect of a particular state and not necessarily restricted to war crimes, is now going to take years and it is obviously not going to be done in a timescale which is remotely defensible.[15]

The ICFY negotiators not only supported the establishment of an international criminal tribunal, they actively supported forensic investigations of mass grave sites. On 26 November, 1992, Vance wrote to UN Secretary-General Boutros-Boutros Ghali on the subject, "Forensic Examination of the alleged mass grave site at Ovcara, near Vukovar." He wrote:

> 1. We consider it of great importance that a forensic examination be made of the alleged mass grave site at Ovcara, near Vukovar, as soon as possible. As a matter of principle it is important that we discover what has taken place. As you know, UNPROFOR set guards at the site several weeks ago and the sooner the forensic examination can be made, the faster it will be possible for UNPROFOR to be relieved of this responsibility. The best expert opinion available indicates that after the winter freeze the evidence might be damaged and therefore lost. Moreover, the risk cannot be excluded that internal forces might attempt to destroy the evidence.
> 2. We have, therefore, been seeking to find the fastest way of initiating a forensic examination of the alleged mass grave site. We discussed this matter with USG Blanca on Monday, November 23. On Wednesday, November 25, I sent (a) cable to the Special Rapporteur of the Commission on Human Rights, Mr Mazowiecki, urging him to authorize a team of forensic experts to do an examination of the site before the onset of the winter freeze.
> 3. We met today, Thursday November 28, with the Chairman of the Commission of Experts, Professor Kalshoven, to make the same point to him, namely that it would be extremely important to have a forensic

15 Full cable in the possession of the author. Dated December 1992, but date unclear.

> examination done as soon as possible. Professor Kalshoven was very helpful and took the view that the examination should be done under the auspices of the Commission of Experts.
>
> ...
>
> ...
>
> 5. I thought I would report to you on my efforts so that you might indicate to all concerned the importance and the urgency of this matter and the need for pragmatic approaches and solutions so as to get the forensic team to the site straight away. I would hope very much that the dispatch of the forensic team would not get caught up in any procedural snags.[16]
>
> The decision to establish a Commission of Experts to gather information on possible international crimes being committed in the conflicts in the Former Yugoslavia was taken by the United Nations Security Council. It had the full support of Vance and Owen from the very beginning. I have seen some accounts arguing otherwise that I consider unfounded and unfortunate.

When reports came in of a mass grave site at Ovcara, near Vukovar, Vance asked this author to contact Physicians for Human Rights for them to do a forensic examination of the site. I did so, using the good offices of a friend in a human rights NGO, who facilitated the contacts. In order for Physicians for Human Rights to proceed with the forensic examination they needed the imprimatur of the Commission of Experts. Again I contacted Professor Kalshoven who readily agreed that Physicians for Human Rights could act under the auspices of the Commission of Experts.

This is how the first forensic examination of a mass grave site in the Former Yugoslavia began. It stemmed from a direct initiative from the UN peace negotiator, Cyrus Vance. By the time the examination actually got under way, Vance had moved on and had been succeeded by Thorvald Stoltenberg. After the Vance-Owen plan was signed by the parties in Athens in April, 1993, Secretary-General Boutros Boutros Ghali had designated Stoltenberg as Special Representative in charge of all UN operations in the Former Yugoslavia, while continuing as Co-Chairman of ICFY. Boutros-Ghali thought that the implementation stage had been reached but, unfortunately, within a week of signing the accords in Athens, the Bosnian Serbs repudiated their signature and Stoltenberg went on, for a year, to double as special representative and as negotiator.

16 Cable in the possession of the author.

As Special Representative of the Secretary-General, Stoltenberg was in charge of the peace-keeping troops, the largest force ever assembled in the history of the United Nations. This author doubled as Director of the International Conference on the Former Yugoslavia and as Director of the Office of the Special Representative. In the latter capacity this author continued to be directly involved in future efforts regarding the mass grave site at Ovcara as well as in efforts to get the peacekeeping troops to play a role on human rights issues.

The examination of the mass-grave site at Ovcara required painstaking work over several months. After the site had been opened up it was important to guard it so as to maintain its integrity and to prevent it from being tampered with. At Stoltenberg's request, this author contacted the UN Force Commander to ask him to provide troops to guard the site. This he did. As the forensic examination proceeded, it would require the emplacement of troops at the site over several months. In the circumstances prevailing at the time, with the pressures on the troops, it took the direct involvement of Stoltenberg to secure that the troops would stay to guard the site over the several months involved.

This was, admittedly, a situation in which the roles of peacemaker had been combined with that of peacekeeper and Stoltenberg therefore had considerable leverage on the force. It does bear out, however, that the direct involvement of the peacemaker can, and did in this instance, play an important role in furthering the process of gathering information into possible international crimes committed during a conflict.

For both peacemakers and peacekeepers in UN peace operations in the former Yugoslavia it was a learning experience to tackle issues of human rights and justice. For the peacemakers the most important assignment was to help negotiate peace agreements and thereby stop conflicts. It was therefore understandable that they gave priority to this task. For peacekeepers, the principal task was to help in the delivery of humanitarian assistance and to help contain and prevent conflicts. UN peacekeepers had their traditions since the early days of the United Nations and they attached importance to principles of neutrality and impartiality.

The former Yugoslavia would challenge them all and the negotiators and peacekeepers would have to come to deal with the stark fact that criminal violations of human rights and humanitarian law were taking place in conflicts in Bosnia and Herzegovina and in Croatia. As this chapter has shown, the peace negotiators and peacekeepers took a principled stance in favour of the establishment of the Commission of Experts and the ICTY and then cooperated with the Prosecutor and staff of the ICTY as well as, in some instances, appearing as witnesses before it.

Conclusion

As we write, there are calls for the Syrian President to be put to trial before an international tribunal for crimes allegedly committed in the civil war in that country. The precedent has now been established that the Security Council, if can reach political agreement among its permanent members, could refer such a case to the permanent International Criminal Court, and there are many commentators who are pressing for this. The point here is that international morality has changed markedly since the times of the Vienna and Paris conferences and even during the Cold War. But for the end of the Cold War the decisions taken by the UN Security Council to establish ICTY and ICTR would never have been taken.

As we saw, the London Conference on Yugoslavia, 1992 and ICFY played parts in the events leading up to the establishment of ICTY and contributed to the eventual establishment of the International Criminal Court. What might we conclude from this for future international peace conferences when it comes to the issue of justice. From Vienna to Paris, during the Second World War, and during the Cold War, political considerations played a role in each instance. That will undoubtedly continue at any future peace conference, and one would need to take a case-by case-approach. But it is important to note that there are now in the international community parallel institutions that might be used. Peace negotiators, or an international peace conference might pursue the cessation of conflicts and political settlements, while in the UN Security Council, if the agreement of the permanent members could be secured, it might be possible to refer cases to the ICC or to establish *ad hoc* tribunals. The Dayton Conference that ended the war in Bosnia said little about the trial of war criminals. But it could do this because ICTY had already been established and had already indicted key leaders and would indict more later.

We cannot, in conscience, argue that international peace conferences must necessarily address issues of justice. A case-by-case approach would be needed. But, depending on the circumstances, peace negotiators or international peace conferences must keep the issue of justice in mind and seek to bring their influence on the justice issue as seems appropriate in the circumstances. This is what Cyrus Vance and Lord Owen did in the International Conference on the Former Yugoslavia.

Conclusion to Part One

This has been an exploratory historical and thematic inquiry into a topic hardly treated before in the literature: international peace conferences. There is no easy way of demarcating what is or is not an international peace conference. We have sought to place the spotlight on conferences with a mandate to negotiate peace but we have recognized that processes such as those of Contadora/Esquipulas on Central America approximated to international peace conferences and we have seen that conferences such as the Bonn Conferences of 2001 and 2011 on Afghanistan helped put down some building blocks for peace, even if the future of that country remains uncertain still. We have taken a flexible approach, letting the evidence speak for itself.

We have come across great peace conferences called to deal with a broad range of situations, such as those of Westphalia, Vienna, Paris, 1919, and San Francisco. We have also come across conferences whose focus was on regions or sub-regions, or particular countries. The Dayton conference on Bosnia was such an example.

We have looked at the institutional architecture of past conferences and identified elements that might be borne in mind in the establishment of future conferences, such as facilities and financing. As Kissinger's response to the question of whether Iran should be invited to an international conference on Syria showed, issues of who participates, and of the organization and ground rules of conferences need to be tackled on a case by case basis.

We have seen grand ideas at international peace conferences for the prevention of future conflicts, such as the Vienna Congress's idea of a concert of major powers to head off disputes that could deteriorate into broader conflict. We have seen the grand ideas of the League of Nations and of the United Nations. We may legitimately conclude that international peace conferences can be springboards for the launch of great ideas for the safeguarding of the future peace.

We have sought to examine whether distinctive elements could be identified in the ways that conferences have approached peacemaking, peacekeeping, peacebuilding, human rights and justice. Basically, peacemaking strategies, whether in a conference setting or outside of it, would be influenced by the parameters of the conflict. Depending on who the parties to the conflict are, it is possible that an international peace conference might serve to mount pressure on the parties to agree to a settlement. But this is not to be taken for granted, especially if different major powers support different parties, as took place in the case of the conflicts in the former Yugoslavia.

 | DOI 10.1163/9789004245907_011

We have seen that the conference setting, because of the fact that the world might be represented at a conference, could facilitate the establishment of peacekeeping or observer operations that could, in turn, help keep the peacemaking process going. This occurred in the case of the International Conference on the Former Yugoslavia, which sponsored the idea of a preventive deployment on the borders between Serbia and Macedonia.

We have seen that international conferences can be platforms to launch new ideas for regional public order, as happened in the case of the Contadora/Esquipulas processes, or foundation blocks for the reconstitution of countries, as happened in the cases of the Bonn conferences of 2001 and 2011 on Afghanistan. This is peacebuilding at work in dramatic ways. In the case of Japan, the San Francisco conference of 1951, where the Japanese peace treaty was concluded, consolidated a process of remaking the nation that had already begun under the Allied/US Administration led by General Douglas MacArthur.

We have seen great human rights ideas come out of the Congress of Vienna, the Paris Conference of 1919 and the San Francisco conference of 1945. The Congress of Vienna agreed on the abolition of slavery, the Paris conference established a treaty-based system for the protection of minorities within the framework of the League of Nations, and the San Francisco conference that established the United Nations sought to anchor the future peace in respect for human rights and fundamental freedoms.

When it comes to bringing perpetrators of crimes against humanity and war crimes to justice, it would be fair to conclude that the main developments came outside of the formal international peace conferences. However the decisions to establish the Nuremberg and Tokyo Tribunals were taken as part of the inter-war peace planning rather than within the framework of particular conferences. We saw that, in the case of the International Conference on the Former Yugoslavia, while the lead mediators supported the idea of international justice in principle, they wanted to maintain a distinction between processes of peacemaking and justice.

It would probably be best to let the evidence speak for itself and not attempt any general conclusions about international peace conferences. Save one: it happens more than once that it is the only option left standing, as in the case of Syria, which we referred to earlier. It has happened more than once also, that even while a conflict rages on and peacemaking is difficult, an international conference might help superimpose a framework of principles and objectives to help steer the quest for peace and mobilise international public opinion behind the framework. And then, there are the inevitable situations where a conference is necessary to hammer out or ratify the peace agreements necessary for a new beginning. Westphalia, Vienna, Paris, 1919, Paris, 1946, and San

Francisco 1951 were examples of such conferences. In the case of San Francisco 1951 the peace treaty with Japan had been painstakingly negotiated beforehand by John Foster Dulles. The conference was necessary to bring the other powers on board and to ratify the treaty.

Diverse uses, flexible formats and procedure, imaginative approaches, great public order blueprints, great peacebuilding ideas, innovative human rights schemes and wrestling with the issue of justice: This is the legacy of the international peace conferences of the past.

Keeping in mind the experiences of international peace conferences we have reviewed in this book, recalling that there was no general peace settlement after the Second World War, noting the contemporary challenges of global governance, and recognizing the numerous problems confronting the United Nations, one might pose the question: has the time come for the convening of a world-wide international peace conference to deliberate on the peace challenges of the present and the future and to recommend an architecture for peace in the twenty-first century? A case could be made for such a conference. However, the idea should first be studied by the academic and research community. Might this be a task that could be initially scoped by an institution such as the TMC Asset Institute in the Hague, named after the great international lawyer and Nobel Peace Prize Laureate?

PART 2

The International Conference on the Former Yugoslavia: The Art of the Possible in UN Peacemaking, Peacekeeping and Humanitarianism

Introduction

The UN Idea and the Art of the Possible

The United Nations idea carries the hopes of humanity that, through international cooperation, the world can be made a more peaceful and prosperous place, with people everywhere enjoying universal human rights in justly governed democratic societies. At the heart of the idea is the principle of solidarity, namely, that one would stand for all and all for one.

When the United Nations Charter was drafted at the San Francisco conference in 1945, there were those who wished that the idea of collective security would take root, that international cooperation could lead to the reduction of poverty, and that the world organization would advance the cause of human rights universally. There was a spirit, and ethos of the world organization that pointed to consensual ways of doing things, harmonising the good in the world's peoples for the betterment of humankind across the globe. United Nations methods are necessarily different from those of a mighty government or alliance that can sweep away considerations of legality or consensualism and marshal power for the ends it seeks.

Due to lack of cooperation, the United Nations idea has never been fully implemented, and is still a work in motion. Even as the Charter was signed and came into force in 1945, the cold war had descended on the world with two alliances squaring off against one another. On the communist side there were so called peoples' democracies that trampled on the rights of their subjects. On the Western side there were claimed democracies that practised colonialism, segregation, and apartheid. Even western powers like the USA had not been willing at San Francisco to give the United Nations the competence to protect human rights as opposed to simply promoting them.

The concept of collective security envisaged in the Charter thus never came into effect, save on a few occasions when Great Powers got their way, as in the cases of Korea in 1951 and Iraq in 1991. The UN would innovate, bringing in the concepts of preventive diplomacy, peacekeeping, development cooperation, humanitarianism, and protection of human rights as best it could through practice. The UN thus pursued its mission by engaging in the art of the possible in the quest for peace, development, and human rights.

This required much inventiveness. Secretary-General Trygve Lie proposed the establishment of a corps of UN Guards in 1947. Secretary-General Hammarskjold came up with the concept of preventive diplomacy and joined with Lester Pearson in developing the concept of UN peacekeeping. Secretary-General U Thant established what was then the UN Disaster Relief

 | DOI 10.1163/9789004245907_012

Organization (UNDRO). Each Secretary-General to date has had to be imaginative in devising approaches for addressing situations of concern or problems affecting humanity as a whole as best as they could, given the political complexion of the United Nations and the diversities of interest in the world body.

Heads of United Nations Departments or Offices similarly had to do the best they could in the circumstances, practising the art of the possible. What could a hapless head of a Disarmament Department do when the arms were in the hands of superpowers determined to keep them. One answer – that, for example, of the late William Epstein, was to keep the idea of disarmament alive and to pursue programmes of practical cooperation wherever possible. What could the Director of the UN Human Rights Division do when the UN Commission on Human Rights declared, in 1947, that it lacked the competence to deal with the thousands of petitions of violations of human rights reaching it from Eastern Europe? Again, the late John Humphrey sought to keep the idea of universal human rights alive and to pursue programmes of practical cooperation to the extent that circumstances permitted at the time.

In the areas of peacemaking, peacekeeping and humanitarianism, including human rights, which are the focus of this book, United Nations peacemakers have sought to do their utmost, invariably in very difficult circumstances, and have fared sometimes well and sometimes have met great odds. Count Folkke Bernadotte lost his life in the effort. The late Ralph Bunche won the Nobel Peace Prize for negotiating an armistice between Arabs and Israelis in 1949. Diego Cordovez in Afghanistan and Alvaro de Soto in Central America, registered signal successes for the United Nations. Cyrus Vance did well in Croatia in 1991 and was stymied in Bosnia. He felt that his own Government and his former Deputy as Secretary of State, had worked against him. He was particularly hurt by what he considered the betrayal by Warren Christopher.

United Nations peacekeeping forces and UNHCR both won the Nobel Peace Prize. They all practised the art of the possible – in difficult circumstances in most cases. There always are media and NGO pundits who know better on the outside what should be done on the inside. They mean well, and are an important part of the UN constituency. But practising the art of the possible is not a straight-forward business and often will involve practical and imperfect solutions. But then, who can do better? NATO forces in Afghanistan and Iraq were hopelessly lost at times, notwithstanding the more numerous firepower they had at their disposal. Many commentators wished the UN had been mandated to take care of the civilian population in Iraq!

United Nations peacemakers, peacekeepers, and humanitarian personnel in the former Yugoslavia gave their guts and their lives in the quest for peace and in the endeavour to save lives and help people in distress. For the United

Nations, Cyrus Vance (with Lord Owen), Martti Ahtisaari, Thorvald Stoltenberg, and Yasushi Akashi strove for peace with as much heart as anyone could. Sometimes they succeeded and sometimes they were obstructed or sabotaged.

The United Nations peacekeeping operation in the former Yugoslavia remains the largest in the history of the world body, numbering close to fifty thousand at one stage. A succession of UN Force Commanders and UN peacekeeping personnel struggled valiantly in the most difficult of circumstances. Mrs Sadako Ogata, UN High Commissioner for Refugees, led the humanitarian effort from 1991 to 1995 and helped millions of people stay alive through deadly circumstances and harsh winters. All of these UN leaders received tongue-lashings from the media and from outside pundits for not having devised perfect solutions in the face of local leaders making up a nest of scorpions.

I have read the book of the late Richard Holbrook, *To End a War*, and he deserves congratulations and gratitude for his efforts. But as a career UN official who served for thirty two years in the human rights, speech-writing/policy, peacemaking, peacekeeping, humanitarian, political, and again human rights areas, I was pained by many things in this book: first, he could draw upon political and fire-power that the UN never could have. I spent three and a half years with UN peacemakers, peacekeepers and humanitarian personnel, seven days a week, without a single day off and I have seen people work even harder than me.

I was present at Dayton when the Accord was signed and I felt that three years earlier we had better peace plans than the one being signed. We could not succeed because of US obstructionism. The only reason why Holbrook succeeded and we did not was because he could draw upon US power. I felt this deeply at Dayton.

Second, in judging the UN and its operatives he is harsh at times, judging them through the lens of a power practitioner able to call upon the assets of the USA. I have seen honourable people like Cy Vance, Thorvald Stoltenberg, and Yasushi Akashi do their utmost but not being able to succeed because they lacked the political and military assets of the USA. I said to myself in reading his book: he was an honourable man but he had no understanding of the predicament of UN leaders.

Third, I read with some anguish about then USG Kofi Annan giving NATO blanket authorisation to go in with their planes without the consent of UN leaders on the ground at a time when Secretary-General Boutros Boutros-Ghali was on a plane and could not be reached. He had clear views to the contrary, which Annan knew. Holbrooke acknowledges Annan's action as the reason why he became UN Secretary-General with American support. I wonder what the great international civil servants such as Ralph Bunche or Sir Brian Urquhart would have thought about this.

Fourth, when I read in his book, his plea to Washington, "Give us bombs for peace," and his encouragement to Presidents Izetbegovic and Tudjman to maintain military offensives against the Bosnian Serbs in Western Bosnia, I could not help thinking that here was a dramatic difference between the UN approach and the approach of a governmental mediator with the backing of American military assets. I could hardly contemplate a UN peacemaker pleading, "Give us bombs for peace." It is not the UN way.

I have therefore written Part Two of this book to make the case that the UN idea on the ground often leads to practising the art of the possible. I shall show that the UN succeeded in conflict containment and prevention in Croatia in 1991, in Macedonia in 1992–1994, in the situation between Greece and Macedonia in 1992–1995, missed in Kosovo, and was sabotaged in the Krajinas in 1994.

I shall argue that UN peacemaking was successful in the situation between Greece and Macedonia, in negotiating a peacemaking regime for the Danube region of Croatia, the Erdut Agreement, the father of which is Thorvald Stoltenberg, and was obstructed in Bosnia as external powers armed the parties and the US bombed the Bosnian Serbs.

I shall show that UN humanitarians were heroic in the face of pervasive inhumanity on all sides of the conflict in Bosnia and Herzegovina and that UN peacekeepers performed valiantly in the face of ingratitude, opportunism, and treachery. Even as UN peacekeepers were saving Sarajevo the Bosnian Government was waging a media war on the UN operation because its aim was to bring about Western military intervention.

I shall show that Thorvald Stoltenberg was skilful in negotiating a new mandate for UN peacekeeping forces in Croatia when President Franjo Tudjman professed to want their departure so that he could move militarily against the Croatian Serbs.

I shall present the challenges of attempting to protect human rights in heart of darkness, as all sides in the Bosnian conflict engaged in brutal conduct. I shall show the inventiveness of UN personnel in this area.

I shall discuss the political leadership of what I believe was the first wartime UN Special Representative of the Secretary-General, when Thorvald Stoltenberg was designated leader of all UN operations in the former Yugoslavia in May, 1993, heading the peacemaking, peacekeeping, humanitarian, human rights and peacebuilding operations. This was quite a challenge, especially in the face of a French UN Force Commander at the time whose personal mission in life was to call in the NATO planes.

In the end I shall submit that the UN served magnificently in the former Yugoslavia through practising the art of the possible. At the end of the day, the

Art of the Possible is what the UN can practice in most instances. In short, I present the story from the perspective of a UN practitioner so that it might be compared with some of the dismissive assessments that one can read from those with the backings of powerful governments. I believe that I stand for the UN idea, practising the art of the possible while they stand for the exercise of power.

CHAPTER 9

Conflict Containment and Prevention

Successes and Misses

Introduction

The United Nations Protected Areas (UNPAS) in Croatia were were meant to dampen the fighting and provide an international presence while peacemaking efforts continued to bring the conflict between Croats and Serbs to an end. Nevertheless, there were shades of protection in the concept and in the implementation given to it by United Nations forces. They practised the art of the possible, which is a hallmark of United Nations peace and humanitarian operations. In this chapter we shall look at the concept, protection efforts on the ground, and the limitations of the operation.

By way of background, it will be recalled that on 27 November, 1991, the UN Security Council had adopted resolution 721 endorsing efforts for the deployment of a UN peacekeeping operation in Croatia, then still a part of the Socialist Federal Republic of Yugoslavia. An implementing Accord was signed in Sarajevo on 2 January, 1992. Six weeks later, on 15 February, 1992, the Security Council confirmed acceptance by all parties of what became known as the Vance Plan and agreed to establish UNPROFOR.

The Vance plan had been the result of a six month negotiation process. The plan's aims were as follows: the cessation of hostilities; the withdrawal of the Yugoslav National Army (JNA) from Croatia; the demilitarisation of areas designated as UN Protected Areas to protect the Serbs and other populations within the UNPAS; facilitation of the return of displaced persons to the UNPAS.

UNPROFOR was initially deployed in Croatia, with its Headquarters in Sarajevo which, at the time, early 1992, before the recognition of its independence, was peaceful. Subsequently, with the spread of civil war in Bosnia and Herzegovina, UNPROFOR's mandate was extended to Bosnia and later, as a preventive deployment, to the Former Yugoslav Republic of Macedonia. In addition, UNPROFOR had an operational mandate in Serbia and Montenegro and a liaison presence in Slovenia.

1 The Concept of UN Protected Areas

The concept for a United Nations peace-keeping operation in Yugoslavia, which was discussed with Yugoslav leaders by the Honourable Cyrus Vance,

 | DOI 10.1163/9789004245907_013

Personal Envoy of the UN Secretary-General and Marrack Goulding, USG for Special Political Affairs (Peacekeeping) in November/December, 1991, envisaged an interim arrangement to create the conditions of peace and security required for the negotiation of an overall settlement of the Yugoslav crisis. The military and police personnel required for the operation would be contributed, on a voluntary basis, by the Government of member States of the UN approved by the Security Council.[1]

All members of the peace-keeping operation would be under the operational command of the UN Secretary-General. They would be required to be completely impartial between the various parties to the conflict. Those personnel who were armed would have standing instructions to use force to the minimum extent necessary and normally only in self-defence.

United Nations troops and police monitors would be deployed in certain areas in Croatia, designated as "United Nations Protected Areas." Those areas would be demilitarized; all armed forces in them would be either withdrawn or disbanded. The role of the United Nations troops would be to ensure that the areas remained demilitarized and that all persons residing in them were protected from fear of armed attack.

The role of United Nations police monitors would be to ensure that the local police forces carried out their duties without discrimination against persons of any nationality or abusing anyone's human rights. As the United Nations Force assumed its responsibilities in the United Nations Protected Areas (UNPAS), all Yugoslav National Army (JNA) forces deployed elsewhere in Croatia would be relocated outside that republic.

The United Nations Force would also, as appropriate, assist the humanitarian agencies of the United Nations in the return of all displaced persons who so desired to their homes in the UNPAS.

The UNPAS would be areas in Croatia in which the Secretary-General judged that special arrangements were required during an interim period to ensure that a lasting ceasefire was maintained. They would be areas in which Serbs constituted the majority or a substantial minority of the population and where inter-communal tensions had led to armed conflict in the recent past. The special arrangements in these areas would be of an interim nature and would not prejudge the outcome of political negotiations for a comprehensive settlement of the Yugoslav crisis. There would be three UNPAS: Eastern Slavonia, Western Slavonia and Krajina. The districts contained in each of them were enumerated.

---

1 Report of the Secretary-General pursuant to Security Council resolution 721 (1991), UN doc. S/23280, Annex III.

The functions of protecting the inhabitants of the UNPAs would be shared between the United Nations Force's infantry units and its civilian police monitors. The infantry would ensure that the UNPAs remained demilitarized. The police monitors would ensure that the local police carried out their duties without discrimination against any nationality and with full respect for the human rights of all residents of the UNPAs.

The infantry units would be deployed throughout the UNPAs. They would be lightly armed but would use armoured personnel carriers and helicopters. They would control access to the UNPAs by establishing check-points on all roads and principal tracks leading into them and at important junctions inside them. At these check-points they would stop and, if necessary, search vehicles and individuals to ensure that no military formations or armed groups entered the UNPAs and that no weapons, ammunition, explosives or other military equipment were brought into them. They would patrol extensively inside the UNPAs on foot, and by vehicle and helicopter. They would also investigate any complaints made to them about violations of the demilitarized status of the UNPAs. Any confirmed violations would be taken up with the offending party and would, if necessary, be reported by the Secretary-General to the Security Council. If serious tension were to develop between nationalities in a UNPA, the United Nations Force would interpose itself between the two sides in order to prevent hostilities.

The civilian police monitors would also be deployed throughout the UNPAs. They would be unarmed. They would have no executive responsibility for the maintenance of public order but they would closely monitor the work of the local police forces. To this end, they would be located with police headquarters in each region and opstina (district) and would accompany the local police on their patrols and in their performance of their other duties. They would investigate any complaints of discrimination or other abuse of human rights and would report to the Chief of the United Nations Force any confirmed cases of discrimination or abuses. They would require free and immediate access to all premises and facilities of, or under the control of, the local police forces.

The United Nations Force would also include a group of military observers. They would be unarmed, in accordance with normal UN practice. They would initially be deployed in the UNPAs to verify the demilitarization of those areas. As soon as demilitarization had been effected, the military observers would be transferred to parts of Bosnia and Herzegovina adjacent to Croatia. Their functions there would be to patrol extensively, to liaise with the local authorities and to warn the Chief of the United Nations Force if inter-communal tension threatened to disturb the peace and tranquillity established by the Force in the

UNPAs. Their good offices would be available to help resolve local difficulties and to investigate allegations of inter-communal tension or aggression.

In accordance with established international principles, the United Nations policy would be to facilitate the return to their homes of all persons displaced by the recent hostilities who so desired. The lead in that matter was taken by the humanitarian agencies of the United Nations. United Nations forces would provide all appropriate support to this effort in the UNPAs. The United Nations police monitors would have an especially important role in this regard.

2 The Practice of Protection

The challenges of protecting the areas, and the valiant performance of UNPROFOR personnel, could be seen in the following illustrative report from Sector West on 5 November, 1993. On the political front, the Civil Affairs Officers reported that the situation in Sector West remained calm but tense. The Croatian Government had repeated its warning to UNPROFOR that it might attack the Serb-controlled part of the Sector. The Serb side was protesting against the presence of around 150 heavily armed Croatian Special Police inside the Sector.

Civil Affairs had nearly succeeded in arranging a further face-to-face meeting between the Croatian and Serb political and police leaders on 3 November but the Serb side had cancelled at the last moment. Civil Affairs would keep trying. Meanwhile, the Sector Commander was contacting the military leaders of both sides, trying to arrange a face-to-face meeting aimed at concluding a ceasefire agreement.

On human rights issues, Civil Affairs and CIVPOL had continued their activities aimed at the protection of human rights of ethnic minorities on both sides of the Sector. On the Croatian side, Civil Affairs had been approached by local Serb citizens who had requested assistance in obtaining citizenship papers and other official documents. In Daruvar, Civil Affairs had started working on the case of discriminatory job dismissal of a Serb woman. In Grubisno Polje, Civil Affairs had visited people requesting humanitarian assistance and old people who wanted to be reunited with their children living in Bosnia. Steps had been taken, in cooperation with UNHCR, to arrange for their medical evacuation through the channels of the ICRC. On the Serb side, Civil Affairs had been taking up the cases of Croats prevented by local authorities from leaving or, in one instance, from coming back, to join families. In each of these two cases the applicants had been waiting for two to six months.

CIVPOL also continued their involvement in the protection of human rights prisoners, both within the Sector, and prisoners taken from the sector to prisons outside the UNPA. This had been accomplished by making periodic prison visits on both sides and interviewing POWS. CIVPOL continued monitoring a wide variety of human rights related investigations in the Sector ranging from murders, sexual assaults, missing persons, harassment, and in cooperation with Civil Affairs, eviction from residences and wrongful dismissal from employment. CIVPOL had also been liaising with UN officials on the excavation of mass grave sites in Sector West.

> On both sides of the Sector, the number of local citizens requesting UNPROFOR's assistance in obtaining documents required for crossing the cease-fire line had increased. Civil Affairs and UNHCR had continued to provide humanitarian assistance for old and sick people on both sides of the Sector.[2] UNPROFOR was doing what it could in the circumstances.

A fair-minded observer would probably grant that UNPROFOR did contribute in some measure to the protection of people in the UNPAS. At the same time, there were limitations to the UN operations and some of these were brought out in a Discussion Paper published by the Refugee Project of the Lawyers Committee for Human Rights in September, 1993.[3] This discussion paper, authored by a highly qualified team of seasoned scholar/practitioners,[4] concluded that a basic underlying assumption to the humanitarian response – that human rights and refugee protection can be provided through the presence of international personnel – was suspect in the situation of the former Yugoslavia. Dedicated UN field personnel had helped many individuals but severe restrictions on access to the concerned populations had rendered many protection activities illusory. "There are no U.N. – imposed guarantors of respect for human rights, the rule of law, or protection for the displaced population."[5] This begs the question, could there be but very rarely "U.N. – imposed guarantors"?

The authors of the report concluded that the original rationale for the four United Nations Protected Areas (UNPAS) had been largely frustrated and that political considerations and objections to disturbing the demographic

2 Document in the possession of the author.

3 Lawyers Committee for Human Rights, Refugee Project. Discussion Paper: Protection by Presence. The Limits of United Nations Safekeeping Activities in Croatia, September, 1993.

4 The late Arthur Helton, Guy Goodwin-Gill, Walter Kalin, Michel Moussali, and Deborah Blatt.

5 Ibid, p. 5.

composition in the UNPAs had caused UN forces at times to neglect human rights and refugee protection principles by rejecting and restricting the movements of asylum seekers at borders. This conflict of interests, they felt, should have been addressed by promulgating explicitly in the mandate of UNPROFOR and other concerned agencies and entities the primacy of human rights and refugee protection.[6] Again, this was an admirable recommendation, but could it have been negotiated in the UN Security Council and who would have enforced it? In the end, it took the air forces of NATO to bring the Bosnian Serbs to heel in 1995. In 1992–93 hardly any Government would have been willing to join in an enforcement operation.

3 Successful Prevention: Preventive Peacekeeping in Macedonia

The initiative for a preventive deployment first came from the Co-chairman of the International Conference on the Former Yugoslavia. They had discussed this idea with President Kiro Gligorov who, in turn, wrote to the Secretary-General of the United Nations on 11 November 1992 asking for such a preventive deployment. In a letter of 18 November 1992, to the United Nations Secretary-General, the Co-chairmen, former US Secretary of State Cyrus Vance and former British Foreign Minister Lord David Owen, told him there was growing need to take preventive measures to avoid the outbreak of violence in Macedonia and Kosovo. They recalled that they had warned the Security Council a few days earlier, on 13 November 1992, that a tragedy of dreadful proportions could occur if conflict were to break out in Macedonia and Kosovo, engulfing the neighbouring countries.

Elaborating upon their idea, the Co-chairmen stated that in terms of preventive diplomacy it would be desirable to put United Nations personnel, under the aegis of UNPROFOR, into Macedonia so as to provide a calming influence for all sides and give a sense of stability. They suggested to the Secretary-General:

> The deployment of a contingent of UNPROFOR personnel within Macedonia, who could have their headquarters in Skopje and be distributed in the main population centres, as well as on the Macedonian borders with Serbia (including Kosovo) and Albania. Their efforts would be complemented by those of the CSCE, which already had a small 'spill-over mission' in Skopje.

6 Ibid, p. 6.

The Co-chairmen suggested that, as a start, about a dozen United Nations military and police officers, with supporting political staff, be sent. They could be stationed in Skopje and could travel to the border areas. In the light of their experience and recommendations, the United Nations presence could be built up as needed. The Co-chairmen were conscious of the scarcity of United Nations resources and they were seeking to indicate a way to implement their recommendation even in the face of that scarcity.

Upon receipt of the Co-chairmen's recommendation, Secretary-General Boutros Boutros-Ghali advised the Security Council that he would be sending an exploratory mission to the FYR of Macedonia to look into the possibility of establishing a preventive deployment of United Nations peace-keepers in the country. Following its visit, the exploratory mission made the following recommendations:

> that a small UNPROFOR presence be established on the Macedonian side of the Republic's borders with Albania and the Federal Republic of Yugoslavia (Serbia and Montenegro) with an essentially preventive mandate of monitoring and reporting any developments in the border areas which could undermine confidence and stability in Macedonia or threaten its territory.
>
> that a small group of United Nations civilian police be deployed in the border areas to monitor the Macedonian border police.

The rationale for the latter deployment was that incidents arising from illegal attempts to cross the border had led to increased tension on the Macedonian side. The Mission believed that the presence of a small United Nations civilian police detachment would have a calming effect.

In December 1992, the Secretary-General reported to the Security Council on the findings of the exploratory mission, together with his recommendations.[7] On 11 December 1992, the Security Council authorized the Secretary-General to establish a presence of the United Nations Protection force (UNPROFOR) in the FYR of Macedonia. The Council requested that the Secretary-General deploy immediately the military, civil affairs, and administrative personnel he had recommended in his report, as well as police monitors.

In mid-December 1992 a United Nations team discussed practical arrangements with the Government in Skopje. The first UNCIVPOL monitors arrived on 27 December 1992. They were eventually deployed along the northern and

7 S/24923.

western borders. On 28 December, a reconnaissance team went to the country to make arrangements for the interim deployment of a Canadian company. On 7 January 1993, a Canadian company arrived in the country pending the arrival of a joint battalion from Finland, Norway and Sweden. On 25 January, Brigadier-General Finn Saermark-Thomsen of Denmark, who had been designated Commander of the Macedonia Command of UNPROFOR, arrived in Skopje. On 18 February, the Nordic battalion took over the operation from the Canadian company.

The Nordic battalion was 434 strong, composed of three rifle companies. It was deployed on the western border from Debar northward and on the northern border up to the border with Bulgaria. At the beginning there were 19 United Nations Military Observers (UNMOs) in the area of operations. The western border south of Debar was covered solely by UNMOs.

From early January 1993, the northern border and the western border north of Debar were constantly monitored from observation posts and by regular patrols, with a view to reporting any activities that might increase tension or threaten peace and stability. The UNMOs conducted regular patrols in their area of operations to monitor the situation. They also carried out a programme of visits to border villages aimed at gaining the confidence of their inhabitants and assisting in defusing possible inter-ethnic tensions.

While carrying out their border visiting programme, the UNMOs were approached by representatives of different ethnic groups who lodged various complaints about alleged discriminatory practices by the authorities. In those cases where the complaints were relevant to the mandate of the mission, they were brought to the attention of the appropriate authorities. Some were also brought to the attention of the competent international bodies, such as the International Conference of the Former Yugoslavia.

UNCIVPOL also conducted regular patrols to specific crossings and the border areas in general on a daily basis. In the course of doing so, it received through local mayors a number of complaints concerning the local border police. In those cases where there appeared *prima facie* to be a basis for the complaint, UNCIVPOL took up the matter with the relevant police authorities.

The Civil Affairs component of the mission established, from the outset, an information programme to explain the role of UNPROFOR in the country. UNPROFOR maintained close coordination with the CSCE mission in the country.

By the middle of 1993, UNPROFOR's assessment was that it had been successful in its preventive mandate in the country. It was concerned, however, about the internal situation and the possibility of instability should there be an increase in the inter-ethnic tensions, a possibility which, it reported, was repeatedly mentioned by local and international sources. A related concern of UNPROFOR was about the deterioration of the economic situation stemming from the implementation of sanctions which, it was felt, could contribute to heightened inter-ethnic tensions.

By September 1993, the Secretary-General reported to the Security Council that the FYROM Command of UNPROFOR consisted of 1,190 military and civilian, including UNCIVPOL personnel. A Nordic battalion was based at Kjojila, east of Skopje, and a United States contingent of 315 troops had arrived in Skopje in early July, deploying to the FYROM side of the border with the Federal Republic of Yugoslavia on 20 August 1993. United Nations Military Observers, UNCIVPOL and Civil Affairs officers were also continuing their activities. UNPROFOR reported: "This first venture in the field of preventive peace-keeping on the part of UNPROFOR continues to be successful, and to enjoy an excellent cooperative relationship with the FYROM Government, and to be fully supported by the people of the country."

The leadership of the preventive deployment would come to conclude that "the increasing internal instability in the FYROM could prove to be more detrimental to the stability of the country than outside threats." UNPROFOR would therefore need "to consider what its role should be, if any, in the event that internal instability results in some form of civil conflict."[8]

Thus it was that the deployment developed the second of its three pillars, as presented by Sokalski, good offices and political action, alongside troop deployment and the human dimension. As Sokalski has written, the mission developed and maintained active contacts with political forces and ethnic groups in the country as a means of promoting domestic stability. Efforts were made to reduce the level of mistrust among the country's political and ethnic actors and UNPREDEP set in place a dialogue on questions regarding the rights of ethnic communities and national minorities. Sokalski has written:

> UNPREDEP was recognized as a significant instrument for facilitating dialogue, restraint and practical compromise between the different segments of Macedonian society. UN troop patrols along the northern and western borders of the country effectively complemented such activities; this outreach had a calming and stabilizing effect throughout the area.

8 Background paper submitted by the FYROM Command to Brainstorming Exercise on the future of UNPROFOR, Zagreb-Mokrice, 15–17 February 1994. Paper in the possession of the author, who participated in the exercise.

> The contingent of UN military observers and the team of civilian police monitors rendered equally invaluable services.[9]

The preventive deployment in the FYR of Macedonia worked effectively – externally as well as internally. The model of United Nations observers patrolling sensitive areas where ethnic tensions were high, receiving complaints, transmitting them to the authorities, and serving as an intermediary and confidence builder is one that clearly has great relevance to situations of ethnic and religious tension, in situations where there are minority populations or in other situations where internal strife or conflict could result in gross violations of human rights. The establishment of a UN rapid reaction force would certainly help facilitate the dispatch of preventive deployment of UN peacekeepers in situations of urgent need.

4 Successful Conflict Prevention on the Tense Geece-Macedonia Situation (1993)

Cyrus Vance and Lord Owen undoubtedly made an invaluable contribution to successful conflict prevention in the dispute between Greece and Macedonia. The situation between the two countries had been tense as a result of the former Yugoslav republic giving itself a name, a flag and an emblem that Greece strongly objected to. Greece also objected to certain provisions of Macedonia's constitution. Greece asserted that all of these things indicated an expansionist policy aimed at creating a Greater Macedonia with areas taken from Greece and Bulgaria. Considering that Macedonia had less than a tenth of Greece's population and maybe a quarter of its resources, the Greek concern possibly stemmed from its experience with the 1946–1949 civil war and the precarious state of its own Government in 1993.

Macedonia was home to a sizeable number of Serbs and Albanians, and their legal and practical situation was of concern to the two other neighbours of the new State. Consequently ICFY's Working Group on Ethnic Communities, Nationalities and Minorities sponsored negotiations between, respectively, the Macedonian Serbs and Albanians and the Macedonian Government. The Working Group helped resolve some points of particular friction such as

9 H. Sokalski, *An Ounce of Prevention: Macedonia and the UN Experience in Preventive Diplomacy*, Washington, D.C.: United States Institute for Peace, 2003, 108. See also, A. Williams, *Preventing War: The UN and Macedonia*, Lanham, MD: Rowman & Littlefield, 2000.

language of schooling, and generally sought to promote the establishment of effective human rights protection institutions, with both domestic and international elements.

When Macdedonia sought to be admitted to the United Nations under the name Republic of Macedonia, Greece rallied support against its admission to the world organization under this name. The Security Council adopted resolution 817 (1993) in which it noted that "a difference has arisen over the name of the State, which needs to be resolved in the interest of the maintenance of peaceful and good neighbourly relations in the region", and "welcomed…the readiness…of the Co-Chairmen of the Steering Committee of the International Conference on the Former Yugoslavia, at the request of the Secretary-General, to use their good offices to settle the abovementioned difference, and to promote confidence-building measures among the parties."

On 12 April, 1993, the Co-Chairmen wrote to the Secretary-General stating their readiness to help settle the differences and to promote confidence-building measures among the parties. They said that they would do so expeditiously and report to the Secretary-General within two months at the latest. The UN Secretary-General formally wrote to Vance and Owen on 13 April, 1993 requesting them to use their good offices to settle the differences that had arisen in connection with the request for admission to membership in the United Nations of the State that was admitted under the name of the Former Yugoslav Republic of Macedonia and to promote confidence-building measures among the parties.

Vance and Owen undertook a month of proximity talks. The Greeks had refused to meet directly with the Macedonians. Immediately after they had written to the Secretary-General on 12 April, Vance and Owen held two meetings with a Greek delegation led by Foreign Minister Papaconstantinou. On the same day, they also met with a delegation from the FYROM, led by Deputy Prime Minister and Acting Foreign Minister Crvenkovski. Vance and Owen met again with the delegations the next day, 13 April.

The discussions took place against the background of earlier work done within the framework of the European Community conference on the former Yugoslavia (the Carrington Conference), and in particular: Opinion No. 6 on the recognition of the Socialist Republic of Macedonia by the European Community and its member States rendered by the Arbitration Commission presided over by Mr R. Badinter: and the Draft Treaty for the Confirmation of the Existing Frontier prepared by Sir Robin O'Neil, Envoy of the President of the European Community.

During the course of the discussions, the two delegations raised issues that they wished Vance and Owen to consider. The two sides also provided written submissions in support of their positions. In particular, the Greek delegation expressed concern about the contents of the Preamble, Article 3 and Article 49 of the Constitution of the 'State represented by the other delegation'. It also made suggestions with respect to the content of the draft Treaty for the Confirmation of the Existing Frontier.

The delegation of the FYROM suggested that the two countries sign an Agreement of Friendship and Cooperation, and provided a draft for the consideration of the Co-Chairmen. Among the specific issues the delegation raised were the need to ensure the free flow of goods, peoples and ideas without discrimination; the need to re-establish as quickly as possible the treaty relations that had previously existed between Greece and the Socialist Federal Republic of Yugoslavia: and provisions of Greek legislation which, it claimed, hindered the exercise of civil, property and legal rights of citizens on the basis of ethnic background.

Following this initial round of discussions, Vance and Owen arranged for technical discussions to be held from 14 to 26 Aptil 1993 between the legal experts of ICFY and the legal experts of the two delegations. The late Paul Szasz and this writer participated for ICFY. During the course of these technical discussions, a working paper was prepared by the ICFY representatives and submitted to the two delegations on 21 April, 1993 for their comments.

Additionally, Lord Owen, accompanied by Mr Vance's Special Adviser, Ambassador Herbert Okun, held talks with the parties in their capitals. On 22 and 23 April, they met with President Gligorov in Skopje and Prime Minister Mitsotakis and Special Envoy Papoulias in Athens.

Further discussions on the ICFY working paper were held with the two delegations between 27 and 29 April at UN Headquarters in New York. On 29 April, 1993, Vance and Owen submitted to the two sides a draft Treaty Confirming the Existing Frontier and Establishing Measures for Confidence Building, Friendship and Neighbourly Cooperation between the two countries.

On 14 May, 1993, Vance and Owen wrote to UN Secretary-General Boutros Boutros-Ghali informing him that on that very day they were transmitting the draft treaty to the Foreign Ministers of the two countries with the request they consult on it and on the proposed name they suggested, "The Republic of Nova Makedonija", in strictest confidence within their respective Governments, and inform the Co-Chairmen as soon as possible of the acceptability of the package.

Vance and Owen thus proposed to the parties a comprehensive treaty that on the one hand gave the Greeks much of what they wanted in respect of the

Macedonian flag and Constitution, and on the other would establish normal and, in principle, close relations that were particularly important to poor and land-locked Macedonia.

However, after every clause in the proposed treaty was settled, the Co-Chairmen were unable to come up with a name acceptable to both parties and the one they finally proposed was, after consideration, rejected by both. However the Greeks, influenced by Vance and Owen, finally offered to negotiate directly with Macdeonia.

Cyrus Vance had decided to step down from ICFY at the beginning of May, 1993, but he continued to mediate in the dispute between Greece and Macedonia. Relations between the two countries deteriorated further in February, 1994, when Greece placed a punitive trade embargo on Macedonia, which lasted for more than eighteen months. The situation calmed down in 1995 when the two sides signed an Interim Agreement in New York. Cyrus Vance continued to assist as UN mediator until 1999 when he was succeeded by Matthew Nimitz.

We shall deal with the further mediation of the dispute in Chapter Ten below. For the purposes of the present chapter, it suffices to reiterate that UN good offices and mediation had helped contain the situation and prevent it from degenerating into conflict between the two countries and possibily pulling in neighbouring countries as well. The UN mediators had truly engaged in the art of the possible.

5 International Monitors on the Drina

ICFY's International Monitoring Mission on the Drina can be considered a successful preventive operation. The background was that the Bosnian Serb leadership had peeled itself off from the leadership in Belgrade when it came to the negotiation of a settlement of the conflict in Bosnia and Herzegovina. In the process the Bosnian Serb military was behaving more and more in a criminal manner leading countries of the NATO alliance to threaten Belgrade with bombing raids unless it brought the Bosnian Serb leadership to book.

Under pressure from NATO countries, President Slobodan Milosevic, then President of the Federal Republic of Yugoslavia, instituted economic sanctions against the Bosnian Serbs: fuel and goods would no longer be permitted to move from Serbia across the Drina River to Bosnian Serb territory. This did not satisfy the NATO leadership. They called for international monitoring of the sanctions. President Milosevic, and probably the Serbian people, were not prepared to countenance the idea of international monitors on Serbian territory.

Thorvald Stoltenberg and Lord Owen met President Milosevic frequently to explore the options for peace and to help defuse dangerous situations. The year was 1993 and the international community was still in quest of peaceful solutions to the conflicts in the Former Yugoslavia. During a meeting with Thorvald Stoltenberg and Lord Owen, at which I was present, President Milosevic intimated that he would look favourably upon the deployment of humanitarian personnel, by humanitarian organizations, to witness the implementation of sanctions against the Bosnian Serbs across the Drina River.

This was a faint opening. That very evening, Thorvald Stoltenberg, a former Foreign Minister of Norway, called his friends, the Foreign Ministers of Denmark, Finland, Norway and Sweden, with a request: would they consider providing, each, ten humanitarian personnel from humanitarian organizations and give a start-up contribution of one hundred thousand dollars for a humanitarian operation to witness the sanctions on the Drina? They all replied positively, either on the spot, or within twenty-four hours.

As Director of the International Conference on the Former Yugoslavia I worked personally on the establishment of this mission and watched over its operations substantively and managerially during its existence. It was an extraordinary effort on the part of all involved and it shows what can be achieved with a sense of daring and innovation: Two Norwegian humanitarian operatives came from Oslo with one hundred thousand Deutschemarks in a suitcase and proceeded to Belgrade. There they secured office-space in a hotel, began to acquire a fleet of vehicles, purchased fuel on the black-market in Belgrade, and laid the ground-work for an operation that would last three years and at one stage would have dozens of international monitors on the ground and hundreds of locals supporting them.

Stoltenberg and Owen designated Brigadier-General Bo Pellnas as Head of the Mission and he was later succeeded by a Finnish General, Tauno Nieminen. Both served the international community with great distinction. We financed the Mission through contributions from a coalition of countries participating in the International Conference on the Former Yugoslavia. Stoltenberg and Owen insisted from the outset on flexibility for the Mission. The UN Director of Administration in Geneva was dead set against this and it fell to me to set up a system, audited by Price Waterhouse, at it then was, outside of the UN framework. I had Price Waterhouse audit the Mission regularly to ensure that it was above board in all respects. Price Waterhouse issued several audit reports certifying the financial soundness of the Mission's administration.

The task of the Mission, in this instance, was to monitor the application of sanctions imposed by Belgrade against Pale and it did this professionally. The precedent, however, is one that could be used, as needed, on specifically human rights tasks where required. The ICFY Mission showed that the mediators, on their own authority, could establish and operate for a period of three years a Mission of hundreds of personnel, operating in a framework of accountability outside of the United Nations administrative rigidity, and render credible reports to the negotiators and the international community. The precedent is one that offers much to peace negotiators wishing to establish or use *ad hoc* international human rights field missions in situations of concern.

6 A Missed Opportunity for a Preventive Deployment in Kosovo?

As we saw in the preceding section, it was an initiative from Vance and Owen on 18 November, 1992 that led to the eventual establishment of UNPREDEP. There is among the ICFY papers a letter from the President of Albania, Sali Berisha, dated 25 December, 1992, addressed to Cyrus Vance as ICFY Co-Chairman, expressing growing concern over the situation then prevailing in Kosovo. President Berisha referred to the idea of a preventive deployment outlined in Secretary-General Boutros-Ghali's report, An Agenda for Peace, and continued:

> The Republic of Albania has hailed the UN Security Council Resolution 795 to send UN forces to Macedonia, as a guarantee of preserving the delicate peace there. Urged by the same ends, I take the opportunity to request from you…the support of ICFY to send these forces to Kosovo. Time is running very fast. Peace is hinging on rapidity and cooperation.[10]

On 29 December, 1992, Vance and Owen replied to President Berisha in the following terms:

> Regarding the specific proposal contained in your letter, namely a preventive deployment in the province, this will require, as you will appreciate, the consent of the Federal Republic of Yugoslavia, followed by an affirmative decision by the United Nations Security Council.
>
> It seems to us that it might be advisable for you to initiate an exchange with the authorities of the Federal Republic of Yugoslavia on measures that all sides could take to maintain calm, to promote confidence and stability and to defuse the situation in Kosovo. Your proposal for a preventive deployment in Kosovo could be raised in that context.

10 Text in the possession of the author.

> You and your government can play a very crucial role in calming the situation by promoting restraint on all sides, particularly the Kosovo Albanian leadership. The positions and actions of your Government are, of course, very important in this regard.[11]

Earlier in the letter, Vance and Owen recalled their meeting with President Berisha in Tirana on 29 October, 1992, in which they had explained to him their view that stability in Kosovo should be secured through genuine autonomy for the province rather than secession or unilateral declaration of independence.

At the end of December, 1992, Vance and Owen, in addition to having proposed a preventive deployment in Macedonia, had invited the leaders of the Federal Republic of Yugoslavia and Croatia, and of the three Bosnian parties, to commence peace talks in Geneva on 2 January, 1993. They thus had their hands full. In addition, President Slobodan Milosevic of Serbia, whose state had jurisdiction over Kosovo at the time, was clearly indicating that he would not agree to the internationalisation of the Kosovo issue.

Whatever the factors that influenced Vance and Owen at the time, given the subsequent history of the province, the grievous human rights violations that took place, the prolonged massive NATO air assault on Serbia, one would be forgiven for asking whether Vance and Owen might have used President Berisha's letter as an opportunity to explore the idea of a preventive deployment in Kosovo and engaged in some diplomacy to this end. Might this, with hindsight, have been a missed opportunity?

One will never know whether the initiative might have made any headway. There had been a CSCE long-term monitoring mission in Kosovo but Belgrade had asked them to leave in July, 1993, following the CSCE's exclusion of Belgrade from the Organization. On 7 April, 1994, the US Permanent Mission in New York gave to the UN Secretariat a paper proposing the deployment of international monitors in Kosovo. They apparently had also raised the idea in Moscow and in the capitals of EU countries. The US initiative proposed a joint EU/Russian/US demarche urging Belgrade to reconsider its refusal to accept international monitors in Kosovo.

According to the US note, "Monitors in Kosovo", the Americans said that they would be willing to show flexibility on the nature of the proposed observer mission. While they would prefer a return of the CSCE, if a CSCE mission remained unacceptable to Belgrade, the US would propose sending monitors from the United Nations. The US made it clear, however, that it was not willing to admit Serbia into the CSCE or improve Serbia's status at the UN as the "price"

11 Text in the possession of the author.

for readmitting CSCE monitors or allowing UN monitors. The US ideas paper given to the UN Secretariat stated however:

> Belgrade can be assured that none of the nations participating in the demarche favors independence – as LDK has proposed – for Kosovo.[12]

At a later stage, in 1994, the Kosovar Albanian leader asked Thorvald Stoltenberg, when they met in Oslo, to facilitate a meeting between himself and President Slobodan Milosevic. Stoltenberg and Owen raised the matter with Milosevic and he agreed on condition that Rugova would approach him directly. Stoltenberg and Owen drafted the following letter and gave it to Rugova for him to send to Milosevic:

> Mr President,
>
> Some time ago I had a conversation in Oslo with Mr Thorvald Stoltenberg, Co-Chairmen of ICFY. We both recognized the importance of dialogue to deal with issues. I have since been informed by the Co-Chairmen, Lord Owen and Thorvald Stoltenberg, that you yourself support such dialogue and would be ready for us to meet. May I therefore suggest that we meet at a mutually convenient time, possibly in the week beginning 28 November, 1994?
>
> Yours sincerely,
> Ibrahim Rugova.[13]

As far as we are aware, Rugova never sent the letter, and an idea that he himself had suggested did not go forward. We believed at the time that Rugova could not persuade the hard-liners in his entourage who preferred a more robust approach to achieving their objectives of the independence of Kosovo.

Conclusion

Without a doubt, one could see from the foregoing serious, substantive, and meaningful efforts for conflict containment and prevention. In the midst of conflict this is no easy thing. Peacemakers, peacekeepers and humanitarian leaders have to be pragmatic and innovative at the same time. Both of these elements were at work in the former Yugoslavia.

---

12 Text of the US paper in the possession of the author.

13 Text in the possession of the author.

CHAPTER 10

Peacemaking

Success on Greece-Macedonia

Introduction

In the preceding chapter we saw how Cyrus Vance and Lord Owen successfully contributed to conflict containment in the dispute between Greece and Macedonia in the spring of 1993. Cyrus Vance stepped down from the Chairmanship of ICFY after the Bosnian Serbs completed the three sides's signature of the Vance-Owen plan at the beginning of May, 1993, but he continued to mediate in the dispute between Greece and Macedonia and his efforts were rewarded with success when the two sides signed on 13 September, 1995, an Interim Accord.[1] The Interim Accord settled many important aspects of the dispute between the two countries, as we shall see below, but the dispute over the name of the Former Yugoslav Republic of Macedonia is still ongong as of the time of writing. Mr Matthew Nimitz has taken over from the late Cyrus Vance as the UN mediator on this continuing problem. However, the Interim Accord negotiated by Vance established the basis for normal relations between the two countries which have endured since 1995 notwithstanding occasional hiccups stemming from the issue of the name. In this chapter we trace the essential features of the Interim Accord, beginning with the hoops that Vance had to jump through to bring the parties to agreement.

I The Party of the First Part and the Party of the Second Part

Because of their dispute over the name of Macedonia, the Accord was concluded between the Party of the First Part (Greece) and the party of the Second Part (FYROM) ! To give effect to the agreements they had reached, the Foreign Minister of Greece wrote a letter to Mr Vance informing him that Greece recognized the Party of the Second Part within its internationally recognized borders with the provisional name of the former Yugoslav Republic of Macedonia pending the settlemet of the difference that had arisen over the name of the

1 UN Treaty Series No. 32193. Greece and the Former Yugoslav Republic of Macedonia. Interim Accord (with related letters and translations of the Interim Accord in the languages of the Contracting parties). Signed at New York on 13 September, 1995.

 DOI 10.1163/9789004245907_014

State. Vance then wrote to the Foreign Minister of the FYROM transmitting the Greek letter whereupon the latter wrote to Vance acknowledging receipt of his letter and of the letter that the Greeks had sent to Vance. There was another exchange from Greece to Vance then on to the FYROM and then from the latter back to Vance about the emblem chosen by the FYROM.

If ever the UN could be seen engaging in the art of the possible, it was in achieving agreement on the Interim Accord.

II Principles

The Interim Accord begain by recalling the principles of the inviolability of frontiers and the territorial integrity of States incorporated in the Helsinki Final Act of the Conference on Security and Cooperation in Europe in 1975. This was Greece's way of obtaining assurance that Macedonia would not pursue territorial ambitions on Greek territory.

The Parties invoked the provisions of the United Nations Charter, particularly those referring to the obligations of States to refrain in their international relations from the threat or use of force against the territorial integrity or political independence of any State. They also invoked the spirit and principles of democracy and fundamental freedoms and respect for human rights and dignity.

They expressed their desire to confirm the existing frontier between them as an enduring international border and also their desire to develop their mutual relations and to lay firm foundations for a climate of peadceful relations and understanding. They affirmed their desire to reach certain interim agreements that would provide a basis for negotiating a permanent Accord.

III Breakthroughs

There can be no doubt that the Interim Accord registered major breakthroughs. Upon the entry into force of the accord Greece recognized the FYROM under this name and the Parties agreed that they would, at an early date, establish diplomatic relations at an agreed level with the ultimate goal of relations at the ambassadorial level. They each agreed to establish liaison offices in the other's capital as promptly as possible.

The two sides, by the treaty, confirmed their common existing border as an enduring and inviolable international border. Each party undertook to respect the sovereignty, the territorial integrity and the political independence of the other Party. Each party pledged not to support the action of a third party directed against the sovereignty, territorial integrity or the political independence of the other party. The parties agreed to refrain from the threat or use of force against one another.

The parties agreed to continue negotiations under the auspices of the Secretary-General of the United Nations pursuant to Security Council resolution 845 (1993) with a view to reaching agreement on the issue of the name of the FYROM. In an important provision in the second paragraph of Article 5, the Parties, recognizing the difference between them with respect to the name of the FYROM, nevertheless agreed to cooperate with a view to facilitating their mutual relations notwithstanding their respective positions as to the name of the FYROM. In this regard, the Parties agreed to take practical measures, including dealing with the matter of documents, to carry out normal trade and commerce between them in a manner consistent with their respective positions in regard to the name of the FYROM. The Parties undertook to take practical measures so that the difference about the name would not obstruct or interfere with normal trade and commerce between them.

The FYROM solemnly declared that nothing in its Constitution and in particular in the Preamble thereto or in Article 3 of the Constitution, could or should be interpreted as constituting or would ever constitute the basis of any claim by it to any territory not within its existing borders.

The Parties undertook to promptly take effective measures to prohibit hostile activities or propaganda by State-controlled agencfies and to discourage acts by private entities likely to incite violence, hatred or hostility against each other.

The Parties undertook to refrain from imposing any impediments to the movement of people or goods between the territory of either Party to the territory of the other. Both Parties undertook to cooperate to facilitate such movements in accordance with international law and custom.

The Parties agreed that the European Union and the United States may be requested to use their good offices with respect to developing practical measures dealing with the matter of documents, and the carrying out of normal trade and commerce between them.

The Parties pledged to be guided by the spirit and principles of democracy, fundamental freedoms, respect for human rights and dignity, and the rule of law, in accordance with the Charter of the United Nations, the Universal Declaration of Human Rights, the European Convention for the Protection of Human Rights and Fundamental Freedoms, the International Convention on the Elimination of all Forms of Racial Discrimination, the Convention on the Rights of the Child, the Helsinki Final Act, the document of the Copenhagen

Meeting of the Conference on the Human Dimension of the CSCE and the Charter of Paris for a New Europe.

Pursuant to the Interim Accord, Greece undertook not to object to the application by, or the membership of the FYROM in, international, multilaterial and regional organizations of which Greece was a member.

IV Treaty Relations

Pursuant to the Interim Accord, the Parties agreed that their relations shall be guided by previous bilateral agreements between Greece and the former Socialist Federal Republic of Yugoslavia, in particular: (a) The convention concerning mutual legal relations. (b) The agreement concerning the reciprocal recognition and the enforcement of judidical decisions; and (c) The agreement concering hydro-economic questions.

Bearing in mind that the FYROM is a land-locked country, the Parties agreed that they would be guided by the applicable provisions of the UN Convention on the Law of the Sea as far as practicable.

V Friendly Relations

The Parties agreed to encourage the development of friendly and good-neighbourly relations between them and to reinforce their economic cooperation in all sectors, including that of water resources management. In particular, they undertook to promote, on a reciprocal basis, road, rail, maritime and air transport and communication links.

VI Economic, Commercial, Environmental and Legal Relations

The Parties agreed to strengthen their economic relations in all fields, to develop and improve scientific and technical cooperation, as well as cooperation in the field of education, for the protection of the environment, and in alleviating the consequences of disaster. The Parties also agreed to cooperate in improving business and tourist travel. They further agreed to cooperate in the fight against organized crime, terrorism, economic crimes, narcotics crimes, illegal trade in cultural property, offences against civil air transport and counterfeiting.

Conclusion

Some may consider the dispute between Greece and the FYROM an unfortunate one, but each side held to its positions strongly. The efforts of Cyrus Vance as the UN mediator undoubtedly contributed to setting the relations between the two countries on the right course. Their dispute over the name of the FYROM continues up to the time of writing. But, on the basis of the Interim Accord, they have developed more or less normal relations and are interacting politically, economically, and socially. Vance's mediation of this dispute was, without doubt, a significant contribution to the cause of peace in the Balkans region. Vance had practised the art of the possible with consummate skill.

CHAPTER 11

Peacemaking: Success on the Danube Region of Croatia

The Erdut Agreement

The Erdut Agreement for the Danube region of Croatia was one of the great successes of United Nations peacemaking in the former Yugoslavia. Thorvald Stoltenberg is the undoubted father of this agreement.

ICFY's main efforts on Croatia had been to put down building blocks for peace one by one and to help work out autonomy regimes for the Croatian Serbs that would guarantee them respect for internationally respected standards of human rights and the rights of minorities. Great credit for the drafting of such a regime must go to our dear departed friend Paul Szasz, who bore the brunt of the drafting of this and many other documents in his capacity as Legal Adviser to the International Conference on the Former Yugoslavia.

This effort to work out a regime of autonomy for the Croatian Serbs would come to naught in the end. Tudjman clearly wanted no part of it because he wanted full integration of the Serbs inside a unitary Croatia. As for Milosevic, when the plan was first presented to him and he had studied it, he told Stoltenberg and Owen, "Gentlemen, please do not ruin today ideas that might work in five years time in the future." He also had other ideas in mind and probably wanted to negotiate with Tudjman an exchange of territory in which he would incorporate into Serbia especially the eastern enclave which was separated from Serbia merely by a river.

ICFY, without a doubt, made foundation contributions to the building of peace in Croatia. The Cease-fire Agreement of 29 March, 1994 was one of its important peacebuilding planks. After the cease-fire agreement, which undoubtedly saved many lives, the issue then arose: how to advance on the political front? The Croatian Government was determined to bring the United Nations Protected Areas within the Croatian constitutional and legal order and let it be known openly that they would go to war to achieve their aims unless progress came through negotiations. President Milosevic of Serbia took the view, formally, that it was a matter between the Croatian Government and the Croatian Serbs. He seemed, however, to be playing for time – to put off having to face the moment when he would have to tell the Croatian Serbs that their future lay within Croatia. The one time he gave a glimpse into his thinking, he told Lord Owen and Stoltenberg that he had in mind an autonomous Croatian

 DOI 10.1163/9789004245907_015

Serb republic within the Republic of Croatia. Whether that would include Sector East he did not say. The Croatian Serbs, as did President Milosevic, encouraged ICFY to address issues of economic cooperation and normalisation of economic life in the United Nations Protected Areas with the thesis that the more there was normalisation and economic cooperation, the more the search for political solutions would be facilitated.

The Croatian Government, the Croatian Serbs, and President Milosevic all agreed that following the cease-fire, one should address economic cooperation and political solutions. The Croatian Government wanted these issues taken in tandem. The Croatian Serbs and President Milosevic wanted them taken sequentially, with economic cooperation coming first and thereafter discussion of political solutions. In the final analysis, ICFY did manage to conclude an Economic Agreement on 2 December, which brought in marked improvements in the quality of life for the population of Sectors North, South, and West in particular.

Even as we were working on the economic agreement, and before it as well, the Co-Chairmen had been discussing with their ICFY colleagues, ideas for a political solution for the four United Nations Protected Areas. They focused on ideas which saw them as integral parts of Croatia but would make arrangements for the protection of human and minority rights and provide for a measure of autonomy with regard to educational and cultural matters.

ICFY colleagues, spearheaded by Ambassador Geert Ahrens of Germany and Kai Eide of Norway, assisted by ICFY legal expert, Paul Szasz, developed detailed ideas on these and other topics.

As ICFY was doing this, and as contacts were taking place with Zagreb, Knin and Belgrade, the American and Russian Ambassadors in Zagreb became involved and the Co-Chairmen eventually decided to constitute an informal group that came to be known as the Z-4 Group, comprising ICFY Ambassador Ahrens and Eide, American Ambassador Peter Galbraith and the Russian Ambassador.

By the autumn of 1994 a detailed blueprint had been worked out and the question was when it would be presented to the parties. The Croatian Government had a fairly good idea of what was being worked upon and began to send signals that there was no need to rush with the presentation. It favoured an integrationist approach and seemed to think that the ideas being developed provided for too much autonomy for the Croatian Serbs. President Milosevic for his part strongly counselled against presenting the proposals to the parties. His reasoning was that ideas that could be sold with more time could be killed by presenting them prematurely.

The American and German governments, however, became more and more insistent that the Z-4 ideas be presented to the parties and, following signature of the Economic Agreement on 2 December,1994, pressure for presentation began building up in Washington and Bonn, and through their Ambassadors on the Z-4 group. The end result was that the Z-4 ideas were presented to the Croatian Government on January, 1995, with less than lukewarm reception. The Croatian Serbs, for their part, refused to receive the document.

The Z-4 document took the form of a draft agreement on the Krajina, Slavonia, Southern Baranja and Western Sirmium. It provided for the indivisibility of Croatia. Nothing in it would be deemed to alter the indivisible nature of the Republic of Croatia. The application of the highest level of internationally recognized human rights and fundamental freedoms provided in the Constitution of the Republic of Croatia, in its Constitutional Law on Human Rights and Freedoms and the Rights of National and Ethnic Communities or Minorities in the Republic of Croatia, and in a list of twenty one international human rights instruments should be ensured throughout Croatia. The Republic of Croatia would become, as soon as possible, a party to each of the twenty one international human rights instruments.

The Republic of Croatia would make arrangements with the Council of Europe for the establishment of a Human Rights Court of Croatia in accordance with Resolution 93(6) of the Committee of Ministers of the Council of Europe. The Government of Croatia would also provide for the appointment of Ombudsmen to assist in implementing the above-mentioned rights and freedoms. There would, in addition, be a Special Constitutional Court.

There would be an autonomous Serbian Krajina. The Government of the Republic of Croatia and the Government of the Krajina would have defined areas of competence. The latter would be responsible for education, culture, housing, public services, business, charitable activities, energy, local land use, protection of the environment of the Krajina, natural resources, radio and television, social welfare, tourism, certification of domicile in the Krajina, creation of corporations and other judicial persons, police, and taxation. The legislature of the Krajina would be elected democratically on a proportional basis for a period of four years. The Krajina would be demilitarised.

The draft agreement also provided for arrangements concerning Slavonia, Baranja, Western Sirmium and Other Areas. It contained proposals for special governance and power-sharing for those areas, for power-sharing, and for demilitarization of the areas. It dealt with Minority Population Areas and with norms for the protection of Minorities.

As regards the transitional governance of the Eastern Area, it envisaged that the Secretary-General of the United Nations should, after consultation with the parties, appoint an Administrator for the Eastern Area. The Administrator would exercise all executive functions in respect of the Eastern Area, in addition to other functions specified in the agreement. The Administrator would help facilitate the return of refugees and displaced persons, would organize and control a uniformed police force, which should as soon as possible come to have a proportionally balanced ethnic composition.

The Z-4 document never took root. The Croatian government thought it provided for too much autonomy and showed no interest in it. The Croatian Serbs, in their unreal state, thinking themselves more powerful than they actually were, eventually scuppered an Economic Agreement at the end of April, 1995, thereby giving the Croatian Government a pretext to act militarily. In May, 1995, the Croatian Government re-took Sector West in a lightning attack. In August of the same year, in another lightning attack, it took Sectors North and South. The Z-4 plan lost its raison d'etre, although ideas contained in it would be drawn upon later in the search for a political settlement for Sector East.

As Co-Chairman of the International Conference on the Former Yugoslavia and SRSG Stoltenberg fervently believed that one should try to prevent conflicts, to negotiate peace, and to support peace agreements through cooperative peacekeeping. In the summer of 1994 he sensed that Croatia would take military action against the Serbs in the Krajinas that would result in a mass exodus of Serbs. The Croatian Government, emboldened by the support it was receiving from the USA, gave the Croatian Serbs an ultimatum: accept Croatian sovereignty within twenty four hours or we shall move against you militarily. This was a dark moment in the Yugoslav peace journey.

Stoltenberg performed one of his great roles in trying to prevent the resumption of conflict. He invited the Croatian government and representatives of the Croatian Serbs to urgent meetings in Geneva and negotiated an agreement whereunder the Serbs agreed to accept Croatian sovereignty in exchange for autonomy and minority rights. He sent a cable to the Foreign Ministers of the principal capitals advising them of this but no one moved. As Richard Holbrook has written, Washington was in favour of, and encouraged, military action and the Croatian government moved twenty four hours later and effectively expelled the Serbs from the Krajinas.

Stoltenberg's effort was one of the most daring attempts at conflict prevention that I had witnessed and participated in. Even though it was sabotaged in the end, what Stoltenberg sought to do must count as a heroic endeavour in the annals of conflict prevention. Stoltenberg also had another heroic role in bringing about the renewal of the mandate of UNPROFOR in Croatia.

Emboldened by American backing, it was only a matter of time before the Croatian Government would move to expel the Serbs from the Danube region of Croatia: Eastern Slavonia and associated areas. In the spring and summer of 1995, Stoltenberg conducted quiet shuttle diplomacy between Belgrade and

Zagreb and, step by step, laid the foundations for an eventual peace agreement signed in Erdut on 12 November, 1995. Under the Erdut Agreement, the UN established a Transitional Administration for the Region that lasted two years and was successfully concluded in January 1998. Stoltenberg's efforts have gone largely unheralded. We relate the story of this remarkable peacemaking exercise.

After Croatia had moved militarily on the Northern, Southern and Western Sectors and ethnically cleansed them clean of Serbs the issue still remained to try for an arrangement for the Eastern Sector. With the weakening of the Serbs because of the intransigence and the stupidity of the Bosnian Serbs that had brought the wrath of NATO upon them, Milosevic could no longer hope to negotiate a deal that would give him this eastern region of Croatia. The ground had shifted.

Stoltenberg here played the third of his great heroic roles for peace in the Former Yugoslavia. While Carl Bildt, who had by the beginning of 1995 succeeded Lord Owen, ran with the Contact Group pack on Bosnia-Herzegovina, Stoltenberg began a patient process of shuttling between Belgrade and Zagreb in an effort to promote a peace deal for the eastern sector. He succeeded, supported later by the US Ambassador to Croatia, Peter Galbraith. But the agreement eventually worked out for the eastern sector owes its genesis and its success to Stoltenberg. I was at his side in this lonely period and I participated in every stage of the effort to piece together an agreement. This is a story I know first hand and I know that the credit for it lies with Stoltenberg.

The Stoltenberg shuttle initially involved him acting as a channel of communication between President Tudjman and his key aide H. Sarinic, on the one hand, and President Milosevic on the other. Stoltenberg, on each of these occasions, met Sarinic one on one and Milosevic one on one. After a number of such shuttle visits to the two capitals Stoltenberg arranged, in the greatest secrecy, for an UNPROFOR plane to take Sarinic to Belgrade for a one on one meeting with Milosevic. An understanding was thereby reached by the two sides for talks to begin in Erdut between representatives of the Croatian Government and the Croatian Serb leadership on a transitional regime in the eastern sector.

En route to the first meeting in Erdut, I had a stopover of five hours at the airport in Frankfurt and it was there that I prepared the first draft of a possible agreement which I took to Zagreb to discuss with Stoltenberg. When we arrived there Stoltenberg and I went over the document and finalized it as a working paper. We learned in Zagreb that the US Ambassador, Peter Galbraith, had also been doing some groundwork on this matter. Stoltenberg shared our background paper with Peter Galbraith and Galbraith's able assistant and I then sat down to put heads together. In the end result, we came up with an agreed short outline of principles that might be put to the sides. Galbraith, being Ambassador to Croatia in Zagreb, ran the draft by Sarinic.

When we went to Erdut for the first meeting the Serb leadership was still playing hard-ball. It was as if they had not understood that the ground had shifted from under their feet and that the Serb position, overall, had been greatly weakened. While Peter Galbraith kept the Croatian side in play Stoltenberg worked on the Serb side and eventually the two sides agreed to a statement or principles that would form the basis for the eventual agreement on the eastern sector. I would be forgiven, I hope, for harbouring the thought, to this day, that the seeds for this Statement of Principles had been planted on my computer at Frankfurt Airport!

The peace journey in Croatia had been a tortuous one. At no stage was one dealing with clean hands on any side, save, I thought, when one was interacting with Croatian Foreign Minister Mate Granic, whose negotiating hand was tough but who gave the impression of personal decency and conscientiousness. Of course one made friends who were personally decent also.

Belgrade had sought to stop Croatia from becoming an independent state, just as it had done in Slovenia. But whereas the war in Slovenia had lasted two weeks, in Croatia the fighting had gone on for months, was brutal, as in Vukovar, and four Serb enclaves had persisted in the heart of Croatia which President Franjo Tudjman was determined to overcome. President Slobodan Milosevic, for his part, had handpicked the leadership of the Croatian Serbs and was controlling them from Belgrade until they peeled off from him to their detriment.

Milosevic and Tudjman mistrusted each other, to say the least, and locked horns in Croatia, probably waiting for the moment when they may have to fight again. At the same time they were working to a game plan by which they would have divided Bosnia-Herzegovina between Croatia and Serbia. That was their game plan, beyond the shadow of a doubt.

Tudjman had allies behind the scene in Austria and Germany. Later he would also have the United States. But Milosevic was the undoubted strongman at the outset of the conflict. He had Orthodox Christian sympathies in Greece and in Russia but this did not amount to much in practice. It was one thing to be backed by Germany and the USA. It was another to be backed by a weakened Russia and by NATO member Greece. In any event, every peacemaker, from Vance to Holbrook, knew that without Milosevic peace could hardly be achieved and they all courted him. This strengthened his hand.

In the midst of all of this, United Nations peacekeepers (UNPROFOR), were stationed around the four Serb enclaves, Sectors North, South, East, and West. Tudjman barely tolerated them. He wanted them to serve Croatian interests and would pile on the pressure whenever it suited him. He let it be known that they were there at Croatia's sufferance and, at one stage, openly threatened not to renew their mandate, something we shall write about later in this chapter.

Then, there were places, such as Vukovar, where crimes against humanity had taken place, without a doubt. The patients at Vukovar hospital had been taken out by Serb soldiers, murdered and buried in mass graves, including at a site in Ovcara. Cyrus Vance had visited the Vukovar hospital before the massacre and he was determined to do his part to help bring to justice those responsible for the murders. At his request I worked personally to help bring about the excavation of this mass grave site.

When the peace journey touched Croatia, then, it had to deal with all of the issues mentioned above: helping to prevent the resumption of war; finding a political arrangement to cover the Serb enclaves, in the face of claims by the Serbs, especially those around Knin, that they constituted a people with an independent State and would never accept Croatian sovereignty; dealing with assertions by the Croatian Government that the Serbs constituted a minority who should be given minority rights, something the Serbs bluntly refused to accept; (in the former Yugoslavia the Serbs were considered a people and they would not accept anything less); dealing with issues of human rights and humanitarian law; and watching over the welfare of United Nations peacekeepers caught in the midst of all of this.

One can make the claim that the efforts of Vance and Owen, and then Stoltenberg and Owen, in facilitating communications between Milosevic and Tudjman helped reduce the risks of the resumption of the war for a considerable while. When the war did resume it was during the watch of Richard Holbrooke and he worked for it because he thought, in the face of Bosnian Serb provocations in Srebrenica and elsewhere, that weakening the Serbs in Croatia would also weaken the Serbs in Bosnia and Herzegovina. Towards the end of 1994 and the beginning of 1995, the USA arranged technical military support for the Croatian Army which, in the end, allowed the Croatian Army to rout the Croatian Serbs and to expel tens of thousands of them from Croatia into Serbia and Montenegro.

Following the Croatian government's re-taking of Sectors North and South, and in the wake of another market-place massacre in Sarajevo, NATO became involved in severe aerial bombardments against Bosnian Serb targets and President Clinton launched an American peace initiative on Bosnia and Herzegovina. Attention on the peacemaking front turned on Bosnia and Herzegovina. Within ICFY Co-Chairman, Carl Bildt and Stoltenberg came to an understanding that while being jointly responsible for all ICFY activities Bildt would focus his efforts on Bosnia and Stoltenberg would focus on the situation in Croatia.

On 3 October, Stoltenberg and US Ambassador Peter Galbraith chaired the first meeting between the Croatian Government and the Serb local authorities in Sector East at the UNHQ in Erdut. The delegation of the Croatian government was led by Mr Hrvoje Sarinic. The delegation of the Serb local authorities was led by Mr Milan Milanovic. The Political and Humanitarian Affairs Coordinator for Sector East, Mr Jesudas Bell, was present at the meeting.

In opening remarks to the delegations they noted the importance of the meeting and their hope that the parties would be able, step by step to produce results that would eventually end in agreement. Stoltenberg and Galbraith then placed before the two delegations some guiding principles for further negotiation which built on the following elements:

- A transition period
- International administration during the transition period
- The stationing of international forces during the transition period.
- The re-establishment of Croatian institutions such as telephone and post office services.
- Establishment of a transitional police force with proportional representation.
- Commitment to respect for human rights.
- The right of refugees and displaced persons to return.
- Restoration/compensation in respect of property
- Assistance in reconstruction of damaged property.
- International guarantees.
- The holding of elections for local administration at the end of the transitional period.

During the prior consultations mentioned above a substantial measure of agreement had already been reached on these guiding principles.

At the meeting, the delegations were moderate and business-like. The leader of the Croatian delegation, Mr Sarinic called for the key questions to be addressed rather than "beating about the bush." The problem, he said, was very simple: "Sector East was, is and will be an integral part of Croatia." The Croatian government was committed to giving the same human rights to Croatian Serbs as was enjoyed by other Croatian citizens. There should be democracy within the laws of Croatia. There should be peace and mutual recognition between Croatia and the FRY. He called for assistance and cooperation on the question of missing persons.

The leader of the Serb delegation, Mr Milanovic, said that his delegation would be reasonable in the search for peace. He called for patience, however, noting that the problems were great and long-standing. It was not easy to create confidence on the part of the population that their human rights and security would be guaranteed in view of what was happening to the Serb population in other parts of Croatia. His delegation was willing to enter into serious negotiations. He would be ready to cooperate on the question of missing persons.

In the light of the Serb delegation's response on the question of missing persons, Mr Sarinic made a pointed request to Stoltenberg as representative of the United Nations and asked for assistance to the two sides in dealing with the issue of missing persons.

Following a recess in the meeting, during which further consultations took place, the meeting reassembled and the two sides agreed to the proposed guiding basic principles. Stoltenberg and Peter Galbraith thereafter issued the following statement:

> At today's meeting agreement has been reached on a first set of guiding basic principles for further negotiations. These basic principles represent an important first step to peacefully resolve the question of Eastern Slavonia. We also wish to emphasise the historic nature of this meeting. For the first time a representative of the Government of Croatia has met with local Serb leaders in an effort to establish a peace. We look forward to the continuation and culmination of this process.
>
> The next phase of these negotiations will be to develop, step by step, precise modalities and thereby agree on a final settlement. During these negotiations we will, as joint chairmen, continue to be guided by the relevant Security Council resolutions and the relevant parts of President Clinton's peace initiative. This means that we seek a negotiated, peaceful settlement within the internationally recognised borders of the Republic of Croatia, on the basis of full respect for internationally recognised human rights and fundamental freedoms and with effective guarantees from the international community.
>
> Mr Sarinic requested, and the Serb delegation agreed, to work for the fastest possible solution to the problem of missing persons.
>
> The next meeting will take place in Zagreb on Monday 9 October.

The agreed principles were as follows:

Guiding Basic Principles for Negotiations on a Settlement of Eastern Slavonia, Baranja and Western Sirmium

1. A transition period shall be established for the region.

2. A transitional authority shall be established by the United Nations Security Council to administer the region during the transition period. Such authority shall include a mechanism to represent the interests of the Government of Croatia, the local Serbs, returning Croatian refugees and displaced persons, and ethnic minorities.
3. International forces shall be stationed within the region during the transition to maintain the peace and enforce compliance with the final settlement. The region shall otherwise be demilitarized during the transition.
4. The transitional authority will facilitate the return of refugees and displaced persons to their homes. It will also take steps to re-establish Croatian institutions in the region (such as telephone service, post offices, banks, utilities, pension offices, passport and citizenship offices, etc.).
5. The transitional authority shall establish a transitional police force in which Croats and Serbs are represented. Other ethnic groups shall also be represented in the police force in the regions where they are present.
6. Internationally recognised human rights and fundamental freedoms will receive the highest respect from all levels of government throughout the Republic of Croatia.
7. All Croatian citizens and persons eligible for Croatian citizenship, including all refugees and displaced persons, have the right to return freely to their places of residence and reside there in conditions of security.
8. All persons have the right to have restored to them any property of which they were deprived by unlawful acts or forced to abandon and to be compensated for any property which cannot be restored to them.
9. The right to return, to recover property, to receive compensation for non-recoverable property, and to receive assistance in reconstruction of damaged property shall be equally available to all Croatian citizens and persons eligible for Croatian citizenship, without regard to ethnicity.
10. The international community will provide guarantees of the terms of and of the human rights protections established in the settlement. These guarantees would include the presence of international monitors for an agreed period of time in the region both during and following the transition. This work shall not be impeded.
11. After the end of the transitional period, elections for local administration shall be held.

On 9 October, Stoltenberg and Galbraith chaired the second round of meetings between the Croatian Government and the Serb local authorities in Sector East at the US Embassy in Zagreb. The delegation of the Croatian government was again led by Mr Hrvoje Sarinic. The delegation of the Serb local authorities was again led by Mr Milan Milanovic. UNPF was represented at the meeting and diplomats from France and Germany also took part.

The approach Stoltenberg and Galbraith followed at that point was to take the eleven principles agreed upon on 3 October and to try to elaborate upon them in light of the positions of the parties. The attitude of the Croatian Government was integrationist, wanting to integrate Sector East into the constitutional and legal order of Croatia and with as few special arrangements as possible. The Serbs for their part emphasised protection and guarantees.

Stoltenberg and Galbraith placed before the parties a Working paper elaborating on some of the eleven principles on issues such as the Transitional Authority, Transitional Administration, the establishment of Joint Commissions, protection of human rights and guarantees.

A practical difficulty that arose at the meeting concerned the meeting place. At Erdut it had been agreed by all sides that the meeting would take place at the American Embassy in Zagreb. However, the Croatian side, in the days before the meeting approached Ambassador Galbraith and asked for the meeting to be held on Croatian territory. Ambassador Galbraith had offered the Croatians an arrangement whereby the meeting would start at the US Embassy and then continue for a working lunch at a down-town Zagreb hotel. The Serb side declined this arrangement, saying that all sides had agreed to meet at the American Embassy and that that arrangement should be respected.

Notwithstanding this difficult situation Stoltenberg and Galbraith managed to get the parties to continue meeting. On Thursday 19 October Stoltenberg saw President Milosevic in Belgrade to brief him on recent developments and to discuss with him the questions that had arisen in connection with the holding of the next round of discussions between the two sides. President Milosevic, while keeping to his oft-stated position that the negotiations on Sector East concerned the Government of Croatia and the Serb local authorities, said that he supported Stoltenberg's efforts and issued a statement to that effect. On the basis of that statement Stoltenberg spoke to Sarinic and Galbraith and the next round of talks between the two sides was set to take place in Osijek on Monday 23 October.

President Milosevic said he would not become involved in negotiations on Sector East during the forthcoming meetings in Dayton USA. He said he had no mandate to do so. However, subsequent statements, attributed to US mediators, said that Sector East would be on the table at the Dayton talks.

President Milosevic thought it unlikely that the Croatian Government would engage in serious talks before their general election was over (29 October). He stressed the importance of the international community providing protection to the Serb population and international guarantees for any agreement reached.

Stoltenberg and Galbraith met with their associates on 20 October and went over the draft agreement they had prepared. There was broad agreement on the document. Through members of Stoltenberg's delegation from France, Germany Russia and the UK, Stoltenberg engaged directly and indirectly in consultation with the capitals of these countries on the draft agreement, particularly concerning the transitional regime; the extent to which it should be involved in the day-to-day running of the region; and what kind of commitment the five countries could make by way of international guarantees. As can be imagined, there were considerable real and formal problems involved on the issue of guarantees.

On 23 October, Stoltenberg and Galbraith chaired a round of talks between the Croatian Government and the Serb local authorities in Osijek. The delegation of the Croatian government was led by Mr Hrvoje Sarinic. The delegation of the Serb local authorities was led by Mr Milan Milanovic. In Stoltenberg's delegation were diplomats sent from Berlin, London and Paris. Stoltenberg had asked the Russian Deputy Foreign Minister Ivanov, when he had met him in Zagreb the previous week to send a person from Moscow. He said he would do so, but the Russian representative did not arrive for the meeting.

At the start of the meeting Stoltenberg and Galbraith presented the two sides with the text of their Draft Agreement building on the eleven principles agreed upon in Erdut on 3 October and taking into account points made by the two sides since then. Stoltenberg and Galbraith, together with members of Stoltenberg's delegation representing France, Germany and the United Kingdom, had gone over the text at a meeting the previous Sunday afternoon. The members of Stoltenberg's delegation had been in close contacts with their capitals on the text of the draft agreement.

After presenting the text of the Draft Agreement to the two sides Stoltenberg and Galbraith gave them time to study it. They thereafter met with the delegations individually and together. The Croatian side made comments on the document as a whole. The Serb side commented on the first three articles and said they would submit further comments later.

The following were the important issues that came up:

Length of the Transition Period: The Croatians moved from one year to eighteen months and the Serbs moved from five years to three years. Stoltenberg and Galbraith sought to hold them to two years.

Appointment of an Administrator: The Croatians, while accepting that there would be a Transitional Authority, were opposed to the nomination of a

Transitional Administrator since, they said, it smacked of colonialism. Stoltenberg and Galbraith suggested, instead, to use the term Transitional Coordinator. Sarinic did not reject this.

UN Representative on the Transitional Authority: The Croatians were opposed to a UN representative on the Transitional Authority. Stoltenberg reported to Boutros Ghali that he was being flexible on this. The real issue, he felt, was to ensure that there was a workable balance between the international and local representatives on the Transitional Authority.

Composition of the International Force: The Croatians wanted NATO while the Serbs wanted the UN.

International Police Component: The Croatians were opposed to the Transitional Authority having a police component. Stoltenberg explored the formula of letting the International Force have an international police component.

As could be seen from the above, the parties were edging towards an agreement. However, in the closing stages, the Dayton conference was in the air and all sides were jockeying for advantages. The Dayton conference was scheduled to begin soon. The UN had not been invited to the conference and Stoltenberg was continuing his contacts with parties on the ground in an effort to take them closer to agreement.

The day before the Dayton conference was due to begin, Stoltenberg received an invitation from the Americans to attend the conference. He was in Zagreb at the time and I was in Geneva. Heavy snow storms had closed down Zagreb airport. There were no commercial planes flying out of Zagreb. Stoltenberg asked me over the telephone to accompany him to Dayton. But how were we to get there.

Here entered into the picture one of the great officials of ICFY, our dear friend Ms Laila Refsnes. She had been Executive Assistant to the Norwegian Prime Minister and Stoltenberg had brought her to ICFY in Geneva as Executive Assistant. She was formidable in her organizational and logistical capacity. She immediately found a solution. The Norwegian Government had made a voluntary contribution to ICFY and Laila explored and found a Charter aircraft willing to fly in to Zagreb and bring Stoltenberg out to London in time for him to connect with a Concord flight to New York and then on to Dayton. This was Executive action of the highest order.

The opening day of the Dayton conference, Stoltenberg and I flew on the Concord to New York to link up with a flight to Dayton. But American airports were also suffering blizzard conditions. To fly out to Dayton, we had to take a flight out of Newark. The Norwegian Permanent Representative to the United Nations met us at JFK and accompanied us in blizzard conditions to Newark.

Flights out of Newark were delayed and, eventually, we took a flight to Dayton that arrived after 1.00 AM in the morning. The first day of the Dayton conference was over.

We learned in Dayton that a communiqué had been issued that Stoltenberg and Galbraith would return to Croatia the next day on the Presidential plane of President Franjo Tudjman to continue their negotiations with a view to completing the Erdut Agreement. Stoltenberg met late that evening with President Milosevic and he made one of his bravado statements that the Croatian issues would not be settled at Dayton.

Stoltenberg and I huddled and we agreed that since the UN had no one else at the Dayton conference I would remain behind and he would return in a week's time. As things turned out, he never did. But, what is more to the point, in the new environment, Stoltenberg and Galbraith were able to clinch an agreement, which was signed on 12 November, 1995. It was effectively the agreement that Stoltenberg had first tabled.

The Erdut Agreement, The Basic Agreement on The Region of Eastern Slavonia, Baranja, And Western Sirmium of 12 November, 1995, provided for a transitional period of 12 months, extendable for another period of the same duration if so requested by one of the parties. It requested the UN Security Council to establish a Transitional Administration to govern the Region during the transitional period in the interest of all persons resident in or returning to the Region.

It further requested the Security Council to authorize an international force to deploy during the transitional period to maintain peace and security in the Region and otherwise to assist in implementation of the Agreement. Article 4 stated:

> The Transitional Administration shall ensure the possibility for the return of refugees and displaced persons to their homes of origin. All persons who have left the Region or who have come to the Region with previous permanent residence in Croatia shall enjoy the same rights as all other residents of the region. The Transitional Administration shall also take the steps necessary to re-establish the normal functioning of all public services in the Region without delay.

Article 5 added:

> The Transitional Administration shall help to establish and train temporary police forces to build professionalism among the police and confidence among all ethnic communities.

The human rights provisions of the Basic Agreement[1] built on earlier human rights drafts of ICFY and on the Z-4 plan for autonomy of the Croatian Serbs. The Basic Agreement provided that the highest levels of internationally-recognized human rights and fundamental freedoms shall be respected in the Region. All persons would have the right to return freely to their places of residence in the Region and to live there in conditions of security. All persons who had left the Region or who had come to the Region with previous permanent residence in Croatia would have the right to live in the Region. All persons would have the right to restoration of any property taken from them by unlawful acts, or that they were forced to abandon, and to just compensation for property that could not be restored to them. The right to recover property, to receive compensation for property that could not be returned, and to receive assistance in reconstruction of damaged property would be equally available to all persons without regard to ethnicity.

Article 10 of the Basic Agreement requested interested countries and organizations to take appropriate steps to promote the accomplishments of the commitments in the Agreement. After the expiration of the transition period, and consistent with established practice, the international community should monitor and report on respect for human rights in the Region on a long term basis. In addition, under Article 11, interested countries and organizations were requested to establish a commission that would be authorized to monitor the implementation of the Agreement, particularly its human rights and civil rights provisions, to investigate all allegations of violations of the Agreement, and to make appropriate recommendations.

The Security Council acted positively on this Agreement and established a Transitional Administration (UNTAES),[2] which did invaluable work on its implementation, and contributed to the promotion and protection of human rights in very challenging circumstances. UNTAES deployed to the area in April, 1996 and continued until 15 January, 1998. It consisted of military, police, civilian observer, and civilian components. The different components all contributed to implementation of the human rights mandate. In early August, 1997, somewhat late, a Human Rights Monitoring Unit of UNTAES became fully

1 Basic Agreement on The Region of Eastern Slavonia, Baranja, and Western Sirmium (The Erdut Agreement), Signed in Erdut, Croatia and in Zagreb, Croatia, November 12, 1995.

2 Security Council resolution 1037 of 15 January, 1996.

functional on the basis of arrangements agreed with the Office of the United Nations High Commissioner for Human Rights.[3]

Conclusion

Stoltenberg, the lonely long-distance runner, had achieved a stunning victory. The UN Transitional Administration in Croatia would successfully implement the Erdut Agreement and normalcy returned to Croatia. Stoltenberg had achieved a stunning success in peacemaking.

3 S/1997/767, Chapter IV, Human Rights.

CHAPTER 12

Peacemaking

Successes and Sabotage on Bosnia

Introduction

UN/EU mediators succeeded twice in getting the Bosnian parties to accept peace agreements: the Vance-Owen plan and the Stoltenberg-Owen plan, also known as the Invincible plan because it was concluded on the British aircraft carrier, the HMS Invincible. Twice the plan was killed by the USA. From May, 1993 to 21 November, 1995, when the Dayton Accords were signed, tens of thousands of people died who would not have done so had the Vance-Owen plan been supported. Again, in September, 1993, the Bosnian parties enthusiastically accepted the Invincible plan only to have the Bosniacs repudiate their acceptance a week later because of American pressure on President Izetbegovic. From then to 21 November, 1995, tens of thousands of people died. Whatever the reasons for US policies, the incontrovertible fact is that they cost tens of thousands of Bosnian lives.

Warren Christopher, Anthony Lake, Richard Holbrook all have written about the US success at Dayton. None of them has chosen to remember that US policies led to the deaths of tens of thousands of people. Objective commentators acknowledge that the Vance-Owen plan was far better than the Dayton Accord. Ivo Dalader, in his book, Getting to Dayton, acknowledges that the Contact Group map was based on the Stoltenberg-Owen map. The Contact Group insisted for months that the Bosnian Serbs must accept the plan as put down and would not talk to the Bosnian Serbs. Six months later they changed their mind and agreed that changes in the plan could be negotiated among the Bosnian parties and agreed to talk to the Bosnian Serbs again. All the people who died between June of 1994 and December of 1994 died because of Contact-Group miscalculations in ruling out negotiated changes and in not talking to the Bosnian Serbs during the period. The facts speak for themselves.

Why did negotiations fail to prevent the violent break-up of Yugoslavia?

Why did negotiations fail to prevent the outbreak of conflict in Bosnia and Heregovina? What are the lessons to be learnt from successive efforts to negotiate a settlement in Bosnia and Herzevovina? These are questions that will be debated for a long time.

 | DOI 10.1163/9789004245907_016

Any Clean Hands?

For three and a half years I saw the principal players in the Yugoslav drama close up: in innumerable meetings in Geneva, New York, Brussels, Washington, Dayton, Belgrade, Zagreb, Sarajevo, Skopje, Tirana, and elsewhere. There is indisputable evidence that Serbs and Croats committed many atrocities on Bosniacs. The Bosniacs also had some share in this dirty business but, admittedly, on a lesser scale.

From what I saw on the peacemaking and peacekeeping sides, however, there were no clean hands on any side of the Bosnian drama. I had, and have, much feeling for the Bosnian President Alija Izetbegovic, who was called upon to protect his people as best he could in very difficult circumstances. No one can understand the burdens on such a person but himself. From what I saw, however, he was more interested in continuing the fight because of his worldview than in concluding a peace agreement.

I shall never forget the moment in August, 2003, when he asked of Radovan Karadzic six concessions which would permit him, he said, to put the peace agreement under discussion to his colleagues in Sarajevo. He would not recommend the peace agreement to them, but would put it to them for their consideration. Owen and Stoltenberg squeezed Karadzic to make the six concessions, which he did. Izetbegovic went away and denounced the agreement. One of his aides, whom I had come to know quite closely, wept on my shoulders. Why would he not choose peace, the person asked me? Does he not know how much we are suffering? This was a searing moment for me. But it was the name of the game throughout.

A few weeks earlier, when Stoltenberg and Owen first broached with Izetbegovic, Milosevic and Tudjman the concept of a peace agreement providing territorial guarantees for the Bosniacs, 'with access from the Sava river to the Adriatic Sea, and with economic viability', Izetbegovic, at a meeting in the Villa Saugy in Genthod, on the outskirts of Geneva, said he was very much interested in the concept and would like to discuss it more. He asked for more details. When he left the meeting and faced the press outside of the Villa he denounced the concept! At the request of Stoltenberg and Owen I had to rush out to the journalists present to correct the record.

A few weeks later, in September, 1993, on the British warship HMS Invincible, Izetbegovic accepted a peace agreement along the lines of the same concept, which became known as the Stoltenberg-Owen peace plan. After the talks on the HMS Invincible we were taken by helicopter to the Croatian town of Split, from whence we flew together in a United Nations place to Zagreb.

Izetbegovic was visibly pleased. So was his Foreign Minister Haris Siladzjic. Siladjic made public comments to the media that there had been a breakthrough and that peace was at hand. When Izetbegovic and Siladzjic went back to Sarajevo they denounced the plan. As we would find out later, the Americans were at that point, along with the Iranians and the Turks, rearming the Bosniacs to continue fighting and the US Ambassador in Sarajevo, Victor Jakovic, was known to be dead set against the plan.

Nothing could save the plan, which I believe was a better one than that eventually concluded at Dayton. Belgian Foreign Minister Willy Claes, who subsequently became Secretary-General of NATO, convened a meeting with the parties in Geneva to see what could be done save the plan. The European Union Foreign Ministers asked that the percentage of territory given to the Bosniacs be increased to fifty one per cent. Stoltenberg and Owen worked on this and secured acceptance from Karadzic and Milosevic. But even that would not lead to peace. Izetbegovic was being further armed to fight. A meeting of the Bosnian parties with European Union Foreign Ministers, in December 2003, ended, literally, in tantrums.

German Foreign Minister Klaus Kinkel was keen to save the plan, which had now become to be known as the European Union plan. In January 2004 he invited Izetbegovic and Croatian President Franjo Tudjman, to a meeting in Bonn to see how a deal could be clinched. Izetbegovic was not interested. Feeling plucky, he told Tudjman at that meeting: "Franjo, there is an ammunitions factory in the town of Vitez. We are going to take Vitez and we will take the ammunitions factory." Tudjman replied, "You will never take Vitez, but if you come close to the town we shall blow up the ammunitions factory."

Peace was far from the mind of Izetbegovic. Even when he did eventually sign a peace agreement in Dayton, he did so under great pressure from the Americans. By then the name of the game had changed for the USA. Presidential elections were looming in the USA and the Clinton team wanted the Bosnian dossier put in order so that Clinton would not be vulnerable in the campaign.

Izetbegovic had, from the outset, used all sorts of ruses to frustrate negotiations, In August, 1992, Vance and Owen had visited the different capitals and secured agreement that the Bosniacs, Croats, and Serbs, would send delegations to Geneva for continuous negotiations until a peace deal was concluded. On the very day that Vance landed back in Geneva he received a fax from Izetbegovic stating that the Serbs had crossed cease-fire lines and he would therefore not be sending a delegation. Vance wrote him a stiff reply: "I cannot believe that a man of honour would go back on his solemn undertaking." Under pressure from Vance, Izetbegovic eventually sent his delegation.

Later, when we would be in negotiations in Geneva or elsewhere, with Stoltenberg doubling as UN mediator and SRSG in charge of the peace-keeping forces, Izetbegovic would stall the negotiations by telling Stoltenberg that the Serbs had committed some breach on agreed lines, and that until they moved back to their previous positions he would not negotiate. I remember once when he complained of Serb troop movements on the Igman mountains. We in the UN had no assets whatsoever that could help us determine whether his claim was true or not. We had to send military observers to the area to look into his claims, which took some three days during which the negotiations were stalled. This was vintage Izetbegovic.

There is also incontrovertible evidence that the Bosniac army deliberately fired from medical centres so as to incite a Serb response on the guns inside the medical centre. The Serbs would then take the blame for firing on a hospital. The UN Commander in Sarajevo had occasion to write to the Bosnian President about this on more than one occasion. On 19 January, 1993, for example, Major General Phillippe Morillon wrote to President Izetbegovic:

> You will I am sure be aware that the firing of weapons from a hospital is against the Geneva Conventions. I regret to inform you that for some time now I have been receiving reports that some mobile mortars have been operating from the vicinity of Kosevo Hospital. This has been sadly confirmed and I now have concrete evidence from witnesses with signed statements that this was in fact the case at 14.30 hours on Monday 11 January.
>
> An 82.mm mortar had been set up on the western side of Kosevo Hospital, within the hospital grounds. This mortar and its crew then proceeded to fire nine rounds, using the hospital as a screen. The direct consequence of this disreputable and cowardly act was that shortly afterwards the hospital came under fire from anti-aircraft gun fire, artillery fire and mortar fire.
>
> I must point out to you the harm that such blatant disregard of the Geneva Convention does to your cause and insist that you take the strongest measures to prevent reoccurrences taking place.

A few days earlier, on 13 January, 1993, General Morillon had written to President Izetbegovic:

> You will no doubt be well aware of the fatal shooting of a British Soldier, a member of UNPROFOR, on United Nations duty in Gornji Vakuf at approximately 1047 hrs this morning...(T)his was a deliberate act of murder of a United Nations soldier by forces either from the HVO or from the army of Bosnian Republic in Gornji Vakuf, possibly with a view to

> inflaming the local situation and preventing UNPROFOR from carrying out its mission....
>
> I demand that you look into this matter personally, initiate an inquiry to ascertain responsibility, both individual and collective, and advise me of the result. I also demand an assurance that you have issued clear direction to all those you command to ensure members of UNPROFOR are no longer put at risk in any way.

Bosniac fighters also, on occasions, deliberately targeted humanitarian workers in order to put the blame on the Serbs. On one occasion Bosniac fighters deliberately targeted and shot to death a Danish driver of a truck in a humanitarian convoy. There is little doubt that this was a deliberate killing, meant to sow confusion – even as the humanitarian operation was seeking to feed mainly Bosniacs of Sarajevo. I accompanied Stoltenberg, as SRSG, to a small town in Denmark where the burial service was held for the slain Danish driver.

He was the only child of his parents. He had decided to work for the humanitarian operation out of noble sentiments. I shall never forget the moment in a Danish church yard where the grieving parents were saying goodbye to their only child. How, I asked myself, was it possible that this generous and good young man was deliberately gunned down in cold blood? What, I asked myself, was passing through the minds of his parents as they laid him to rest? How could the United Nations be expected to provide humanitarian assistance and help make peace in these circumstances? These are sobering moments and reality checks for all of us.

The state of affairs that one had to deal with was well summarized by General Rupert Smith in a meeting with Stoltenberg and Bildt in Sarajevo in June of 1995. "Gentlemen," Rupert Smith told Stoltenberg and Bildt, "There is no peace to keep here and I do not think my force should even be here. The Serbs have achieved their objectives and are interested in a settlement that would ratify their gains. The Croats would like to take more territory from the Bosniacs. The Bosniacs would like to avenge their losses against both sides. They are determined to keep fighting. If, as politicians, you ask me to remain here, I shall have to fight."

He went on to explain this and would, indeed, eventually reconfigure his forces into a Rapid Reaction Force to fight the Bosnian Serb Army which had, by then, gone completely out of control. Rupert Smith was an impressive General to whom must be given a great deal of the credit for moving the international community from a posture of watching helplessly as the Bosnian Serb army moved to insanity to taking them on and defeating them.

The Croat leadership was, like that of the Serbs, a murderous bunch. Franjo Tudjman and Slobodan Milosevic, without a doubt, both had in view to split up Bosnia between them. Let me deal first with Tudjman. Very early in the peace negotiations, Vance and Owen had invited Tudjman as President of Croatia, and Dobrica Cosic, as President of Yugoslavia, to a meeting in Geneva to set down the bases of future cooperation for peace. Vance and Owen sought to build heavily on this Belgrade-Zagreb relationship. At the end of the meeting, while a communiqué was being typed up, Tudjman and Cosic went on chatting about the conflict. My interpreter kept interpreting in my ears. Tudjman told Cosic, "You know, Dobrica, that the only solution is for us to divide up Bosnia between us." Cosic replied, "It is the only way"!

The Croats played the cleverest hand throughout the peace negotiations and achieved many gains. In the end, however, they were pushed by the USA into a Bosniac-Croat Federation in Bosnia-Hercegovina which stopped them from gobbling up large parts of Bosnia and incorporating them into Croatia. At the outset of the negotiations, from September, 1992, I had gotten to know the Bosnian Croat leader Mate Boban fairly well. He was an affable killer. He played his cards cleverly, appearing cooperative and in support of peace, even as his forces on the ground sought to take more territory from the dwindling areas of the Bosniacs in Central Bosnia. The massacre at the Medak Pocket was a classic case of the modus operandi of the Croats.

When it comes to the Bosnian Serbs, there is no doubt that they declared war on innocent civilians and ethnically cleansed large parts of Bosnia-Herzegovina, killing Bosniacs by the tens of thousands. The hands of Radovan Karadzic and Ratko Mlaldic dripped with blood.

Unholy Terror

The Yugoslav dossiers were not easy to comprehend. There were many historical, legal, political, economic, social and cultural factors. Peacemaking was so complex, and one never knew who came to the process with good faith or not. The Bosnian dossier was an especially treacherous one.

John R. Schindler, Professor of Strategy at the US Naval War College, has written a well researched and finely documented book that undoubtedly sheds new light on major aspects of the Bosnian conflict of the 1990s. It justifies no less than an overhaul of many of the core tenets of the war as presented by pundits at the time.[1]

---

1 Unholy Terror. Bosnia, Al-Quaida and the Rise of Global Jihad, Zenith Press, St Paul, Minnesota, 2007.

Schindler, a historian by training, is well-versed in several languages, which gave him first hand insight into original sources about what took place prior to, during, and after the conflict. He had served for several years as a National Security Agency intelligence analyst and counter-intelligence officer, and lived for a number of years in the Balkans region. He writes about events he has studied at close range and with much authority.

Going back to the Ottoman occupation of Bosnia for some five hundred years Schindler points out that life for the Christians – Serbs and Croats had been cruel and oppressive. Converts to Islam enjoyed all the spoils of the conquerors and, as the Ottoman Empire was disintegrating in the nineteenth century, fought to retain their position of dominance. The Serbs, a rural community, suffered the most.

During the German occupation of the then Royal Yugoslavia, Croat Ustashas had joined forces with the Nazis and, aided by Muslims, had terrorized the Serb population in concentration camps such as that at Jasenovac. There was much ethnic cleansing, even genocide against Serbs.

As Tito's Yugoslavia was breaking up at the end of the 1980s it was therefore understandable that the last thing the Serbs of Bosnia would wish was to be in an independent Bosnia under Muslim domination. The Bosnian Croats, for their part, desired to join their brethren in Croatia.

Alija Izetbegovic belonged to a generation that was determined to reinstate Muslim ascendancy in Bosnia. He sought the establishment of an Islamic Bosnian state run in accordance with Islamic law. He had fought all his life for this and his writings bore ample evidence of this. As Yugoslavia broke up and he pressed the case for an independent Bosnia under Muslim rule, he knew that the Serbs would never accept this but he pressed on regardless. It mattered not to him that war would come. He in fact courted war. He was an Islamic Internationalist and his central concern was the establishment of an Islamic state in Bosnia no matter the cost.

He presented two faces to the world: the moderate multiculturalist to the Western world and the ardent Islamist to the Islamic world. He visited many Islamic countries, sought and obtained billions of dollars before, during and after the conflict in support of the Islamic cause in Bosnia. Schindler's documentation of all this is meticulous and unassailable.

When, in 1991, the Portuguese Presidency of the European Union proposed a loose confederation for Bosnia constituted of Muslim, Serb and Croat provinces, Izetbegovic accepted the plan and then repudiated his acceptance. War was inevitable thereafter but it was as if Izetbegovic preferred war. His aim was Muslim control of the Bosnian State. He was ready to partition Bosnia if needed once he could have Muslim control over the majority of the State.

In the year before the outbreak of the war in 1992, Izetbegovic, supported by international Islamic countries and forces, had established, trained and equipped an army. Beginning then, and throughout the war, thousands of Islamic fighters from different parts of the world descended on Bosnia from Afghanistan and elsewhere, fought in the war, and stayed on in Bosnia to launch further jihadist campaigns in places such as Algeria, Western Europe and North America. Osama bin Laden and Ayman al Zawahiri and many similar figures were in Bosnia. Many infamous names wanted for terrorist activities had been in Bosnia as well. Mujahiddin elements slit throats, beheaded people and committed other depravities.

Schindler documents that Izetbegovic was willingly at the centre of all of this. Inside his SDA party there was in inner core group that was devoted to the establishment of an Islamist state. Any moderate figure was eliminated. Fikrit Abdic and Mohammed Filipovic were targeted for assassinations.

Corruption, smuggling, crime, nepotism and assassinations swirled around Izetbegovic. He was the ring-leader. Billions of Islamic dollars poured into Bosnia and large parts of it went into the pockets of crooks. With the acquiescence, and at times encouragement of the USA, arms flowed into Bosnia for the Muslims from Iran, Turkey and Pakistan. The USA made or organized clandestine flights for arms shipments. Jordanian and Malaysian peacekeeping contingents funnelled arms to the Muslims. Germany slipped arms to the Croats.

Where Izetbegovic and his associates succeeded remarkably was in persuading the USA and the West that a defenceless Muslim people was the subject of genocidal violence by the Serbs. The Muslims hired a leading Washington public relations firm to promote their cause and their Ambassador to the UN, Mohammed Sacirbey, subsequently exposed as a gambler and embezzler, was devastatingly effective in his presentation of the case of Muslims being slaughtered. The Serbs had no match for this public relations blitz and they suffered for it.

True enough, they committed war crimes and crimes against humanity but, Schindler points out, all sides did. The Muslims, like the Croats, had their fair share of atrocities, but the Western media had eyes only for Serb violence. The Muslims fired from near hospitals to incite counter fire from the Serbs. There is good evidence to believe that infamous 'Serb' bombing massacres were in fact committed by Muslim forces to paint the Serbs in a bad light.

Izetbegovic's key strategy was to secure American intervention on his side and he succeeded when the massacres at Srebrenica took place. But, Schindler documents, there is good reason to believe that Izetbegovic knew that Muslim forces were committing atrocities against Serbs from their base in Srebrenica and that General Mladic would launch an offensive on the town. Aware of this, he withdrew the Muslim military leadership of Nasser Oric and left Srebrenica to its fate. His objective was precisely to facilitate a massacre. He got it and US intervention!

Izetbegovic was never interested in peace as such and he rejected successive peace plans, preferring to fight on. He had his Islamic aims, financing and jihadists, and his real objective was to make Bosnia an Islamic base in Europe. In September 1993 he secretly signed a partition plan with the Serbs and then repudiated it. Partitioning Bosnia was never a problem for him. He wanted a compact Muslim State, living by Islamic law, and he wanted Bosnia to be an activist Islamic base in Europe.

All of these 'findings' of Schindler are superbly documented and in most instances irrefutable. The propaganda game waged by the Muslims and their supporters was spell-binding and plain wrong. The numbers killed were vastly overstated and all sides suffered casualties and atrocities. Evidence of Serb rapes of Muslim women showed far smaller numbers than thrown around, and Serb women were also raped by Muslims, but Western correspondents were not interested in this. Journalists had become prosecutors for one side.

Schindler writes: "Westerners ought to heed the lessons of what happens when governments are overly influenced by 'public intellectuals' who have no idea what they are talking about. In the future, what entertainers and celebrities say about complex international issues, particularly ones involving deep-seated ethnic and religious conflicts, should be discarded out of hand and probably considered the converse of the truth."

In the concluding part of the book Schindler documents that thousands of jihadists obtained Bosnian passports. From a Bosnian base they reached out to places such as Algeria, France, Canada and the United States. The man who was arrested in Seattle, coming from Canada, with explosives to blow up Los Angeles airport, was a Bosnian jihadi graduate.

Schindler ends the book with the following caution: "If Bosnia, the most pro-Western society in the *umma*, can be converted into a Jihadistan through domestic deceit, violent conflict, and misguided international intervention, nowhere in the Muslim world can be judged safe from dangerous radicalization. The lesson of Bosnia was that it happened."

And this, at heart, was the Izetbegovic project.

Great Powers Take Sides

Whatever might have been the proper policy from the point of view of justice, or morality, the Security Council had laid down policies calling for a cessation of hostilities, instituting a ban on arms, calling for negotiations, putting peacekeepers on the ground to 'protect' enclaves and 'safe areas' and establishing processes that would lead to the establishment of the International Criminal Tribunal for the Former Yugoslavia.

The London Conference, held in August, 1992, basically confirmed these policies. It added principles such as non-recognition of territorial acquisitions achieved through use of force, respect for human rights, and negotiations for peaceful outcomes. More than thirty Governments participated in the London Conference and in the Steering Committee of the International Conference on the Former Yugoslavia that it established to negotiate peace for the Former Yugoslavia.

Yet, even as the Security Council and the London Conference put down these markers for peace negotiators, led by Cyrus Vance and Lord Owen initially, the Great Powers had ranged themselves on the sides of the parties and were to do so even more with the arrival of the Clinton administration.

Lord Carrington is on record as having protested against German recognition of Croatia and Slovenia in the midst of his negotiating efforts. He considers that this German policy ruined his efforts. Germany tilted, throughout the period when the search for peace was underway, towards Croatia. So did Austria.

Russia, an enfeebled power at the time, was very much mindful of its historical affinities with Serbia and it was conscious that a new East–West line seemed to be emerging along the Drina River. There were elements of culture, history, and politics in this. The Croats were Catholics and therefore emotionally close to Austria and the West. Serbia was Orthodox and had more affinities with the Orthodox world of Russia and Greece. Russia was never a decisive player in the Yugoslav conflicts but it tilted towards the Serbs. In the end, however, this did not count for much as Russia was mainly interested in coming to an accommodation with the United States on economic issues. One unfortunate consequence of this was that there was no balancing element that could work in favour of the peacemakers. The United States could, and did, pretty much what it wished.

The United States of George Herbert Walker Bush and James Baker wanted very much to leave the Yugoslav mess to the Europeans. There were those in Europe who were arguing for a European defence force under the aegis of the Western European Union while the United States insisted that NATO was the European security organization and that it should not be compromised. James Baker, in his memoirs, relates how the first Bush administration decided to leave the problems of the Former Yugoslavia to the Europeans.

That, however, would change dramatically with the arrival of the Clinton Administration, which opted for a policy of 'lift and strike': lift the arms embargo on the Bosniacs and help them to strike at the Serbs. When it could not persuade its European partners to adopt such a policy it went ahead nevertheless, clandestinely supplying arms to the Bosniacs.

What's a poor peace negotiator to do in such circumstances? The Security Council and the London Conference called for negotiations but major powers took sides in the conflict and, in effect, obstructed negotiations. There is no doubt, with the evidence that emerged subsequently, that the USA sabotaged the negotiating efforts of Vance and Owen and Stoltenberg and Owen.

I do not wish to be misunderstood on this point. The Clinton Administration had come to believe that a great injustice had been done to the Bosniacs and that they should be given the means to fight and defeat the Serbs. The result of this, however, is that whereas the conflict might have been brought to a negotiated end in 1993, the stance of the United States led the Bosniacs to fight on until the Fall of 1995. During that time thousands of people died and Srebrenica would occur. The Stoltenberg-Owen peace plan of the Fall of 1993, as amended by the European Union Ministers, gave the Bosniacs fifty one per cent of contiguous territory, with access to the Sava River and the Adriatic sea. It can by no stretch of the imagination be argued that the Dayton Peace Accord was a better deal than the Stoltenberg-Owen plan of two years earlier. Perhaps it was right on moral grounds to insist that the Bosniacs should be given arms to fight and that the conflict should last another two years. The people who died in 1994 and 1995 are not able to express their views on this and we shall never know if they might have chosen life over death, if given a chance. One is clear, though: had the conflict been brought to an end in the Fall of 1993, Srebrenica would not have taken place.

It is not my purpose, in these pages, to re-open the issues of war versus peace argued at the time. The actress Liv Ullman made a magisterial case for peace in a speech she delivered in Paris at the time. What I seek to show here is that, for better or for worse, the major powers at the time took sides in the conflict and that resulted in a situation in which they would decide when peace would be made, as occurred at Dayton, in November, 1995.

As for the Americans, Candidates Clinton and Gore, in the Presidential campaign of 1992, had taken the Bush Sr. Administration to task for failing to protect the Bosniacs. The Bosniacs and their supporters in the USA had done a great deal of work with Vice-Presidential candidate Albert Gore and he was known to be particularly strong in his views that the Bosniacs must be defended.

Another factor that influenced the positions of the Clinton team related to the fact that their's was the first Democratic Administration in twelve years, after President Reagan had defeated President Jimmy Carter. Cyrus Vance had been the Secretary-of-State who had resigned from the Carter Administration over the ill-starred rescue attempt to free the American hostages in Iran. One sensed that the Clinton people, including the incoming Secretary-of-State, Warren Christopher, who had been Vance's Deputy at the State Department, wished to put distance between themselves and Vance, especially taking into account that the Vance-Owen Peace Plan, unveiled just before President Clinton was inaugurated in January 1993, had been taking flak in the media for allegedly rewarding ethnic cleansing in Bosnia-Herzegovina. Their posture towards Vance was one of non-engagement.

Shortly after President Clinton had been elected, I prepared at the request of Vance and his adviser, my good friend Ambassador Herbert Okun, a briefing file for Christopher, who was then leading the Clinton transition team. It included the background papers and considerations that had led up to the Vance-Owen Peace Plan, and was sent to Christopher with a personal letter from Vance.

A few weeks later, I put together another briefing file and worked with Ambassador Okun on speaking notes for Vance for a meeting that he had with incoming National Security Adviser Anthony Lake at Vance's New York apartment. Vance and Okun meticulously went over the factors and considerations that had led to the Vance-Owen plan. At that stage, it had been accepted by two of the Bosnian parties, the Bosniacs and the Croats, but the Serbs had refused to come on board. Vance sought United States backing to help bring the Serbs on board. The Clinton Administration did not lift a finger to help bring this about.

Instead, shortly after President Clinton's inauguration, when Secretary of State Christopher came to New York for a working visit, he was openly critical of the Vance-Owen plan in a press conference that he gave at the United States Permanent Mission to the United Nations. He had chosen to ignore the briefing materials Vance had sent him. This was a bitter experience for Vance. Lord Owen, the more pugnacious of the Vance-Owen team, shot back at Christopher in remarks to the press.

The Vance-Owen plan was doomed because of the intransigence of the Bosnian Serbs and the lack of support of the United States. In fact, however, it was unfortunately doomed from the start. Izetbegovic accepted the plan in the belief that the Bosnian Serbs would reject it. His was therefore an acceptance of convenience. So was that of the Croats. Their real aim was to annex large parts of Bosnia-Herzegovina adjacent to Croatia.

President Slobodan Milosevic understood the motives of President Izetbegovic and President Tudjman and he wished for the Bosnian Serbs to accept so as to place them in a better light and to force the hands, especially, of President Izetbegovic.

President Milosevic lost out in the end in the high stakes game in the Former Yugoslavia but he was, without a doubt, the shrewdest among the Yugoslav leaders. His problem was that his chosen surrogates in Bosnia and Croatia decided to go their own way and, in the end, both ended up being beaten, taking Serbia and Montenegro along with them.

The Owen-Stoltenberg policy of progressive implementation of the Vance-Owen plan would be dealt a death blow by the Russian Foreign Minister, Kozyrev. In May, 1993, after the Athens meeting and the Bosnian Serb repudiation a week later, I accompanied Stoltenberg and Owen on visits to Croatia, Byelorussia, Ukraine, and the Russian Federation, seeking support for progressive implementation. I was present in the meeting with Kozyrev in Moscow at which he enthusiastically embraced the approach of progressive implementation. After the meeting he spoke to the press and publicly supported progressive implementation. The very next weekend Stoltenberg and Owen met him in Split, Croatia, in transit to a meeting in Washington, and he again strongly endorsed progressive implementation.

Unfortunately, however, at a meeting in Washington the next week, Kozyrev, in a meeting with Christopher and others, endorsed a diametrically opposed approach in a Joint Action Plan.

Stoltenberg and Owen had to recognize that progressive implementation had died in Washington. The fighting continued on the ground and more and more people died. Stoltenberg and Owen sought to pick up the pieces and went on a series of visits to different capitals probing for a new approach. The one they finally decided to test was close to the Cutileiro plan for Bosnia – Herzegovina: a loose confederation of three republics, each with its defined territory, with an economically viable territory for the Bosniacs assuring access to the Sava River and the Adriatic sea.

Milosevic, Tudjman, and Izetbegovic all expressed support for such an approach and, at a meeting with Stoltenberg and Owen at the Villa Saugy in Genthod, just outside Geneva, Izetbegovic gave the green light to Stoltenberg and Owen to pursue this approach. However, in vintage Izetbegovic fashion, upon leaving the meeting he denounced the ideas that had been put to him by Stoltenberg and Owen to the media waiting outside. It fell to me to go out and explain to the media that he had, in fact, expressed much interest in the ideas presented to him and wanted to continue discussing them. Izetbegovic was emboldened at the time because, as we now know, he was then receiving arms from the USA, Turkey, and Iran. We also now know that Osama bin Laden was then active with his band in Bosnia-Herzegovina.

We now know from Congressional testimony in Washington about what was actually happening behind the scenes at the time, with arms flowing to the

Bosniacs. It is important to make the point that the aim in giving arms to the Bosniacs was not to improve their bargaining hand on the ground – which would have been an understandable position, but was in fact a policy opposed to negotiations. The idea was for the Bosniacs to continue fighting so as to avenge their losses and to defeat the Serbs.

Put simply, the United States opted for a policy of continued fighting instead of a policy of working out the best deal attainable through negotiations.

Responsibilities of the Parties

Let there be no mistake about it: the mess in Yugoslavia came about and continued because of the failures – and sometimes crass stupidity - of its own leaders. How could these leaders have let loose the demon of nationalism in such a vulnerable land? How could it have happened that these leaders were willing to go to war because they could not arrive at compromises among competing demands for federalism, and confederalism? How can one explain that the leaders in Bosnia and Herzegovina allowed a war to continue for two years after the only difference separating them was over the allocation of, at most, one or two percent of territory? One often gets the impression that the responsibility for achieving peace is not on the leadership of the warring parties but on the international community. This was one of the great distortions at large in the propaganda campaigns being waged about conflict in the former Yugoslavia.

Errors of Judgment

The failures of leaders in the former Yugoslavia were decidedly compounded by errors of judgment on the part of influential outside actors. Without a doubt, former German Foreign Minister Genscher miscalculated when he pushed for recognition of the former Yugoslav republics. But for that the Carrington-led process might have achieved its objective of a Yugoslav community of laws, human rights, and economic cooperation. Another serious miscalculation was when the newly-installed Clinton Administration choose not to support the Vance-Owen peace plan which had been largely worked out by February, 1993. By keeping the Bosniac leadership at bay and sniping at the plan, precious time was lost and the momentum for peace snuffed out. Another grievous error of judgment was made between September 1993 and January 1994 when the "Invincible-Package," revised into the European Union Action

Plan, was lost although it had been painstakingly negotiated among the three Bosnian parties for months and when everything else had been agreed upon save for the fate of a few cities representing at most one to two percent of territory. The story goes that the Bosniac military advised their political leadership that more could be won on the battlefield. External advice also urged the Bosniac leadership to withhold consent – something that they could well come to regret deeply with the passage of time. Those who rendered such advice have much blood on their hands. But what of the negotiators themselves and their negotiating strategies? How do they come out of the story?

Negotiating with Honour

The story of the European Community Conference, or the Carrington Conference as it has come to be known, has been told elsewhere. Briefly stated, Carrington sought to negotiate among the constituent republics of the former Yugoslavia a framework convention that would have provided for a mixture of federal and confederal relations among them; would have regulated legal and economic relations; would have provided guarantees of respect for human rights, including the rights of minorities and communities; and would have set the country along a new path of cooperation. With the exception of Serbian President Milosevic, who expressed reservations on a portion of the draft convention dealing with the degree of autonomy, the Carrington draft Convention met with substantial agreement. That was in the late fall of 1991. Carrington was proceeding on the basis, known to governments of the European Community, that the issue of recognition would not be broached until work on his draft convention was completed. By the middle of December, 1991, the German Government was pressing for recognition of Croatia and Slovenia. Carrington and the then Secretary-General of the United Nations wrote to German Foreign Minister Genscher strongly pleading with him not to push for recognition and warning of the consequences of premature recognition. This was to no avail. By the middle of January, 1992 the European Community, under German pressure, agreed to recognise successor republics. Less than four months later conflict broke out in Bosnia and Herzegovina. Carrington considered that European Community recognition before work on his draft convention was completed knocked the basis out of that work. He practically suspended his efforts and resigned honourably later in the year at the London Conference, which passed the task on to the International Conference on the Former Yugoslavia. Carrington had served with dignity and left with honour.

Under the aegis of the Carrington Conference, Portuguese Ambassador Cutileiro had held numerous rounds of talks with the Bosnian parties, between January and July of 1992 – starting before the outbreak of conflict in April 1992. Cutileiro worked with them on a plan according to which three constituent peoples would be recognised in Bosnia and Herzegovina, organised along confederal lines, with guarantees of respect for human rights and the rights of minorities. Each constituent people, Croats, Muslims and Serbs, would have a republic, with their population coming from different concentrations where they were the majority. Leaders of the Bosniacs, Croats, and Serbs all accepted a Statement of Principles in March of 1992. A few weeks later the Bosniac leader Alija Izetbegovic repudiated his acceptance. Shortly thereafter conflict broke out at the beginning of April, 1992 and Cutileiro tried his best to stop it – to no avail. Cutileiro persisted in his efforts until the London Conference, when he also stepped down. He also had served with dignity and left with honour. The spirit of his plan would return later.

The negotiating processes engaged in by Carrington and Cutileiro had a number of features worthy of note: They did superb technical groundwork; drew upon very qualified experts; opted for discreet negotiations; and had clear objectives – which they very likely would have achieved but for the ground being removed from their feet by the German Government. Cutileiro's blueprint was an imaginative combination of pragmatism and principle. History will probably conclude that Alija Izetbegovic was guilty of a capital blunder when he repudiated his acceptance of the March 1992 Statement of Principles.

ICFY

The London Conference of August 1992 was held for variety of reasons. The newly elected Secretary-General of the United Nations had had a messy encounter with the Carrington Conference when it concluded an agreement on the control of heavy weapons and sought to entrust supervision of its implementation to the United Nations. The protests of the Secretary-General were inelegant to say the least. The European Community, for its part, was in a quandary and wished to pass the Yugoslav dossier to the United Nations. In the end result, Prime Minister John Major in his capacity as President of the Presidency of the European Community and the Secretary-General of the United Nations co-chaired the London Conference held in August, 1992. That Conference was more in the nature of a parliamentary than a negotiating exercise. Pages of do's and dont's were legislated for parties on the ground in the former Yugoslavia to observe – with scant regard for the willingness of the parties to observe them. An International Conference on Former Yugoslavia was established at London, to be based in Geneva and to be steered jointly by the distinguished former U.S. Secretary-State Cyrus Vance and the former U.K. Foreign Secretary, Lord Owen.

Vance and Owen arrived in Geneva on 3 September and set about their tasks with gusto – with a meeting of the Steering Committee of the Conference that very day. In less than two weeks they were on mission in the Former Yugoslavia and by the end September, they had assembled the Bosnian parties for continuous talks in Geneva. On 30 September they brought together the Presidents of Croatia and of Federal Republic of Yugoslavia for talks. The two leaders issued a joint communique providing for the resolution of outstanding disputes and laying down steps for future cooperation between them. A further meeting was held between these leaders in October. During that month also, a meeting was held between the Presidents of Bosnia and Herzegovina and the Federal Republic of Yugoslavia. They too issued a joint statement. Missions to Macedonia, Albania, Slovenia, Croatia, Bosnia and Heregovina and the Federal Republic of Yugoslavia sought to develop the outlines of blueprints for peace.

On the Bosnian question, Vance and Owen, assisted by Martti Ahtisaari, later the President of Finland, sought to write on a clean slate. Ahtisaari first invited the Bosnian parties to offer their views on the framework for a settlement. The Croats and the Serbs argued for a return to the Cutileiro Statement of Principles. The Muslims argued for a unified, integral, multi-ethnic Bosnia and Herzegovina. Ahtisaari asked them to submit maps indicating majority areas of the main population groups. Numerous meetings were held with the three delegations individually between the end of September and the middle of December, 1992 to discuss a constitutional framework and maps. Joint meetings could not be held because the Muslims took the position that they would not meet with the Serbs led by Radovan Karadzic.

In the last week of December, 1992 a joint meeting of Croat and Muslim leaders was held in Geneva on the eve of all-party talks scheduled to open in Geneva on 2 January, 1993. A constitutional framework was discussed providing for the establishment of ten largely-autonomous provinces within a unified Bosnia and Herzegovina, and maps were discussed. What was at work, in effect, was the development of an alliance strategy on the eve of all-party talks: an alliance of Croats and Muslims supported by the Co-Chairmen. The mediators were acting politically. In the light of experience one can pose the question whether political mediation against one of the parties could be successful mediation. Earlier in December, the Co-Chairmen, Vance and Owen had publicly invited the electorate in the Federal Republic of Yugoslavia to vote against

Slobodan Milosevic and for Milan Panic in Serbia's Presidential elections. It was a high-risk strategy.

Fortunately for the duo, Cyrus Vance had developed relations of confidence with Milosevic when Vance had mediated an end to the conflict in Croatia the previous year. So when the Bosnian parties assembled in Geneva on 2 January, 1993, in the presence of the Presidents of Croatia, the Federal Republic of Yugoslavia, Montenegro and Serbia, Vance got Milosevic to bring immense pressure to bear upon Radovan Karadzic to get him to accept a constitutional framework for Bosnia and Herzegovina providing for ten largely autonomous provinces within a unified country. This brought the Vance-Owen process to a new stage: from consultations to alliance, to politicking to pressure. Radovan Karadzic, acting under severe pressure from Milosevic, joined the Croat leader Mate Boban, and the Bosniac leader Alija Izetbegovic, in signing the constitutional framework in January, 1993. It was only a framework; the map depicting ten provinces had to be agreed upon; arrangements for implementing a cessation of hostilities had to be negotiated.

Vance and Owen put down a map which was signed by the Croat leader Mate Boban. Karadzic and Izetbegovic wanted changes. Vance and Owen decided to move the negotiations to New York where they could be nearer to the Security Council. The thinking was that the members of the Security Council could be marshalled to bring pressure to bear upon the Muslim and Serb leadership to settle the map and to proceed with implementation of the plan. To the Vance-Owen methods of negotiation could now be added attempts to marshall pressure upon recalcitrant parties. It would appear to work after some time but then fail, thus inviting the question: If pressure tactics are overused are they doomed to failure?

The Clinton Administration versus the Mediators

After President Clinton was elected, Vance, a respected former Democratic Secretary-of-State, under whom Secretary-of-State Christopher served as Deputy, personally briefed senior members of the Clinton transition team on the nature of the Bosnian problematique and on the lines being pursued in the search for a settlement. After President Clinton was inaugurated Vance personally sent to Secretary Christopher copies of plans and maps under discussion with the Bosnian parties. Before long the Clinton Administration, Secretary Christopher included, began to snipe at the Vance-Owen plan and to take swipes at Vance himself. Vance, a dignified, honourable, disciplined person if ever there was one, kept his cool and refrained from replying in public.

Cy Vance and Lord David Owen had done their utmost to devise a peace plan for Bosnia and Herzegovina that would maintain the integrity of the country and would reverse ethnic cleansing by the Bosnian Serbs. I was present in many conversations with them in which they both expressed their determination to help reverse ethnic cleansing and to make sure that the Serbs returned territories they had taken by force.

The Vance-Owen plan (VOPP) contained constitutional arrangements and a map of ten provinces designed to respect the cosmopolitan nature of Bosnia and had extensive provisions on the protection of human rights.

After President Clinton was elected in November, 1992, I prepared a letter that Cy Vance sent to the head of the Transition Team, Warren Christopher, explaining the rationale of the VOPP and enclosing a full set of the documents. Vance and his adviser Herb Okun met in Vance's New York appartment with the incoming Deputy National Security Adviser, Sandy Berger, to explain the thinking behind the plan to him. I also prepared a set of the VOPP documents for him.

When Vance and Owen moved the negotiations from Geneva to New York at the end of January, 1993, they maintained contacts with the new US Administration. Unfortunately, senior Administration officials were sniping at the VOPP and when Vance and Owen met Warren Christopher, then Secretary of State, at the US Mission in New York he was far from supportive of the plan.

Articles critical of the plan cited Administration officials and Vance and Owen came in for bitter personal attacks. While, with Vance's blessing, Lord Owen publicly defended the plan, Vance remained quiet publicly but the attacks on him hurt him and he felt that he was being let down by people from his own party.

In the spring of 1993, sometime in the month of March, Vance came to work early, as he usually did. I also usually came in early to prepare for the day's work. Vance and I were alone in his office and he needed to get something off his chest. I had a good relationship with him and he spoke with feeling to me.

He was convinced, he said, that Warren Christopher had never read or paid any attention to the letter and papers he, Vance, had sent to him on the VOPP. Christopher was not only uninformed about the VOPP but was being deliberately unhelpful.

Vance said that his wife, Gay, had no respect for Christopher and did not trust him. He told me the story about the time, during the hostage crisis in Tehran, when he was Secretary of State and Christopher was his deputy. Vance was opposed to a military rescue mission and had made this clear to President Carter and others. Christopher knew this well.

The weekend when the decision was made to send in the military rescue mission, Vance had taken a weekend break in Florida. He had told Christopher where he would be and left his coordinates.

When President Carter called the meeting that weekend to decide on the rescue mission, he continued, Christopher made no effort whatsoever to contact him. "He knew where I was and that I opposed a military rescue mission. He made no attempt whatsoever to contact me. I would have returned to Washington for the meeting." Nor did Christopher try to contact him to tell him that the President had decided on a rescue mission.

Vance continued that after he had resigned he nevertheless recommended to President Carter that Christopher succeed him.

Returning to the VOPP, Vance thought that Christopher was being deliberately unhelpful and nasty. I could feel that he felt that he had served the Carter Administration faithfully as Secretary of State and that his former Democratic colleagues, notably his deputy Christopher, were ostracising him. This discreet and proud man was hurting and felt that he was being hung out to dry by his former associates.

Worse for the peace process, however, the Clinton Administration's special envoy for the Bosnian talks, Ambassador Reginald Bartholomew began to play the role of advocate for the Bosniac side, and to press for more territory to be allocated to the Muslims in the allocation of territory among the ten provinces. It was precisely on this issue that Vance and Owen were endeavouring to persuade Radovan Karadzic to come on board the map they had put down – as Izetbegovic engaged in a stand-off to see what more Bartholomew could obtain for him. When Bartholomew did succeed in getting the map changed to allocate more territory to the Muslims, Izetbegovic signed in March. But the reasons for Izetbegovic's signature were the very reasons why Radovan Karadzic stayed further away from the map. Pressure from the United States in favour of one side, however well-intentioned, pushed another side away from the peace table.

Conclusion

We have set out in some detail in this chapter the honourable efforts of peacemakers. Unfortunately, their efforts were sabotaged by dishonourable parties and by misguided do-gooders. Thousands died because of their "do-goodery"!

CHAPTER 13

Humanitarianism

Heroism in the Face of Inhumanity

Introduction

Human rights were at the heart of the situations that humanitarian actors had to deal with in the former Yugoslavia. The lead humanitarian UN agency, designated as such by the UN Secretary-General, was the Office of the UN High Commissioner for Refugees. Under the inspired leadership of Mrs. Sadako Ogata, it sought valiantly to address the challenges of protection and assistance. Mrs Ogata and UNHCR kept drawing attention to the human rights root causes of the problems in the former Yugoslavia, calling on the warring parties to stop their violations, and calling on the international community and the designated peacemakers in the ICFY to work out political solutions to the conflicts. Mrs Ogata and her colleagues pointed out that humanitarian operations were being used by the international community as a 'fig leaf' to cover their failure to stop the conflict. I have among my papers submissions from UNHCR to me as Director of the ICFY pleading that the Co-Chairmen should take action to bring violations to an end and should see to it that there were political solutions.

Unfortunately, in this conflict the point was registered forcefully that parties with the will to fight and the means to fight will fight. Yugoslavia had broken apart and the three communities in Bosnia and Herzegovina wanted to have their share of the land of the country. On top of that, for whatever historical or other reasons, universal standards of human rights had no influence on the Serbs, who kept pointing to their treatment under the Ottomans and vowing never to live under Muslims again. The Croats wanted to take areas of Central and Western Bosnia into Croatia and were quite brutal themselves. And the Muslims wanted to avenge injustices at the hands of the Serbs and the Croats and committed their share of inhuman actions. No one was willing to abide by civilized standards of conduct.

UNHCR was thus left to cry in the wind as it sought to assist and protect people as best it could. I cannot honestly say that the international community, or we in ICFY, responded in a timely manner or fittingly to Mrs Ogata's calls for effective action to stop human rights violations or to devise political solutions as she sought. Mrs Ogata would conclude in her Memoirs:

 | DOI 10.1163/9789004245907_017

> Operating in war-torn countries in the Balkans for nearly a decade, we saved innumerable lives and mitigated human suffering. We strove and came up with new approaches and new hypotheses to address constantly evolving situations. We often had to deal with problems that were beyond what we could achieve. The humanitarian 'fig leaf' filled the gap that political and military action failed for so long to address.[1]

Still, she presented the human rights dimensions of the situation with clarity and forthrightness. In this chapter we shall present UNHCR's analysis of the situation, the place it accorded to human rights in its analysis, and how it thought human rights approaches could be used to help protect people at risk. The significance of UNHCR's analysis is that it stands historically as an attempt to rally the international community to human rights ground and provided ideas that might be considered on a future occasion.

I The Centrality of Human Rights in A Comprehensive Response to the Humanitarian Crisis in the Former Yugoslavia

As United Nations involvement in the former Yugoslavia intensified in 1991–1992, the UN Secretary-General designated the United Nations High Commissioner for Refugees as the lead agency for assistance to 1.8 million refugees and displaced persons as well as some 850,000 persons affected by the ongoing conflict in Bosnia-Herzegovina. Following the deployment of the United Nations Protection Force (UNPROFOR), and in accordance with the UN peacekeeping plan, UNHCR was entrusted with the design and implementation of a scheme to facilitate the voluntary return of the displaced to their homes in the UN Protected Areas in Croatia.[2] UNHCR undertook its activities in close cooperation with UNICEF and WHO, and in close cooperation with UNPROFOR as well as with the ICRC.

Against the background of a large-scale and complicated refugee situation, the High Commissioner, following consultations with the UN Secretary-General and a number of governments, convened in Geneva on 29 July, 1992, an informal international meeting at the Ministerial level, with the objective of launching an initiative to address the immediate humanitarian needs of the victims and receiving States, and to intensify action in search of lasting

1 S. Ogata, The Turbulent Decade, Confronting the Refugee Crises of the 1990s. New York, W.W. Norton, 2005, p. 171.

2 See UN doc. S/23592.

solutions to the plight of the victims of the conflict. In a note that the High Commissioner submitted to the meeting, she urged concerted and coherent action towards a comprehensive approach that would serve to (1) enhance respect for human rights and humanitarian law (2) strengthen efforts to prevent or contain displacement; (3) provide refuge and material assistance for those in need of international protection; and (4) initiate action to create conditions, including for the socio-economic rehabilitation of affected areas, in order to encourage refugees and displaced persons to return home.[3]

The presentation of the High Commissioner focused on the centrality of human rights in the comprehensive humanitarian strategy of UNHCR.

A *Respect for Human Rights and Humanitarian Law*

The High Commissioner noted that the situation in the former Yugoslavia had been "characterized by widespread atrocities, disregard for humanitarian law and massive violations of human rights, particularly targeted against civilians on grounds of national, ethnic or religious origin. Some of the most preoccupying features include systematic expulsions, forcible relocations, assassinations and occupation or destruction of homes, particularly in Bosnia and Herzegovina and parts of Croatia. International relief workers have also been subjected to attacks" The High Commissioner underlined in her report that:

> The reaffirmation of basic human rights and humanitarian law principles must be an essential element of a comprehensive humanitarian approach, and demands for their respect should be pursued vigorously at the highest political levels. The commendable efforts of the ICRC to negotiate agreements respective of the provisions of the 1949 Geneva Conventions and their Additional Protocols must be supported. The States emerging from the former Yugoslavia should be strongly encouraged to develop legislation and build institutions for the protection of human rights, particularly those of minorities.[4]

B *Preventive Protection*

The High Commissioner thought that an important objective of humanitarian action in the former Yugoslavia had been, and should continue to be, to prevent and contain displacement, to the extent possible, by providing protection and assistance to victims of the conflict who might otherwise feel compelled to move. However, preventive protection should not prejudice the right to seek

3 UN doc. HCR/IMFY/1992/2, 24 July, 1992.

4 Ibid, para. 6.

asylum. In her assessment, a preventive strategy appeared to have had some effect in containing the problem in the former Yugoslavia. "Therefore it is incumbent on the international community to pursue every opportunity for preventive action in order to reduce the factors which compel displacement and ease the way for early resolution of the problem."[5]

Preventive protection, aimed both at areas where conflict had broken out and also where tensions were mounting, could, in the assessment of the High Commissioner, be undertaken through such activities as monitoring of the treatment of ethnic minority groups, mediation between parties, exposure of the practice of forced relocation and other measures to improve respect for human rights and humanitarian law. Such action was being carried out by UNHCR in cooperation with other organizations but required greater support and encouragement of the international community as well as the parties concerned, both politically and financially. The presence of international organizations and NGOs for the purpose of providing relief could help to build confidence in fragile security situations. "International presence to provide relief to affected population should be increased to enhance preventive protection, in addition to addressing humanitarian needs."[6]

C *Humanitarian Access*

The High Commissioner stressed that humanitarian access at all times to those in need of protection and assistance, whether in conflict or non-conflict areas, must be upheld by all parties and the international community, as must respect for the freedom of movement of the individuals and their right to seek protection and assistance. Principles must be established to ensure respect for the safety of relief workers and staff of international humanitarian organizations as an important aspect of humanitarian access.[7]

D *Special Humanitarian Needs*

The High Commissioner noted that concern had been voiced by a number of Governments, NGOs and others about the evacuation of critical medical cases, notably children from Bosnia and Herzegovina. Given the limited resources and extremely precarious security conditions, she thought that the utmost efforts should continue to be made to reduce the need for evacuation by providing adequate medical supplies and equipment for local treatment.[8]

---

5 Ibid, para. 7.

6 Ibid, paras. 8–9.

7 Ibid, para. 10.

8 Ibid, para. 11.

E *Temporary Protection*

The High Commissioner stressed that, since the outbreak of the Yugoslav conflict, it had been the position of her Office that persons fleeing from the former Yugoslavia who were in need of international protection should be able to receive it on a temporary basis. Because of the large numbers involved, UNHCR believed that it was not practical to use individual asylum procedures, although persons who had a valid claim under the 1951 Convention relating to the Status of Refugees should not be precluded from applying for it if they wished. The concept of temporary protection would require further elaboration in the light of national legislation and procedures. It should include, as a minimum, admission to the country where such protection was being sought, respect for the principle of non-refoulement and basic human rights (the elements of which had been outlined in Conclusion 22 (XXXII) of the Executive Committee of the High Commissioner's Programme), and repatriation when conditions so allowed in the country of origin. The determination of the duration of temporary protection would require an ongoing assessment of the situation in the country of origin on the basis of reliable and up-to-date information. Appropriate mechanisms should be established for the collection, analysis and dissemination of such information, and for consultations among concerned Governments and UNHCR.[9]

F *Material Assistance*

Because of the dramatic daily increase in the number of refugees, recently some 10,000 per day, and the constantly evolving situation on the ground, the High Commissioner pointed out that the magnitude of the needs went far beyond the target of the appeal of the previous May, as well as the capacity of UNHCR and a few agencies. It would require the massive mobilization of the entire United Nations humanitarian system and the international community at large.[10]

G *Return and Rehabilitation*

Temporary protection and international assistance, the High Commissioner explained, could not be allowed to become protracted and must be linked clearly to the pursuit of lasting solutions, which, in turn, must respect the rights of the individuals concerned, including their right to return home in safety and dignity. A mechanism should be developed for regular and reliable information exchange on conditions prevailing in the areas to which persons could return, dialogue, including through Tripartite Commissions involving

9 Ibid, paras. 12–13.

10 Ibid, para. 17.

the parties and UNHCR, to create conditions conducive to return, and promotion of guidelines and arrangements for return in keeping with internationally recognized safeguards.[11]

H *Modalities for a Comprehensive Approach*

The High Commissioner recommended that a comprehensive approach should be accompanied by the creation of an international coordinating mechanism at the political and technical level that would allow regular exchange of information, dialogue and consideration of options for concerted action in relation to prevention, protection and return, as well as for the mobilization of international assistance and support for humanitarian action. Such a coordinating mechanism should comprise a core group of States directly concerned with the problem, including both receiving States and donor governments, as well as interested organizations, and could be convened under the auspices of UNHCR.[12]

I *Inter-agency Cooperation*

The High Commissioner considered that the coordination mechanism established by UNHCR as the lead agency with UNICEF, WHO, IOM, ICRC, and the International Council of Voluntary Agencies (ICVA), and the cooperation established with ICRC to meet the requirements of the relief operation, should be reinforced. The Inter-Agency Standing Committee established pursuant to General Assembly Resolution 46/182, under the auspice of the UN Department of Humanitarian Affairs, should be utilized to mobilize the enormous material and financial resources necessary for the short-term assistance, as well as the longer-term rehabilitation needs which may call for the involvement of lending and development-oriented agencies.[13]

In her Memoirs, The Turbulent Decade, Mrs Ogata provided a dramatic account of her efforts to promote protection and assistance for refugees, displaced persons, and threatened civilian populations in the former Yugoslavia. The following points may be singled out:

A Protection through presence

Addressing the problems of internally displaced persons, Mrs Ogata wrote:

> In the absence of adequate legal principles or effective enforcement mechanisms that covered internally displaced persons, international

11 Ibid, paras. 18–20.

12 Ibid, para. 21.

13 Ibid, para. 22.

> presence proved to be the only available tool for their protection. UNHCR's presence would also respond to the concerns of those who had not yet moved from their homes but feared they might be removed. UNHCR had to place colleagues in conflict zones instead of evacuating them out from insecure situations. We posted large contingents of field protection officers throughout Bosnia and Herzegovina and opened as many as twenty seven suboffices. Their functions ranged from responding to the safety and assistance needs of the fleeing people to negotiating with the local authorities to counteract displacement and to publicly denouncing abuses as a last resort.[14]

B Protection for people where they lived

Mrs Ogata recapitulated the origins of the idea of establishing safe areas in Bosnia-Herzegovina and UNHCR's response to the concept. A UNHCR Working Group on International Protection had examined the organization's basic position on safe areas and concluded that "the overriding principle in Bosnia and Herzegovina should be to bring safety to the people rather than to bring people to safety." She explained:

> In other words, the first policy priority was to improve the level of safety and to provide assistance in the place where people were. Since suffering and displacement were caused by armed conflict, a genuine and durable cessation of hostilities should be the goal. UNHCR would be against the establishment of safe areas that might distract from the necessity to bring all fighting to an end. Where displacement in Bosnia and Herzegovina was caused by ethnic persecution, special measures should be taken to improve the conditions of the remaining minority groups through three means: deployment of peacekeeping forces, human rights monitoring, and humanitarian assistance. Failing the cessation of hostilities so that admission to safety became necessary, UNHCR's priority was to seek entry to neighbouring countries or to relatively secure regions of Bosnia and Herzegovina. To UNHCR, the establishment of one or more clearly delineated safe areas under military protection should be only a last option.[15]

C Release of prisoners and detainees

Because the ICRC had suspended its presence in Bosnia and Herzegovina at one point due to attacks on its personnel, UNHCR was called upon to help

---

14 The Turbulent Decade, op. cit., p. 55.

15 Ibid, p. 90–91.

ameliorate the situation of peope detained in the conflict and to help dismantle the detention centres that had become infamous.[16] The ICFY Humanitarian Issues Working Group that Mrs Ogata chaired dealt with the dismantling of the detention centres, with representatives of ICRC joining the negotiating meetings in Geneva. Within this framework, the ICRC was able to reach agreement for the simultaneous release of five thousand detainees by all three sides from ten different locations. "Some thousand detained persons were released on October 19" (1992).[17]

D Pressing for political solutions

Mrs Ogata wrote:

> I had been long convinced that the humanitarian problems would not be solved without an overall political settlement for Yugoslavia. The ICFY came as a challenge to seek and promote solutions to the conflict.[18]

Unfortunately, she "recognized more than ever the limits of the Security Council. Its concern was primarily political, with limited heed to humanitarian consequences."[19] She "noted an increasing gap between the Security Council and the Secretary-general in New York, and UNHCR in the field, on the understanding of the needs of these 'safe' areas. The reality was that we could carry on humanitarian action only within the range allowed by the war situation."[20]

The peacemakers did what they could. Cyrus Vance told a meeting on the 'Comprehensive Response to the Humanitarian Crisis in Ex-Yugoslavia', on 4 September, 1992:

> Let us all work together to bring the day nearer when we may never more hear expressions such as 'ethnic cleansing', or see the daily suffering of hundreds of thousands of displaced persons." Exhortations, however, did not suffice, and Mrs Ogata was left to fend for the victims as best she could, with remarkable innovativeness, courage, and perseverance.

16 Ibid, p. 70.

17 Ibid, p. 73–74.

18 Ibid, p. 71.

19 Ibid, p. 89.

20 Ibid, p. 93.

Conclusion

Without a doubt, UNHCR carried a heavy burden during the Yugoslav conflicts. It had to raise funds for assisting such large numbers of people and its operatives had to work in the most difficult of conditions. I have in my mind's eye a twenty-eight year old Japanese colleague who moved in and out of dangerous areas, interacting with the leaders of warring parties, pleading with them to help alleviate the suffering of the people, and sending to Headquarters the most moving of reports about the plight of the civilian victims.

Nicholas Morris, the Special Envoy of the High Commissioner, Mrs Ogata, spoke to me on different occasions, as Director in the Office of the SRSG and as Director of the ICFY, that humanitarian personnel were operating in the most unsafe conditions of any UN humanitarian operation to date. I asked him to document this and included this in a report from the ICFY Co-Chairmen to the UN Security Council. Nicholas also made strong representations to me that humanitarian assistance was being diverted for military purposes on all sides of the Bosnian conflict. It was harder to make a case about this in a report to the Security Council and, eventually, we did not.

Nicholas Morris made poignant representations to Dr Radovan Karadzic to bring ethnic cleansing to an end. So did the SRSG in Zagreb, all to no avail. UNHCR had to operate in the most difficult environment, doing what it could to protect people in distress while pleading for political solutions and for effective action on the part of the international community to protect the human rights of people at risk.

We shall see in subsequent chapters the efforts of the UN Special Rapporteur on human rights in the former Yugoslavia, as well as efforts by the peacemakers and the peacekeepers to help protect human rights. Unfortunately, we have to recognize that though they did what they could in the circumstances, it was not enough. In fact, only negotiated solutions could bring an end to the suffering of the people. The Vance-Owen plan might have stopped the conflict in Bosnia and Herzegovina in the spring of 1993, two and a half years earlier than the Dayton peace accords. The USA, however, wanted to, and did arm, the Bosnian government so that it could continue fighting and take back territories lost to the Bosnian Serbs.

Whatever the moral rationale for this US policy, the fact of the matter is that countless people died and suffered in the conflict from the spring of 1993 to November, 1995. While UNHCR was calling for political settlements, the most powerful country in the world was arming the Bosnians to fight. We also had peace agreements such as the Invincible package a full two years before Dayton. President Izetbegovic and Foreign Minister Haris Silajdzic accepted this agreement on the HMS Invincible and then repudiated it a week later under US pressure. History will judge the Invincible package a more stable one than that concluded at Dayton. Again, the question arises, why did so many people have to die and to suffer in the two years between September, 1993 and November 22, 1995, when the Dayton accords were signed?

There was a moment in August, 1993, when President Izetbegovic asked for, and obtained, six concessions from Dr Karadzic. Lord Owen and Thorvald Stoltenberg secured these concessions but Izetbegovic would still not sign. One of his close aides, in a private moment, wept on my shoulder and asked, "Why does he not sign? Does he not know how much we are suffering?"

I relate the above not to be accusatory, or judgmental. Rather, it is to address UNHCR's plea that everything be done to bring about a political solution, and to protect the rights of the victims. The sad fact of the matter is that a solution to the Bosnian conflict could not be achieved until the US government was ready. And it was only in the summer of 1995 that the US was ready to bring about a solution. And, in the meantime, in the words of the song by Elvis Presley, singing about the plight of the victims in the slums of Chicago, "And his Momma cried."

By a strange quirk of circumstances, I was present at Dayton when the accords were negotiated and signed. The US team, under criticism in the media, kept briefing journalists that what was being worked out was the best that could be attained in the circumstances. When Vance, Owen, Ahtisaari and Stoltenberg did this a full two and half years earlier, the US Government and the media pundits all came down hard on them. Well, in fact, there were better peace agreements long before Dayton, negotiated by the ICFY negotiators. Uncle Sam chose to let the conflict continue. And the victims cried. And UNHCR cried. And we cried.

CHAPTER 14

Peacekeeping in the Face of Ingratitude, Opportunism, and Treachery

Introduction

United Nations peacekeeping changed for ever in the former Yugoslavia. At the outset of UNPROFOR the peacekeeping doctrine was the classical one: that UN forces were interposed between warring parties who wished them to help keep a peace that they had agreed to. With a stretch, one could say that there was such an agreement in respect of the deployment in the UNPAs in Croatia.[1] One could not, however, say this of the subsequent deployments in Bosnia and Herzegovina and the Former Yugoslav Republic of Macedonia. The leadership of the peacekeeping force was reluctant to have to deal with human rights issues. From the very outset of the deployment of UNPROFOR, however, it would be called upon to contribute to the human rights effort. As the duration of the Force's deployment increased it would come to accept a role in reporting on human rights violations, in speaking out on human rights violations, and in being ready to use force if needed for the protection of those at risk. Yugoslavia established the principle that UN peace forces had a duty to contribute to the defence of human rights.

In an earlier Chapter, we saw how UNPROFOR discharged its mandate as a protection force in the UNPAs in Croatia. In this chapter we shall see how the human rights-related role of the force would develop dramatically over time. For background, we provide an overview of the contributions ofe of UN peacekeeping forces in the former Yugoslavia.

I The Contributions of UN Peace Operations in the Former Yugoslavia

In a briefing to the UN Security Council, meeting in Informal Consultations on 23 February, 1995, Thorvald Stoltenberg, Co-Chairman of the ICFY and, during 1993, the SRSG in charge of all UN operations in the former Yugoslavia, addressed head on criticism of UNPROFOR in the media and proceeded to provide a

1 See on this, M. Goulding, Peacemonger, London, John Murray, 2002.

 | DOI 10.1163/9789004245907_018

dramatic account of the force's contribution in the area. Noting that there had been charges that the UN and UNPROFOR had not fully implemented their mandate, he admitted that, to a certain extent, this had been true. But, he pointed out, a UN withdrawal from areas of the former Yugoslavia would make the world realize that what it had accomplished there had been of 'capital importance'. Since the Council's adoption of resolution 713 in September 1991, 62 resolutions had been adopted and more than 50 Presidential statements had been issued. UNPROFOR, whose authorized strength was 50, 433 personnel, barely mustered 43, 547. Its casualties then stood at 1,340, 139 of them fatal.[2]

The UN High Commissioner for Refugees, he continued, had spent more than 1 billion in direct assistance to some 4 million refugees and displaced persons. The Sarajevo airlift was the longest in history. UNPROFOR units were stationed along the 712 kilometre cease-fire line in Croatia, along a 1,205 kilometre line inside Bosnia, and along the 290 kilometre FYROM border. ICFY monitors were operating in a 500-kilometre arc between the Federal Republic of Yugoslavia (FRY) (Serbia and Montenegro) and Bosnia and Herzegovina and along a 245 kilometre line between Croatia and the FRY. There were no UN personnel along the 850 kilometre border between Croatia and Bosnia and Herzegovina.

There had been close to 100 ceasefire agreements in Bosnia and a dozen in Croatia. Those figures, Mr Stoltenberg said, illustrated the seriousness of the threat that would arise if UNPROFOR were compelled to withdraw from Croatia. There had been successes in that country through the five successive blueprints for an overall regional settlement and the two plans for Croatia, the latest of which was the "Z-4" Plan emanating from a Zagreb group in which ICFY participated. An economic agreement between Croatia and the Croatian Serbs had led to the re-opening of the highway between the Croatian and Serbian areas of Croatia, permitting renewed contacts among people and among families. Four thousand five hundred vehicles were then using the highway daily. The oil pipeline had been opened on 26 January, 1995, and agreement reached on its joint operation by Croatia and the Knin authorities. The Croatian authorities had recently delivered the spare parts needed for the Obrowsz power plant, which would resume operation in a few weeks. Mine-clearance operations had begun along two railway tracks.

On the political front, Mr Stoltenberg continued, the "Z-4" document was a basis for political negotiations. The parties were all familiar with the

2 See UN Secretariat Note: Proceedings of the Security Council. Thursday 23 February 1995. Informal Consultations. Briefing by Mr Stoltenberg. Members of the Council welcomed this briefing as 'comprehensive' and 'comprehensible'.

document's contents and with time he was confident that talks would take place on them. What might result from them was a new mandate for UNPROFOR and possibly a new deployment and reinforcement.

Turning to Bosnia and Herzevovina, the bulk of the negotiations at that stage was being carried out by the Contact Group, with ICFY's support and assistance. The most significant event inside Bosnia had been the creation of an ICFY Mission on the Bosnia-FRY border after the FRY had indicated its willingness to isolate the Bosnian Serbs by sealing that border. Within hours of Mr Milosevic's decision, ICFY had received his consent for its border mission, as well as financial and manpower support from donor countries. Within a week, the first 60 ICFY personnel were in place. With 190 personnel from 17 countries manning 21 border posts, the mission acted promptly on all information received.

Mr Stoltenberg next drew the Council's attention to the Former Yugoslav Republic of Macedonia (FYROM), where the situation was of serious concern. Domestic tensions were high because of differences between Macedonians and Albanians and also because the country was under severe external pressure due to the effects of sanctions against the FRY; and because of a critical economic situation following a Greek embargo.

Nevertheless, one of the most positive and stimulating aspects of UN action in the FYROM had been the preventive deployment of UN troops, which could serve as a model for future operations. Stoltenberg added that he had reached agreement with the FYROM Government on holding tripartite talks between the Government, the Albanian opposition, and the Albanian party taking part in the Government. At a meeting in Geneva that week, donor countries and governments had indicated their readiness to support multi-media Albanian broadcasts. A few weeks before that, at an educational conference in the Hague, education in the FYROM had specifically been discussed, in concert with ICFY and UNESCO. Participants were hopeful that their discussions might lead to the establishment of an Albanian Pedagogical Institute in Skopje, which would be of great importance to the Albanians.

Stoltenberg continued that he had checked with President Milosevic regarding Mr Rugova's interest in meeting him in order to discuss the situation in Kosovo. President Milosevic had replied in the affirmative. That had been conveyed to Mr Rugova who had said that he would have to discuss it with his people.[3]

---

3 Note by the author: Rugova made this request and after Stoltenberg informed him of Milosevic's positive response he said he would have to discuss it with 'his people' and never came back to the subject.

We have set out the content of this briefing in some detail because it provides a dramatic snapshot of UN peace operations in the former Yugoslavia, taken from the notes on the proceedings of the UN Security Council.

II Development of a Human Rights Role

Thorvald Stoltenberg, who, at one stage, served simultaneously as ICFY Co-Chairmen and SRSG in charge of all UN operations in the former Yugoslavia, played a decisive part in bringing about a human rights role for United Nations peacekeepers in the midst of a conflict – the first time this had ever been done. How this came about is a story not well known.

Professor Torkel Opsahl, a member of the Commission of Experts gathering information into possible crimes in the Former Yugoslavia, was a fellow Norwegian and a good friend of Stoltenberg. He had served brilliantly as a member of the European Commission on Human Rights, on the UN Human Rights Committee, and on other international human rights bodies. This writer had been fortunate to have him as Director of Studies when the author participated in the Research Centre of the Hague Academy of International Law and he and the author had done a United Nations mission together to visit prisoner of war camps in Iran and Iraq in 1988 during the war between those two countries.

Opsahl, a man of principle, was outraged by the atrocities being committed in the former Yugoslavia and he conveyed his views with some passion to Stoltenberg. When Stoltenberg became the SRSG in charge of all UN operations, including the peacekeeping forces, he asked this author, as Director of his office as SRSG, to look into what might be done by the peacekeepers on the human rights front.

It will be remembered that the force had been established initially as a protection force and carried the name the United Nations Protection Force (UNPROFOR). The concept was that it would be placed around the Serb enclaves in Croatia with the idea that there would be protection through presence. The main role in human rights related issues was played by the Civilian Police (CIVPOL) but this was, again, largely a role of protection through presence.

The United Nations peacekeeping doctrine at the time did not envisage an active human rights protection role for United Nations peacekeepers and the UN Department of Peacekeeping Operations was far from having made the intellectual or policy leap into the notion that peacekeeping troops could play a role on human rights matters. The cable traffic in the early days of the force bears this out.

This prevailing culture came out very much in this author's meetings with the Force Commander, Deputy Force Commander and other senior peacekeeping personnel when the author met with them to discuss the issue of a human rights role for the peacekeepers. The first meeting was in May, 1993, with the Deputy Force Commander, Major-General Gaudreau of Canada and other senior leaders at the force headquarters in Zagreb. It was a cooperative and constructive meeting. The Deputy Force Commander, a seasoned UN peacekeeper, explained that peacekeeping forces had never been called upon to gather information and report on atrocities committed by the parties among whom they were stationed. If it became known that they were doing this it would make their relations with the parties on the ground difficult. Moreover, across the former Yugoslavia, the force, though cumulatively large, was thinly distributed on the ground.

This author, in turn, explained that we were dealing with a situation that had not arisen before. The forces were on the ground and serious violations of human rights were taking place in their midst. Members of the international community were harsh in their criticism and the situation we were in was untenable. We had to be seen as attentive to the human rights issues involved.

The Deputy Force Commander was a gentleman and he clearly absorbed these arguments even though he maintained his position during the meeting. This author sought to make the case for the forces to at least report on what they were aware of, confidentially. One could see the discomfort of the peacekeeping leaders over the idea that they should report on violations to non-peacekeeping entities and that this would become known to the parties on the ground. They were thinking about the fact that they had to operate among the very parties on the ground and they were, at the end of the day, vulnerable, being so thinly spread out. This author nevertheless pressed the point for at least reporting.

It must be said that one was dealing with leaders of goodwill and they reflected on our discussions. In the end one could see a softening of their position on reporting, even if there was not an immediate change. Eventually, Yasushi Akashi took over as SRSG following Stoltenberg's request to Boutros-Ghali that he be relieved of the SRSG position so that he could concentrate on the negotiations, and a unit was established in the Office of the SRSG to gather information on violations of human rights and to report thereon to the SRSG. Thus it was that the first human rights component was established in a United Nations peacekeeping force operating prior to the conclusion of a peace agreement. It was a small step, but an important one. It began with the insistence of a peacemaker/peacekeeper, Thorvald Stoltenberg.

Stoltenberg was in a strong position because he doubled as SRSG and chief UN negotiator and therefore had considerably more leverage. But there are ways for the peacemaker to exert influence on people of goodwill in charge of peacekeeping forces. A peace negotiator who comes to the conclusion that there is need for human rights monitoring on the ground, even while peace negotiations are carried on, can and should exert such influence.

III Peacekeepers Report on Atrocities

On 13 May, 1993, the Force Commander, General Wahlgren, sent a communication to Kofi Annan, USG for peacekeeping, on alleged Bosnian Croat (HVO) forces atrocities in the Lasva Valley. He provided advance notice of the outcome of investigations conducted in central Bosnia by the human rights staff of the related bodies based with UNPROFOR. In brief, they were reporting a major, well-coordinated and planned exercise in ethnic cleansing conducted by the HVO at various locations in the valley of the river Lasva, including Vitez and Ahimici, involving hundreds of Muslim civilian deaths "in circumstances which will certainly be described as atrocities, and may involve breaches of the Genocide Convention. The evidence is detailed, extensive and convincing."

According to Wahlgren's report, a major sequence of events took place from 16 – 20 April. They had been witnessed by about 60 identified persons, of whom many had given statements, including members of the British battalion, who seemed fully informed. The purpose was to drive all Muslims out of a number of towns and villages physically and by terror. HVO burned villages, telling the Muslim inhabitants that the area under the Vance-Owen plan was to become a part of Croatia.

The communication continued that the pattern of alleged behaviour was "tragically familiar, but entails especial levels of barbarity." 18 HVO members were specifically accused. The number of persons killed was unknown as, in some villages such as Ahimici, several hundreds of persons were said to be missing still. Grenade and petrol-bomb attacks on houses were said to have been followed in some instances by house to house massacres. "It is concluded by the investigators, who had Britbatt protection and logistical assistance throughout their work, that the practice was to spread terror by engaging in public massacres, followed by vigorous pressure in the area to leave it." The communication continued that some later retaliation by Bosnian forces had taken place, but not on a large scale.

The foregoing was also contained in a report given to the Centre for Human Rights in Geneva for the attention of the Special Rapporteur.[4]

On 21 December, 1993, Stoltenberg as SRSG in charge of UNPROFOR sent a communication to Kofi Annan, USG in charge of the Department of peace-keeping operations on alleged massacres committed by Bosnian Presidency forces. On the night of 14 September, 1993, the Mayor of Prozor had requested UNPROFOR to witness the results of an alleged massacre by Bosnian Presidency forces in the village of Kriz. A company of UNPROFOR had attended the scene on 15 September and reported that it appeared that, the previous day, an attack had been made by 70 – 100 Bosnian Presidency forces whose aim was to pin down HIV troops on their frontline positions and to draw the remainder of the men out of the village of Kriz. During the offensive, an HVO command post had been located and attacked in the village and, as the Bosnian troops withdrew back through Kriz, they had systematically killed a number of civilians. A total of 35 civilian bodies had been identified including elderly men and women, and a fourteen year old female. Some of the elderly had been killed in their beds or while cowering for cover elsewhere. The majority of those killed had been shot but a small number had been stabbed, one had possibly been axed to death, and a number of bodies burned. There were reports of 'Mujahideen' involvement.

The communication noted that Special Rapporteur Mazowiecki had written to President Izetbegovic on 15 October to condemn this and other unacceptable massacres of civilians by Bosnian forces and had urged an investigation of the matter and punishment of the perpetrators. UNPROFOR had no information of any action on this front by the Bosnian Presidency.[5]

IV Peacekeepers Speak Out about Atrocities

On 6 October, 1993, Stoltenberg, in his capacity as SRSG in charge of UNPROFOR, sent a communication to the Secretary-General transmitting a report drawn up by Civil Affairs Sector South on behalf of various components of UNPROFOR in respect of the incursion into the "Medak pocket" by the Croatian Army on and after 9 September, 1993. The report had been endorsed by Force Commander Jean Cot and the Head of Civil Affairs Cedric Thornberry. The report described a series of grave breaches of international law.

4 Communication in the possession of the author.

5 Communication in the possession of the author.

Stoltenberg informed the Secretary-General that he endorsed the report's recommendation that it be transmitted to the Human Rights Commission's Special Rapporteur, Mr Tadeusz Mazowiecki, and to the Commission of Experts on War Crimes for their consideration. The report had been hand-carried to these two recipients in Geneva that very day. Stoltenberg approved a press statement on the grave breaches.

Stoltenberg further informed the Secretary-General that a copy of the report was being transmitted to the Croatian Minister of Defence Mr Susak, in Zagreb, requesting appropriate action on his part. Furthermore, UNPROFOR had details of the senior command structure of the units responsible for the actions described in the report which, as could be seen from the report, "appear in large measure to have been premeditated and planned."[6] The press statement issued by UNPROFOR was blunt in its content and tone.

Another occasion when UNPROFOR spoke out forthrightly occurred later that month. On 27 October, 1993 UNPROFOR issued the following remarkable press release on a massacre that had taken place in the Muslim village of Stupni Do:

> UNPROFOR troops succeeded in entering the Muslim village of Stupni Do on the afternoon of 26 October 1993 and have confirmed that a massacre has occurred there.
>
> Stupni Do...was attacked by Croatian Defence Council (HVO) troops on Saturday, 23 October, allegedly as a reprisal for a Muslim attack on the nearby Croat village of Kopjari on Thursday, 21 October, during which all the inhabitants were driven out of the village.
>
> The Nordic Battalion (Nordicbat) of the Bosnia-Herzegovina Command of UNPROFOR found that all 52 houses of the village had been burned to the ground. At last report, the UNPROFOR soldiers had searched half the houses and had found the bodies of 15 persons who had either been shot or burned to death. This included a group of women holding each other's arms, who had been shot. In addition, two young women from a group of 25 refugees who escaped from the village have made accusations of rape.
>
> The whereabouts of many of the village's inhabitants is still unknown, but it is believed that some succeeded in escaping into the surrounding hills.
>
> The UNPROFOR troops initiated attempts to reach Stupni Do almost immediately after the HVO attack began on 23 October. Throughout the

6 Communication in the possession of the author.

> three-day stand-off with the HVO, they were constantly blocked by the Bobovac Brigade. The UNPROFOR troops were threatened with rocket-propelled grenade anti-tank weapons, small arms and anti-tank mine barriers. Several of the UNPROFOR armoured personnel carriers (APCs) were damaged by small arms fire and grenades.
>
> UNPROFOR's Force Commander General Jean Cot, said: 'Despite the valiant efforts of Nordicbat, the HVO troops systematically prevented the UN soldiers from entering the village of Stupni Do for three days. It is unacceptable that we were forced to delay our entry into the village for such a period. It is clear that the HVO troops were attempting to hide from us the atrocities they had committed.
>
> At the same time, UNPROFOR is deeply concerned about the safety of more than 200 Muslims being held in two school buildings in the town of Vares. There has been some evidence of mistreatment of some of the prisoners by HVO soldiers. UNPROFOR troops with APCs are stationed near these locations.
>
> The Force Commander said these tragedies impeded moves towards reconciliation among the parties involved. He said it was another example of the need for all the parties to the conflict to make a solid commitment towards the protection of minorities within the areas they controlled.
>
> The investigation into the massacre and the collection of further evidence regarding war crimes will continue. UNPROFOR troops, UN Civilian Police, members of the European Community Monitoring Mission, representatives of UNHCR and other humanitarian agencies will visit the village.[7]

On 5 September, 1994, UNPROFOR issued the following Press Statement by the SRSG for the former Yugoslavia, Yasushi Akashi on "Recent Mass Expulsions and Other Severe Violations of Human Rights in Bosnia and Herzegovina":

> I am deeply concerned by reports over the past several days of the continued mass expulsion of people from the Bosnian Serb controlled areas of Bijeljina and Banja Luka. I strongly condemn these extremely serious violations of international humanitarian law and universally recognized principles of human rights.

7 Statement signed by Shannon Boyd, UNPROFOR Spokesman, Zagreb HQ, 1800053. Text in the possession of the author.

> Since the middle of July, over 2,400 people are believed to have been expelled from the Bijeljina area to Tuzla as part of a deliberate policy of rendering the area ethnically homogeneous. These expulsions have continued throughout the past six weeks but have increased dramatically in size in recent days. On Sunday 4 September alone, more than 750 people were reported to have been expelled from the Bijeljina area to Tuzla. Smaller numbers of people are also reported to have been expelled from the Bijeljina area to central Bosnia.
>
> More than 750 people have also been forcefully expelled from Banja Luka over the past two weeks and of these, 500 are now at the camps of UNPROFOR's Jordanian and Nepali battalions in Sector West of the United Nations Protected Areas of Croatia. 250 others, mainly ethnic Romany, have crossed into Croatia proper.
>
> Many of those who have been expelled have reported the systematic practice of forced labour in the areas from which they have arrived, as well as other severe human rights violations including torture, rape and sexual assault, arbitrary arrest and detention and arbitrary deprivation of property.
>
> Recalling the Security Council Presidential Statement on Bosnia of 2 September 1994 as well as other relevant presidential statements and Security Council resolutions, I demand the immediate cessation of these practices and remind those who commit these violations of international humanitarian law that they are personally responsible.[8]

On the same day, 5 September, 1994, Nicholas Morris, the Special Envoy of the UN High Commissioner for Human Rights for the former Yugoslavia, wrote the following letter to Dr Radovan Karadzic, the Bosnian Serb leader:

> Dear Dr Karadzic,
>
> Already this month, over 1,300 members of the minority communities in the Bijeljina area have been forced to leave their homes by your authorities and expelled towards Tuzla. Similar departures continue from the Banja Luka region to Croatia: almost 1,000 in the last two weeks. The expulsions from the Bijeljina area are combined with the exaction of significant sums of money (reportedly by a man known as 'Vojkan') and take place in circumstances that create great hardship for, and sometimes threaten the lives of, the old and the vulnerable. Able-bodied males are separated from their families and apparently detained by your authorities.

8 Statement in the possession of the author.

> On many occasions UNHCR has expressed the gravest concern to you at these practices. The ICRC has done likewise. We have been assured by you and your colleagues that resolute correction action would be taken by your authorities, yet the expulsions continue and even intensify. Once more, I write to urge you to take immediate action to provide proper protection to the minorities in the areas that you control, and for whose safety you are directly responsible.
>
> Yours sincerely,
> Nicholas Morris.

On 6 September, 1994, SRSG Akashi wrote to USG Annan and USG Gharekan that he had raised with Dr Karadzic at their last meeting in Pale the ongoing abuses of human rights around Bijeljina. At that time, Dr Karadzic had attributed the problem to criminals and had undertaken to replace the Chief of Police due to what he had acknowledged was a very unsatisfactory situation in the area with respect to security and crime.

Akashi continued that he had subsequently learned that the Chief of Police had indeed been replaced. The UNHCR office in Tuzla nevertheless continued to report the arrival of large numbers of refugees who had been forced to leave the Bijeljina area. As a result he had issued the statement reproduced above.

He continued that he had telephoned Dr Karadzic to ensure that he was aware of the events around Bijeljina, and to express strong concern. He reported: "Dr Karadzic has advised me that he has taken measures to identify, arrest, and prosecute those responsible. I urged immediate action as the frequency of expulsions indicates that more are likely to follow. I also advised him of my statement of yesterday and that a statement might also be issued from Geneva by the ICRC."[9]

V The Rapid Reaction Force (RRF)

On 28 February, 1994, NATO planes fired the first ever shots in the history of the military alliance when it shot down four Serb jets flying in a no-fly zone. The Serb jets had ignored orders to land or be shot down. Two other planes escaped. The Serb planes had apparently gone on a bombing run against a Bosnian Muslim ammunitions factory in Novi Travnik.[10] According to NATO sources the

9 Communication in the possession of the author.

10 Four Serb Jets Shot Down by Nato, The Times, London, 1 March, 1994.

no-fly zone had been violated hundreds of times by all three warring factions using helicopters to ferry men and materiel and to evacuate the wounded. But NATO's Admiral Boorda reportedly said that the incident involved the first confirmed violations by fixed-wing aircraft since NATO, acting under Security Council authorization, began operating Operation Deny Flight. Russia supported NATO's action in shooting down the planes.[11] This could be classified as part of a conflict containment strategy, rather than a protection strategy as such.

The following year would see UNPROFOR's establishment of a Rapid Reaction Force (RRF) after Bosnian Serb forces had attacked UN safe areas and chained UNPROFOR personnel to military installations to deter NATO response to their aggression. Like the policing of the No-Fly Zone, the RRF was more of a conflict containment measure but it did have more of a protection dimension inasmuch as it acted to deter future Bosnian Serb attacks against Muslim positions.

The setting up and deployment of the RRF was authorized by Security Council resolution 998, voted after the hostage problem following earlier NATO air strikes against Bosnian Serb targets. The purpose of the RRF was to permit UN peace forces to support theatre forces in conducting their peacekeeping mandate. It consisted of three main units: a multinational brigade, a 24-hour airmobile brigade reinforced by Royal Air Force helicopters, and a French brigade on alert in France.

Its general mission was to be prepared to conduct operations in order to enhance the security of UN forces, to facilitate freedom of movement in Bosnia and Herzegovina and thereby maintain the credibility of the UN peace forces. The concept of operation took account of the political environment (the need for impartiality, the risk of escalation in the war, and the element of reversibility of operations.). The RRF was considered a second echelon element while the in-theatre forces made up the first echelon. The second-echelon was meant to support the first-echelon in the achievement of its mandate. The RRF was under the overall command of Force Commander General Janvier based in Zagreb and the operational command of General Rupert Smith in charge of UN forces in Sarejevo.

To begin with, the multinational brigade was deployed mainly in Bosnia, particularly Mount Igman . The airmobile brigade was deployed to Ploce. The French brigade remained on alert in France. The multinational brigade had 1000 troops deployed on Mount Igman and, during the night of 27th to 28 July, 1995, conducted successful deterrent action in order to dislodge Serb

11 Ibid.

encirclement of the locality of Krupac. The RRF conducted a silent infiltration of the area which obliged Serb forces to withdraw. The RRF thus carried a distinct preventive protection function in this instance.[12]

VI Protection from Ethnic Cleansing

On 13 October, 1992, USG for peacekeeping, Marrack Goulding, sent the following cable to General Satish Nambiar, the Commander of UNPROFOR, based in Zagreb:

> 1. At a meeting with SecGen this morning Mr Vance expressed his grave concern about continued abuses by the Bosnian Serb authorities in and around Banja Luka. Large numbers of Muslims were being rounded up and bussed to the Travnik area and made to walk through no-man's land into Muslim-controlled territory, many being shot as they went. Mr Vance felt that early deployment of UNPROFOR troops could help to deter such activities. This would be achieved when the new Canadian contingent was deployed for humanitarian protection duties. Meanwhile, was there any possibility of temporarily detaching some elements from Canadian battalion in Sector West to Banja Luka, ostensibly as advance party for new Canadian battalion?
> 2. SecGen agreed that your views should be sought on this idea.[13]

UNPROFOR would come to accept, over time, that it should take account of considerations such as these in its deployment, operations, and strategies.

VII Cooperation with the Commission of Experts

On 23 November, 1992, USG for peacekeeping, Marrack Goulding sent a cable to UNPROFOR Force Commander Nambiar on the subject "Human Rights." It read as follows: "Following the establishment of the Commission of Experts under Security Council resolution 780, I should be grateful if you would ensure that any information relating to human rights matters is passed to Geneva for

12 This account is based on a "Rapid Reaction Force Brief," circa August, 1995 in the possession of the author.

13 Communication in the possession of the author.

the attention of both the Special Rapporteur and the Commission. Please relay such material directly through your Geneva LO, keeping us informed. X and Y (names withheld by BGR) are hereby authorized to serve as UNPROFOR liaison to the Commission, whose Secretary, Ms. J. Dauchy, will contact (them) later this week."[14]

UNPROFOR gave its fullest support to the Commission of Experts.

VIII The Human Rights of the Peacekeepers

While pushing for a human rights role for the UN peacekeeping forces, UN leaders were not unmindful of the human rights of peacekeepers themselves as could be seen in a cable from Vance to the Secretary-General on 14 September, 1992. Reporting on a Mission to the former Yugoslavia, from September 9 to 13, 1992, Vance informed the Secretary-General:

> We left Izetbegovic in no doubt about our concern over attacks on UNPROFOR personnel and called on him to bring the perpetrators of such attacks to justice. This he agreed to do.[15]

Conclusion

From the foregoing, it could be seen that the challenges facing UN peacekeepers were formidable. UN peacekeeping evolved to incorporate a role in the protection of human rights. The methods used were reporting, investigations, statements of concern, condemnations. In the end, UN forces were forced to go into fighting posture in order to help uphold the principles of the Universal Declaration of Human Rights. That was perhaps the most important lesson for UN peacekeeping and the defence of human rights that came out of the Yugoslav experience.

14 Communication in the possession of the author.

15 Report in the possession of the author.

CHAPTER 15

Peacekeeping

Negotiating the Peacekeeping Mandate in Croatia

The United Nations Protected Areas (UNPAS) in Croatia were meant to dampen the fighting and provide an international presence while peacemaking efforts continued to bring the conflict between Croats and Serbs to an end.

Throughout its existence in Croatia, both sides had used the presence of UN forces for their own advantage. The Serbs had sought to engage in ethnic cleansing under the very noses of UNPROFOR. The Croatian Government, for its part, treated UNPROFOR as though it were doing the United Nations a favour in having UNPROFOR within its midst. UNPROFOR had served with tenacity and honour through all of this. It had been supported in its endeavours by the dynamism and ingenuity of ICFY personnel. In a highly volatile situation, ICFY negotiators, led by Stoltenberg and Owen, and ably supported by Knut Vollebaek, Geert Ahrens, General V. Eide, and K. Eide, had helped bring about the Cease-Fire Agreement of 29 March, 1994 and an Economic Agreement of 5 December, 1994. These were important peace stabilisation and peacebuilding agreements. Nevertheless, there had been numerous breaches of the ceasefire agreement and the Economic Agreement was being used by one side or another for bargaining leverage.

On 12 January, 1995, President Tudjman announced that Croatia would withdraw its support for UNPROFOR's continuing role in Croatia. Following President Tudjman's announcement, the 'Zagreb-4' ambassadors, comprising the United States and Russian ambassadors to Croatia and Ambassadors Ahrens and Eide from ICFY, presented a "Draft agreement on the Krajina Slavonia, Southern Baranja and Western Sirmium" to both sides on 30 January 1995. The Secretary-General reported to the UN Security Council on 22 March, 1995 that "While the Croatian Government accepted it as a basis for negotiation, the Serbs in Knin refused to receive it until the future presence of UNPROFOR was assured. Subject to the renewal of UNPROFOR's mandate, the Serbs expressed their readiness to enter into political discussions from 1 April."[1] The Secretary-General's report was overly generous. President Tudjman had no interest whatsoever in the Z-4 document.

1 S1995/222 and Corr.1, para. 11.

 DOI 10.1163/9789004245907_019

Boutros-Ghali reported to the Security Council on 22 March, 1995 that the total withdrawal of all UN peacekeeping forces from Croatia would result immediately in a grave threat to peace and security extending beyond the borders of Croatia. The probability of major renewed conflict was high.[2] In the circumstances, the maintenance of a reduced force in Croatia under a new mandate seemed the only way to reduce the risks of a renewed major war, while permitting continued progress in implementing the economic agreement and beginning political negotiations. He welcomed a joint announcement on 12 March 1995 by President Tudjman and US Vice President Gore "which opened the way to a solution along these lines."

After the US authorities provided the Secretary-General with the necessary information about their negotiations with the Croatian Government, he "instructed Mr Thorvald Stoltenberg, acting as my Special Envoy, to conduct negotiations with the parties in order to define the mandate of a future UN peace-keeping force in Croatia that I could recommend to the Security Council in the knowledge that both parties would commit themselves to cooperate with the force in the implementation of its mandate."[3]

When Stoltenberg saw Tudjman on the matter he was breathing fire and thunder. When we went to see the Croatian Serb leader, Milan Martic, in Knin, it required an overland route of six hours in a blizzard during which our party got lost and one was fearful that one might freeze to death in an armoured personnel carrier. After this arduous journey, when we sat down with Martic and his collaborators at his headquarters in Knin he greeted us thus: "Gentlemen, I know that you are poor civil servants who have to earn their pay; let us therefore get along with it and hear what you have to say." Stoltenberg, in a vintage line, replied to him, "Thank you for a very interesting intervention. Now let us get on with the business at hand." He was unruffled by Martic and was as cool as ice! It had nothing to do with the blizzard we had come through.

Stoltenberg, in the light of the frosty attitude of both sides, decided not to try to negotiate a written agreement between the two sides but to maintain contacts with them and to submit proposals to Boutros-Ghali for the mandate of the UN force in Croatia that the Secretary-General would then advance in a report to the Security Council. Boutros-Ghali reported to the Security Council on 22 March, 1995 that it had become apparent from Mr Stoltenberg's negotiations that an undestanding on the details of the new mandate and the modalities of the United Nations would require further work. "The gulf between the positions of the Government of Croatia and the Krajina Serb authorities on the

2 S1995/222, para. 68.

3 Ibid, para. 70.

role and functions fo the new force remains wide, and I am not yet in a position to inform the Council that the parties would accord it their practical cooperation. Further negotiations are therefore necessary."

Based on the advice of Stoltenberg, SRSG Akashi, and DPKO, Boutros-Ghali continued:

> "I am however, able to report that, in my view, the basis could be established for an agreement that the mandate of the force should include the following functions:
>
> (a) Support for implementation of the cease-fire agreement of 29 March, 1994;
> (b) Support for implementation of the economic agreement of 2 December 1994;
> (c) Implementation of those elements of the existing United Nations peacekeeping plan for Croatia that are accepted by both parties as having continuing relevance. These would include, but not be limited to, maintenance of a United Nations presence on the international borders of the Republic of Croatia and confidence-building and humanitarian tasks, such as assistance to refugees and displaced persons, protection of ethnic minorities, mine clearance and convoy assistance."[4]

The elements advanced by the Secretary-General would provide the basis for a new peacekeeping operation established by the Security Council on 31 March, 1995 in its resolution 981. The mandate of the UN Confidence Restoration Operation included the following:

- Performing the functions envisaged in the cease-fire agreement of March 29, 1994;
- Facilitating implementation of the economic agreement of December 2, 1994;
- Facilitating implementation of all relevant Security Council resolutions;
- Assisting in controlling by monitoring and reporting, the crossing of military personnel, equipment, supplies and weapons, over the international borders between Croatia and Bosnia and Herzegovina, and Croatia and the Federal Republic of Yugoslavia (Serbia and Montenegro) at the border crossings;

4 Ibid, para. 72.

- Facilitating the delivery of international humanitarian assistance to Bosnia and Herzegovina through the territory of Croatia; and
- Monitoring the demilitarisation of the Prevlaka peninsula.

Once again, Stoltenberg's diplomatic groundwork had helped pave the way to the removal of a major roadblock in the quest for peace in the former Yugoslavia.

Conclusion

Two comments may be made about Stoltenberg's achievements on this dossier: first, his hall mark quiet and confidence-building diplomacy. Second, his relationship of trust and confidence with Secretary-General Boutros Boutros-Ghali who valued him highly as a partner and turned to him on this, as on other precarious occasions, to perform special missions for him.

CHAPTER 16

Human Rights: How to Protect in the Heart of Darkness?

The UN Special Rapporteur

Introduction

The Special Rapporteur initially appointed by the UN Commission on Human Rights to investigate the situation of human rights in the territory of the former Yugoslavia, Mr Tadeusz Mazowiecki, former Solidarity Prime Minister of Poland, was undoubtedly a stirring voice of conscience on behalf of the victims of abuses in the former Yugoslavia. His successors continued in the path he had mapped out in highlighting the plight of the victims. In this chapter we review the endeavours of the Special Rapporteur and discuss his relations with the peacemakers and peacekeepers.

By way of background, it is useful to recall the message Cyrus Vance and Lord Owen sent on 30 November, 1992 to the second special session of the Commission on Human Rights. Vance and Owen welcomed the Commission's decision to convene a second special session to consider the serious situation of human rights in the area of the former Yugoslavia, especially in Bosnia and Herzegovina and declared:

> Regrettably, the disgraceful practice of ethnic cleansing has not ceased and violations of international norms on human rights and humanitarian law are rampant. We condemn these violations in the most categorical terms.

They added that in their efforts to promote peace with justice in the area of the former Yugoslavia, they had placed emphasis on the provision of humanitarian assistance; the strict application of sanctions; helping to bring about a cessation of hostilities in Bosnia and Herzegovina; and the preparation of a constitution for Bosnia and Herzegovina. They had also sought to promote preventive measures to avoid the spread of the conflict. They continued:

> We urge the distinguished members of the Commission on Human Rights, all Member States of the United Nations, and non-governmental organizations, to do everything possible to support and to strengthen the

 | DOI 10.1163/9789004245907_020

endeavours being undertaken in accordance with decisions of the Security Council of the United Nations.

We hope that your session will help in bringing an end to the violations of human rights and humanitarian law taking place. We also hope that you will give attention to the important question of protecting the rights of minorities. This issue is of great importance to the future stability and security in the area of the former Yugoslavia.

I Mandate of the Special Rapporteur

At its first special session on the former Yugoslavia, the Commission on Human Rights had adopted resolution 1992/S-1/1 on 14 August 1992 in which it requested its Chairman to appoint a special rapporteur to investigate first hand the human rights situation in the territory of the former Yugoslavia, in particular within Bosnia and Herzegovina, and to receive relevant, credible information on the human rights situation there from Governments, individuals, intergovernmental and non-governmental organizations, on a continuing basis, and to avail himself or herself of the assistance of existing mechanisms of the Commission on Human Rights. The Chairman of the Commission appointed Mr Tadeusz Mazowiecki, former Prime Minister of Poland, as Special Rapporteur.[1]

II Initial Report

The Special Rapporteur visited the region from 21–26 August and, in his first report to the Commission,[2] submitted the following conclusions to the Commission based on the information that he marshalled in his report: Massive and grave violations of human rights were occurring throughout the territory of Bosnia and Herzegovina. Human Rights violations were being perpetrated by all parties to the conflicts. There were also victims on all sides. However, the situation of the Muslim population was particularly tragic. They felt that they were threatened with extermination.

1 Amnesty International's Conception of the Role of the Special Rapporteur was as follows:

The Special Rapporteur 'should play a central role in documenting the human rights situation and making recommendations about preventive measures' – Amnesty International, Open Letter, 27 October, 1992.

2 The UN Secretary-General circulated the report to the UN General Assembly and the Security Council on 3 September, 1992: UN doc. A/47/418; S/24516.

Acts of violence, he continued, were tolerated and often even encouraged by responsible authorities. Consequently, the rule of law did not exist. The situation of people being detained in camps and staying in refugee centres was particularly dramatic. The indoctrination of a large part of the population that was taking place encouraged national and religious hatred. In spite of the high level of commitment of the United Nations personnel – UNPROFOR and UNHCR – they were unable adequately to protect the affected population and in many circumstances were helpless to prevent violations of human rights. There was urgent need for immediate concerted action. Even when peace was achieved, serious violations of human rights were likely to continue due to the intensity of mutual distrust and hatred.[3]

The Special Rapporteur made a number of ground-breaking recommendations that would influence UN policy and lead to innovative developments. He recommended that the United Nations, without delay, issue a peremptory warning to the authorities controlling the different parts of the territory of Bosnia and Herzegovina that, with respect to their duty to safeguard the security of the civilian population, they may, in accordance with the norms and standards of international law, be brought to justice not only for the direct perpetration but also for the toleration of acts of atrocity, violence and other violations of human rights. The United Nations, he wrote, should continue firmly to call upon the competent authorities to abandon the policy of ethnic cleansing in all its forms. Every victim of this policy should be guaranteed the possibility of claiming his/her rights under international supervision.

The Special Rapporteur considered that it was indispensable not only to increase the size of UNPROFOR but also to expand its mandate in three areas: First, the mandate should cover the whole territory of Bosnia and Herzegovina; second, UNPROFOR personnel should have the right to react directly to the human rights violations committed in their presence and to assist the victims; third, UNPROFOR personnel should be given the mandate to collect information and receive complaints concerning human rights violations occurring also on the territories which at the time were not covered by UNPROFOR's mandate. This should include access by the UNPROFOR civilian police to places of detention. Their findings should be communicated not only to the local police but also to the competent juridical authorities.

The Special Rapporteur considered that there was an urgent need to establish an investigative commission, under the auspices and in cooperation with the competent United Nations bodies, vested with the task of determining the fate of the thousands of persons who had disappeared after the seizure of

3 Ibid, paras. 51–57.

Vukovar as well as of other persons who had disappeared during the conflicts in the former Yugoslavia.

The Special Rapporteur emphasized that the need to prosecute those responsible for mass and flagrant human rights violations and for breaches of international humanitarian law and to deter future violators required the systematic collection of documentation on such crimes and of personal data concerning those responsible. He recommended that a Commission be created to assess and further investigate specific cases in which prosecution might be warranted. This information should include data already collected by various entities within the UN system, by other intergovernmental organizations and by non-governmental organizations.[4]

The Special Rapporteur considered that further implementation of his mandate required the appointment of staff based in the territories of the former Yugoslavia in order to coordinate the monitoring of human rights violations together with the other UN bodies. He recommended the creation of an adequate professional and logistical infrastructure within the Centre for Human Rights (now the OHCHR). It also required the establishment of a working relationship with other multilateral initiatives, in particular the Co-Chairmen of the International Conference on the Former Yugoslavia.[5]

These were innovative recommendations of the Special Rapporteur, all of which would come to be implemented in the subsequent months. The Special Rapporteur thus made a major contribution to UN and international policy in the former Yugoslavia, particularly the pursuit of justice in respect of war crimes and crimes against humanity.

III The Special Rapporteur and the Peacemakers

The Co-Chairmen, Vance and Owen, saw Mr Mazowiecki on Friday 4 September, within days of their arrival in Geneva. On that occasion he indicated that he saw his mission as an integral part of their efforts. Subsequently he submitted a detailed memorandum to the UN Secretary-General, which he copied to the Co-Chairmen, concerning his mandate. Among other things, he advocated putting human rights monitors on the ground.

In a letter to the Co-Chairmen he proposed the designation of contact persons. He designed Professor Roman Wieruszewski. In their reply the Co-Chairmen designated Mrs Ogata and Ambassador Ahrens.

4 Ibid, paras. 58–70.

5 Ibid, paras. 72–73.

On 22 September, 1992, the Office of the UN Secretary-General consulted Cyrus Vance on the following policy proposals, which Vance endorsed. In his reply to the Secretary-General, Vance explained that they had already been implemented:

- Mr Vance would bring to the attention of the Steering Committee of ICFY the recommendations which the Special Rapporteur might make for their consideration, as part of the effort to address the crisis in the former Yugoslavia in all its aspects.
- Similarly, Mr Vance would encourage Mr Mazowiecki's participation in the Working Group on Humanitarian Questions chaired by the UN High Commissioner for Refugees.
- Provision was being made for making available to the Centre for Human Rights five professional posts so as to assist the Special Rapporteur. While it was not the usual practice for support personnel of Special Rapporteurs to be posted in the field, allowance could be made in this case having regard to the high priority given by the Commission on Human Rights to the mission entrusted to Mr Mazowiecki.
- The Special Rapporteur was answerable to the Human Rights Commission. His reports were also being published as Security Council documents. Provision would be made for Mr Mazowiecki to report in person to the General Assembly when the item came up in the Third Committee of the General Assembly.[6]

The Office of the Secretary-General also suggested that the attendance of Mr Mazowiecki in the periodic meetings of the Steering Committee of ICFY as an observer, an idea which Mr Vance supported, should be put to the members of the Committee when they met next. Some senior officers in ICFY did not support this recommendation on the ground that there were no observers on the Steering Committee. This was an unfortunate position. Giving Mr Mazowiecki the opportunity to brief the Steering Committee would have been a way of highlighting the human rights issues in the Steering Committee.

In a briefing paper that a senior advisor wrote for the Co-Chairmen for their second meeting with Mr Mazowiecki on 8 October 1992, he suggested that, in the future, their relationship with Mr Mazowiecki could be placed on the following basis:

6 Communication from De Soto to Vance dated 22 September, 1992, in the possession of the author.

> (a) If he has information on specific events that he feels would be useful to you, he could send specific briefing notes to you.
> (b) If he has specific issues he would like to consult you on, he may indicate them to a member of your staff and you would try, if possible, to get back to him.
> (c) He should understand that the Co-Chairmen, as peace-makers, have to maintain a discreet posture and, therefore, the roles of the Co-Chairmen on the one hand, and the Special Rapporteur on the other hand, would need to be kept distinct.[7]

The briefing paper continued:

> It might be a good idea for you to indicate, from your vantage point, some issues that Mr Mazowiecki might look into. The following come to mind:
>
> - What are his perceptions about any forms of cooperation that could be pursued by the Republics of the former Yugoslavia to promote and protect human rights in the area?
> - Does he have any thoughts to offer on a mechanism or mechanisms that could be developed to ensure protection for human rights in BH?
> - Would he see a role for an International Verification Commission on Human Rights in the region or in BH, for, say, a five year period?
> - Could he provide the Co-Chairmen with his reflections on issues of group rights that would need to be addressed in the area of the former Yugoslavia in the future, and what are his recommendations.[8]

In the actual meeting on 8 October, which lasted forty-five minutes, Mr Mazowiecki informed the Co-Chairmen that he would be undertaking a mission to the area of the former Yugoslavia in the coming week and he wished to have an exchange of views with them. He raised the following issues: information on gross violations of human rights; the latest situation in Bosanski Brod and Sarajevo; developments regarding the proposal for a no-fly-zone over Bosnia and Herzegovina; developments in relations between the Bosnian Croats and the Bosnian Serbs.

Lord Owen suggested that it might be helpful if the Special Rapporteur could get in to Kosovo and help bring a wide international presence to that

7 Background Notes for the Co-Chairmen's Meeting with Mazowiecki, 8 October 1992, 10 A.M. Document in the possession of the author.

8 Ibid.

area. Mr Vance followed up on his request for assistance during his forthcoming field mission.[9]

The Special Rapporteur operated in the Polish language. Conversations were therefore through an interpreter. As a former Prime Minister he saw himself operating on this plane. He had little practical experience on human rights matters and therefore could not engage in a discussion on issues such as minority and group rights. One had the impression that there was never really a substantive dialogue between the Special Rapporteur and the Co-Chairmen.

I *The Special Rapporteur and the Peacekeepers*

As we saw earlier, the Special Rapporteur, in his first report, considered that it was indispensable not only to increase the size of UNPROFOR but also to expand its mandate in three areas: First, the mandate should cover the whole territory of Bosnia and Herzegovina; second, UNPROFOR personnel should have the right to react directly to the human rights violations committed in their presence and to assist the victims; third, UNPROFOR personnel should be given the mandate to collect information and receive complaints concerning human rights violations occurring also on the territories which at the time were not covered by UNPROFOR's mandate. This should include access by the UNPROFOR civilian police to places of detention. Their findings should be communicated not only to the local police but also to the competent juridical authorities.

II *The Special Rapporteur Leads a Campaign to Expose Ethnic Cleansing*

Counting interim reports, including reports to the General Assembly and the Security Council, Mr Mazowiecki submitted sixteen reports.[10] One of his major contributions was his campaign to alert the international community to the practice of ethnic cleansing in the former Yugoslavia, especially Bosnia and Herzegovina. He highlighted this theme in report after report submitted to the Commission on Human Rights and the General Assembly. In his report of 17 November, 1992, Mr Mazowiecki defined the practice as follows:

9 Note on the Meeting in the possession of the author.

10 On 27 July, 1995, following the Bosnian Serb attacks upon and occupation of United Nations safe areas of Srebrenica and Zepa, Mr Mazowiecki resigned his mandate with an emotional appeal to the international community. See the International Herald Tribune, 28 July, 1995, p. 1.

> The term ethnic cleansing refers to the elimination by the ethnic group exerting control over a given territory of members of other ethnic groups.[11]

In his second periodic report, Mr Mazowiecki stated "that the principal objective of the military conflict in Bosnia and Herzegovina is the establishment of ethnically homogenous regions. Ethnic cleansing does not appear to be the consequence of the war but rather its goal."[12] In his third report he elaborated that "the continuation of ethnic cleansing is a deliberate effort to create a *fait accompli* in flagrant disregard of international commitments entered into by those who carry out and benefit from ethnic cleansing."[13]

In his sixth report, submitted on 21 February 1994, Mr Mazowiecki referred to the various manifestations of 'ethnic cleansing' and population transfers,

---

11 A/47/666-S24809. In the first interim report submitted by the Commission Experts established pursuant to Security Council resolution 780 of 6 October, 1992 to investigate grave breaches of the Geneva Conventions and other violations of international law committed in the territory of the former Yugoslavia, the Commission stated: "The expression 'ethnic cleansing' is relatively new. Considered in the context of the conflicts in the former Yugoslavia, 'ethnic cleansing' means rendering an area ethnically homogenous by using force or intimidation to remove persons of given groups from the area. 'Ethnic cleansing' is contrary to international law."

Based on the many reports describing the policy and practices conducted in the former Yugoslavia, 'ethnic cleansing' has been carried out by means of murder, torture, arbitrary arrest and detention, extra-judicial executions, rape and sexual assaults, confinement of civilian population in ghetto areas, forcible removal, displacement and deportation of civilian population, deliberate military attacks or threats of attacks on civilians and civilian areas, and wanton destruction of property. Those practices constitute crimes against humanity and can be assimilated to specific war crimes. Furthermore, such acts could also fall within the meaning of the Genocide Convention: S/25274.

In its final report to the Security Council, the Commission of experts concluded that it was a deliberate policy to instill terror so as to induce persons to leave. Among the coercive means used to remove the civilian population were: "mass murder, torture, rape and other forms of sexual assault; severe physical injury to civilians; mistreatment of civilian prisoners and prisoners of war; use of civilians as human shields; destruction of personal, public and cultural property; forced expropriation of real property; forceful displacement of civilian population; and attacks on hospitals, medical personnel and locations marked with the Red Cross/Red Crescent emblem": S/1994/674.

12 E/CN.4/1994 of 19 May, 1993, para. 6.

13 E/CN.4/1994 of 26 August 1993, para. 135.

in particular the terrorization of Muslims and Bosnian Croats in Serb-held territory. He reiterated his outright condemnation of such practices "which violate fundamental human rights including the right to life, integrity of the person, property, privacy and family life, freedom of thought, conscience, religion and of movement, to earn one's livelihood, to nationality, and rights as a member of an ethnic or cultural group."[14]

He deplored the escalation in the rate of 'ethnic cleansing' in Banja Luka, where there had been a sharp rise in repossessions of apartments, whereby Muslim and Croat tenants were summarily evicted. Almost all non-Serbs had lost their jobs in Banja Luka and he estimated that only 3 per cent of non-Serbs continued to hold employment within the territories administered by the Bosnian Serbs. The authorities in Banja Luka had removed all physical traces of the presence of a Muslim community through the demolition of all of the municipalities' 202 mosques and four other mosques/mausoleums had been razed. On 15 December 1993 the remains of a 16th century Ferhadpasina mosque and four other mosques/mausoleums had been razed. The site had since been turned into a car park.[15]

In the same report, Mazowiecki drew attention to the terrorization of Muslims and Bosnian Serbs in Bosnian Croat held territory, in particular in Mostar: "A result of the 'ethnic cleansing' of Serbs is that their population in Mostar has been reduced from a pre-war figure of 30,000 to just 400."[16] He also deplored the killing in Mostar on 18 October, 1993, of a well known Muslim doctor and members of her family, apparently by members of the Bosnian Croat Defence Forces.[17]

Mr Mazowiecki continued that displacements of populations had been effected by three means: involuntary population exchanges between municipalities under the control of opposing belligerents; private arrangements for emigration to the territory of another of the belligerents; and the forced and immediate expulsion of communities from their places of residence. The various forms of displacement were often accompanied by extortion and theft. Displaced persons leaving Serb held territory were routinely subjected to strip searches at the frontier and to the confiscation of all valuables.[18]

14 E/CN.4/1994/110, paras. 7 ff.
15 Ibid, 8–13.
16 Ibid, paras. 15–19.
17 Ibid, para. 17.
18 Ibid, paras. 40–48.

In his seventh report, Mr Mazowiecki reported on the destruction of Gorazde by Bosnian Serb forces, including a deliberate "scorched earth policy."[19]

III *Documenting the Violations*

Following horrible massacres of Muslims in Bosnia and Herzegovina, Mr Mazowiecki resigned as Special Rapporteur during 1994 because he felt that the international community had not done enough to protect human rights in Bosnia and Herzegovina. He sought, by his resignation, to draw attention to the plight of the victims in Bosnia and Herzegovina. He was succeeded, in turn, by Elizebetn Rehn of Finland, Jiri Dinstbeir of the Czech Republic, and Jose Cutileiro of Portugal. All of these special rapporteurs, through their reports to the Commission on Human Rights, the General Assembly, and the Security Council, documented as best they could the criminal violations of human rights that had taken place in the former Yugoslavia. They therefore made a historic contribution in alerting the international community to what had taken place.

Conclusion

However, as we stated in the conclusion to the previous chapter on humanitarian operations, there could really be no serious possibility of stopping the violations without stopping the conflicts through negotiations. Whatever the Special Rapporteurs documented and reported on, and whatever they recommended, the violations and atrocities would continue once the conflicts continued. That was the nature of the conflict. One was not dealing with political or military leaders who were mindful of international human rights and humanitarian law. In the absence of countervailing force, only negotiated solutions could hope to alleviate the plight of innocent civilians. This is why it was so terribly wrong for the USA to support the continuation of the conflict between 1993 and 1995 while people died or were ethnically cleansed in large numbers.

There were those who said that the peace negotiators should not negotiate with the leaders of the warring factions but with leaders of civil society supportive of peace. No one could explain how these leaders of civil society would overwhelm the fighting forces or their military or political leadership. At the end of the day, peace has to be made through those with fighting forces on the ground.

19 E/CN.4/1995, para. 15.

The Special Rapporteurs of the Commission on Human Rights served an important function inasmuch as they acted as the voice of conscience and justice. This was their greatest contribution. At the end of the day, however, it was the peace negotiators who had to try to stop the conflicts, provided that major powers, notably the USA, would let them do their job. The Americans never gave the ICFY negotiators on Bosnia a chance because they blocked peace agreements and armed the Bosnian Muslims and the Croatian government.

CHAPTER 17

Political Leadership

The First War-Time SRSG

Introduction

UN envoys and mediators have existed almost from the inception of the United Nations. Count Folke Bernadotte lost his life trying to end the Arab-Israeli conflict. The late Ralph Bunche won the Nobel peace prize for his successful mediation of an armistice between Arabs and Israel. UN envoys helped in the search for peace in the Congo in the 1960s and elsewhere. Martti Ahtisaari implemented the peace plan that brought independence to Nambia. UN envoys and mediators thus functioned in war-time or in a combination of peace-time and war-time.

But the concept of Special Representative of the Secretary-General is of more recent vintage. In the past, UN Force Commanders were responsible for UN peacekeeping operations on the ground in their theatres of responsibility. They headed UN operations, military and civilian. In the case of the implementation of the peace agreement for Cambodia, the Secretary-General appointed Yasushi Akashi as Special Representative for that country and he led in the implementation of UN activities in that country. This brought in the concept of an SRSG with broad-based responsibilities.

In 1993, Secretary-General Boutros Boutros-Ghali brought in a major innovation in the concept of SRSG. He appointed Thorvald Stoltenberg as his Special Representative and entrusted him with responsibility for all UN operations in the former Yugoslavia, peacemaking, peacekeeping, humanitarian, peace-building, human rights. Henceforth, the Force Commander came under the authority of the Special Representative. So did Civil Affairs, and humanitarian operations on the ground, including the Special Envoy of the UN High Commissioner for Refugees. Every UN operation in the former Yugoslavia came under the authority of the SRSG. This was the first time in the history of the United Nations that such a concept came into operation.

At the time there was much fighting in Bosnia, a fragile ceasefire in Croatia with intermittent breakdowns into conflict, and the danger of spill-over of conflict to Kosovo and Macedonia. For reasons that will be touched upon below, Stoltenberg served simultaneously as SRSG and as Co-Chairman of the International Conference on the Former Yugoslavia and in that capacity participated in UN peacemaking and conflict prevention efforts throughout the

 | DOI 10.1163/9789004245907_021

former Yugoslavia. This meant, from May, 1993 to January, 1994, being, as SRSG, the head of all UN operations in the former Yugoslavia while conflict raged on the ground in Bosnia and conflict flared up from time to time in Croatia. Stoltenberg was thus the first war-time SRSG in the history of the United Nations with responsibilities for UN peacekeeping operations in Bosnia, Croatia, and the Former Yugoslav Republic of Macedonia. The UN peacekeeping operation in the former Yugoslavia was the largest ever in UN history, with actual forces numbering some 45,000 and an authorised complement of 50,000. Managing this operation, while simultaneously serving as peace mediator, was the greatest of challenges. In this Chapter we shall relate how the first-ever UN war-time Special Representative managed the many issues that he had to face.

Co-Chairman and SRSG

The International Conference on the Former Yugoslavia (ICFY) had been established by the London Conference in August of 1992. The Co-Chairmen of its Steering Committee, the principal peacemakers, were the late Cyrus Vance and Lord Owen. They appointed Martti Ahrisaari, who subsequently won the Nobel Peace Prize for his contributions to peace in different parts of the world, as lead negotiator on Bosnia and Herzegovina. Ahtisaari met with the three Bosnian parties successively in Geneva from September to December, 1992. Vance, Owen and Ahtisaari convened the Bosnian leaders and other leaders in the former Yugoslavia to peace negotiations in January, 1993. Vance, Owen and Ahtisaari presented the Bosnian parties with a peace plan in January 1993 consisting of a constitutional arrangement for Bosnia founded on an integrated republic of ten provinces with a corresponding map of the provinces. The Bosniacs (Muslims) and Croats accepted the plan but the Bosnian Serbs withheld their approval.

Vance,Owen and Ahtisaari then moved the process from Geneva to New York from February to April, 1993 in the hope that pressure from the UN Security Council would lead the Bosnian Serbs to accept and also help hold all parties in place during the implementation phase. Continuing Bosnian Serb recalcitrance led Western powers to raise the threat of sanctions against the FRY (Serbia and Montenegro). President Slobodan Milosevic, who had wanted the Bosnian Serbs to accept the Vance-Owen plan, very much wanted to avoid sanctions against his country. He therefore brought pressure upon the Bosnian Serbs to accept the Vance-Owen plan and approached Vance and Owen to reconvene the peace talks in Athens at the beginning of May, 1993.

While this was taking place, Vance's tenure as Co-Chairman was coming to an end. He had indicated to Secretary-General Boutros-Ghali from the outset that he would be serving for a limited period and planned to step down at the end of April. Thorvald Stoltenberg accepted an appointment to succeed him as ICFY Co-Chairman.

At the beginning of May, 1993, the Bosnian Serbs accepted the Vance-Owen plan at the Athens conference and eyes were then turned to implementation, which would require an even larger UN peacekeeping operation. Stoltenberg, who was due to take over from Vance, attended the Athens conference along with Vance and Owen. It was proposed to him that he should, while continuing as Co-Chairman, simultaneously serve as SRSG. He reflected on whether one could be simultaneously peacemaker and SRSG and was persuaded to accept the double assignment by Vance, who thought that his position as Co-Chairman would strengthen his hands as SRSG and vice versa. Vance stepped out of the picture after the Athens conference. Thus it was that Stoltenberg came to wear the two hats simultaneously. By the end of 1993 he would conclude, as fighting intensified on the ground, and as the parties put pressure on him in his capacity as negotiator for things under his responsibility as SRSG, that he should give up the functions of SRSG and did so during January, 1994, when Yasushi Akashi took over from him as SRSG.

Within a week of their acceptance of the Vance-Owen plan in Athens at the beginning of May, the Bosnian Serbs repudiated their acceptance a week later. Stoltenberg was thus left in the situation of having to strive with Owen for implementation of the Vance-Owen plan in the predominantly Muslim and Croat provinces under the Vance-Owen plan, leaving open the possibility of implementation in the majority Serb provinces later. In the second half of May, 1994, he and Owen went to Russia, Byelorussia, and Ukraine in search of peacekeeping troops for the progressive implementation of the Vance-Owen plan. This effort would shortly afterwards be scuttled by the Americans at a meeting in Washington that came up with a document known as the Joint Action Plan. Russia, economically weak at the time, changed its stance of support for the progressive implementation of the Vance-Owen plan to support for the Joint Action Plan.

While Stoltenberg was on the road in the quest for peace during May, 1993, issues came up to him from UNPROFOR and from other UN components in Zagreb for his decision as SRSG, and he had to lead the UN operations as an itinerant SRSG. He was able to do so with the support of a core team of political, military, and operational advisers.

In June, 1993, Stoltenberg arrived as SRSG in Zagreb. This was a culture shock for the Force Commander, an experienced Swedish peacekeeper, General Wahlgren and other UN leaders on the ground. Stoltenberg had to deal with the following major issues as SRSG:

(a) **Taking Charge as SRSG and Establishing the Office of SRSG, Conceptually and Physically:** Stoltenberg, a former Norwegian Defence Minister, had to register with the Military and civil affairs leadership that there was henceforth political leadership of all UN operations. He had to put down a concept of the SRSG. He also had, literally, to construct physical offices. The Force Commander wanted him to rent office space in down-town Zagreb!

(b) **Clearing up major Administrative Problems left over.** The Head of Administration, Mr Baldie, reported to Stoltenberg when he took over that there were major administrative and financial problems that he himself had inherited from the previous Head of Administration. Under Stoltenberg's leadership the Administrative and Financial affairs of UNPROFOR were put into order.

(c) **Managing Peacemaking and Peace and Humanitarian Operations simultaneously.** Stoltenberg had to travel much in his capacity as a peacemaker. This meant that he had to be accompanied at all times by a Military Adviser and a Director of his Office who helped him lead the peace operations while he was on the road.

(d) **Integrating Human Rights in a Peacekeeping Operation for the first time in UN history.** Stoltenberg injected into UN peacekeeping operations for the first time the idea that UN peacekeepers should be ready to share information on violations of human rights to which they were witnesses. This was something that UN peacekeepers were not used to. The peacekeeping tradition was enhanced in this respect because of Stoltenberg.

(e) **Supporting War Crimes Investigators:** As SRSG, Stoltenberg directed that UNPROFOR should provide back up and support for the excavation of mass grave sites, for example, the site at Ovcara, near Vukovar.

(f) **Providing Political Leadership to the Humanitarian Operations.** There was clear evidence that humanitarian assistance was being diverted by the warring parties for military purposes. Stoltenberg had to hold steady nerves so that humanitarian assistance would continue notwithstanding this. He also had to hold steady nerves when the humanitarian leadership presented him with representations that humanitarian personnel were facing the highest security threats in any UN operation to date.

(g) **Maintaining the Integrity of Humanitarian Operations:** At one stage the Force Commander, General Cot, proposed that his troops be entrusted with the task of delivering humanitarian assistance. Stoltenberg had to hold the line that humanitarian activities must retain their integrity from the military.

(h) **Establishing a policy for the implementation of Security Council resolution 836:** Security Council resolution 836 authorised the calling in of air power in support of UN peacekeepers. This was a major, and controversial issue. Stoltenberg strongly advised that the decision to call in the planes should be that of the UN Secretary-General.

(i) **Setting up a System for Managing Requests from the Force Commander for the Use of Air Power:** It took considerable staff work from the military and civilian advisers of Stoltenberg to set up a system for the management of requests from the Force Commander. According to the system established, regardless of where in the world Stoltenberg was, a request from the Force Commander would have to be processed within an hour of receipt, and the SRSG would have to decide whether to advise the Secretary-General to call in the planes or not. The Force Commander landed Stoltenberg with a number of surprise simulations, sometimes in the midst of peace negotiations.

(j) **Guiding an Erratic Force Commander:** Week after week, the Force Commander would send urgent cables to Stoltenberg seeking his directives on mundane issues. One had to reply to him professionally, asking him to use his professional judgment on day to day matters.

(k) **Controlling a Force-Commander. Determined to Use Air Power.** The Force Commander, General Cot, was reprimanded by Secretary-General Boutros-Ghali in January 1994 for publicly advocating the use of air power. Throughout Stoltenberg's tenure as SRSG he had to be vigilant on this issue. That meant spending Christmas week of 1993 at UNPROFOR Headquarters in Zagreb to head off any situation in which the Force Commander could act on his own on the pretext that the SRSG was absent.

(l) **Motivating the Forces and Building Support among Troop Contributing Countries.** UN peacekeeping forces were giving their lives while the Bosnian parties attacked them on different occasions. This meant that Stoltenberg had to consciously strive to motivate the forces and to retain support from their countries.

(m) **Comforting the Parents of Humanitarian personnel assassinated on the ground.** When humanitarian personnel were killed, Stoltenberg had to go to their parents to comfort them. The case of Bjarne Nielsen of Denmark was one such instance. The only child of his parents, he was deliberately shot by Muslim forces while driving a truck with humanitarian supplies. Stoltenberg went to Denmark to comfort his parents.

(n) **Acting as a Shield for the UN Secretary-General.** Stoltenberg consciously took the position that the Secretary-General had appointed him to take the responsibility for situations. He went to the Secretary-General only when he felt that a problem was sufficiently serious to warrant the Secretary-General's attention.

(o) **Gaining the confidence of the UN Security Council.** Stoltenberg had to liaise with the Security Council in order to assure their continuing support for the peace operations. He did this through reports, informal briefings, and contacts with capitals.

(p) **Negotiating solutions to operational problems on the ground.** There were occasions when problems on the ground, such as the suspension of humanitarian relief operations, had to be managed through negotiations. Stoltenberg steered the negotiation of such problems.

(q) **Steering Fact-Finding Exercises into Allegations of Atrocities and Massacres.** When atrocities and massacres took place, fact-finding was done by UNPROFOR under the direction of Stoltenberg. The investigation of a massacre at Medak was one such instance. Stoltenberg sent up a major report to UN headquarters and to the War Crimes.

(r) **Steering Relations with NATO.** UN-NATO relations required careful political management, especially at a time when certain elements in NATO were trigger-happy. Stoltenberg, as former Defence Minister of a NATO country, helped in the management of this relationship. In this task he was assisted greatly by Norwegian General V. Eide, a former Chairman of NATO's military committee.

(s) **Guiding Relations with NGOs and Humanitarian Organizations:** Numerous NGOs and humanitarian organizations were active on the ground. Relations with them had to be nurtured and managed. One issue that came up, for example, was what NGOs and humanitarian organizations would do in the event of a UN withdrawal from the area. The management of relations with NGOs and humanitarian organizations had to be carefully handled.

(t) **Providing Political Guidance to a UN Peace Operation:** Stoltenberg was conscious throughout that the principal role of an SRSG was to provide political leadership to the UN operations. His was the first experience in the application of this concept.

Close Air Support

The issue of Close Air Support, the use of NATO planes in support of UN peacekeeping forces was a particularly intricate one that Stoltenberg had to wrestle with. On 7 July, 1993, within a month of his installation in Zagreb, Stoltenberg sent the following Memorandum to Secretary-General Boutros-Ghali on "Legal and Policy Questions" :

> "Further to our last discussion, my subsequent contacts have brought even more pointedly that we shall need to have legal and policy answers to the following questions:

> 1. What is the extent of the right to self-defence of United Nations Peacekeeping Forces? Specifically, can resort to air support for self-defence be made in places that are not "within or near" to the safe areas?
> 2. In the event that it is felt on the ground that air support is needed for purposes of self-defence, what margin do the forces or their commanders have to avail themselves of air support?
> 3. In your report to the Security Council on the implementation of the safe area concept you stated that you would make the first decision whether to use air support for the protection of UN forces in the safe areas. This conforms to my own view that the decision to cross the line to the use of air support should be made by the Secretary-General. The question has arisen in discussions: Can the Force Commander, in the event of a serious threat to the security of the forces, call in air support on the ground that the emergency was such that he had to act immediately?
>
> My assessment is that these questions may come up more and more in the field and quite likely also in the circles of the Security Council. It would be helpful if the Legal Counsel could take a look at these questions and provide his opinions so that we may have an opportunity to consider them when next you and I meet."[1]

Resolution 836 of the Security Council had brought in the option of close air support should United Nations peacekeepers seeking to defend the safe areas come under attack from any of the parties. But how was this concept to be put into practice? Our good friend Brigadier General John Wilson, Stoltenberg's Military Adviser, and I would spend many hours trying to put together a policy for the Special Representative, who would be called upon to decide on the recommendation of the Force Commander whether to advise the Secretary-General to call in the planes.

UNPROFOR Force Commander Jean Pierre Cot was an energetic, and volatile Force Commander. He, on his side, set about the development of a system within UNPROFOR to send forward to the Special Representative a recommendation for transmittal to the Secretary General on the use of NATO planes in close air support. From the outset of his appointment Cot had been an avid advocate of close air support. Shortly after his appointment he came to Geneva on 30 June for a dinner with Stoltenberg at which Lord Owen and I were present. Cot ardently championed the use of aerial support.

1 Text of the Memorandum in the possession of the author.

He considered that air support was the only means he had to intervene on behalf of his battalions. In a cable to Stoltenberg on 6 July, 1993, he stated, "As a military commander, my responsabilities (sic) dictate me to be ready at the earliest to insure security for the men I have under my command. It is my duty to consider the worst possible scenario...It remains clear that the initial decision of use would be taken by the Secretary-General in close coordination with you and me, the chain of decision, carefully designed, should be as quick as possible."

General Cot took an aggressive approach to the use of close air support. His early position papers required careful scrutiny on Stoltenberg's part and this placed a heavy burden on me as the Director of Stoltenberg's office, effectively his chief of staff, and on Norwegian General Viglik Eide and Brigadier General John Wilson. Eide, a former Chairman of the Military Committee of NATO, had been appointed by Stoltenberg as his Deputy in Zagreb. Wilson, as previously indicated, was Stoltenberg's Military Adviser.

Even after several sessions backwards and forwards, General Cot's "Concept of Employment of Air Power," of 18 August, 1993, remained strident. It read in parts, "The troops available to the Force Commander UNPROFOR for the performance of the mandate are fully committed to the task at hand; the Force Commander does not have a strategic reserve at his disposal. Air support therefore is the only means he has available to react to serious incidents....(T)he overriding concern of the Force Commander is for the security of his ground troops in any eventual use of air support. Consequently, air support will be used as a deterrent for as long as possible. If employed, use will be in a measured response, proportional to the threat and mindful of the danger of escalation."

General Cot's concept of employment of air power continued: "The first use, if undertaken, must be a success, and therefore must have as its aim to achieve significant effect on the aggressor with no collateral damage." What kind of aggressive attack would call in air power? Cot set out the following circumstances "(a) A hostile action whose deliberate nature is established without doubt; and (b) Attributable with accuracy to the aggressor position. The probability of provocation and deception has to be considered." After employment of air support, Cot added, UNPROFOR would attempt to return to the deterrence phase as soon as possible.

Cot's system called for the Special Representative to respond to his recommendation to call in the planes within an hour. John Wilson and I advised Stoltenberg that this was reasonable and we proceeded, with the assistance of a Finnish Major, our good friend Pasi Koronen, to set in place a system to make this possible. At the time Stoltenberg, while Special Representative of the Secretary-General, was also Co-Chairman of the International Conference on the Former Yugoslavia and, as such, immersed in the negotiations for peace.

He was thus constantly travelling in theatre in the Former Yugoslavia and in different parts of the world. I as Director of his Office, and John Wilson, his Military Adviser, invariably travelled with him. Pasi Koronen assured coverage of the Stoltenberg's office as Co-Chairman of the International Conference on the Former Yugoslavia.

With the lack of technical assets that characterized United Nations peacekeeping at the time, a system had to be devised to allow Stoltenberg to receive Coded UN Cables wherever he might be in the world so that he would be constantly reachable by the Force Commander. We also had to develop procedures and criteria within the Office of the Special Representative to process a recommendation from the Force Commander to the Special Representative, to advise the Special Representative on his response, and to ensure that the decision of the Special Representative was sent back to the Force Commander within the hour. The credit for the development of such a process must go to Pasi Koronen and John Wilson.

Pasi Koronen drafted a policy paper which he, Wilson and I went over carefully and we recommended to Stoltenberg a procedure with the following elements:

- A representative of the SRSG's Office, Zagreb, would be included as a member of the UNPROFOR Headquarter Air Report Validation Team.
- The UNPROFOR requesting officers on the ground would include Stoltenberg's Office in Geneva as an information addressee on their air support request. The Geneva Office would treat the request as early warning of the operational circumstances but would not act on the document.
- The SRSG's Geneva Office would be advised, by secure telephone, that an advice from the Force Commander for first use was in preparation and a secure cable/fax would be anticipated. Should the secure telephone not be manned, e.g. because the advice was forthcoming out of working hours, contact would be made wherever the SRSG, his Director (BGR), or close staff were located.
- The secure cable/fax would be forwarded to the Communications Room in the Palais des Nations in Geneva through the normal UN communications system, with an information copy to the UN New York Situation Room. UN New York would not act on the information copy, treating it as early warning pending receipt of the SRSG's recommendation.
- If the SRSG could not be contacted, then the senior staff of the SRSG would liaise with the Deputy Special Representative in Zagreb, General V. Eide, who would act on behalf of the SRSG.

The instructions ended, "Speed and accuracy in the decision-making process are imperative as, in the real situation, a great number of human lives may be at stake." What a responsibility it was to be the Chief of Staff of the SRSG in the development and operation of such systems and to be at his side wherever he went. The United Nations was in uncharted waters and one was given a chance to help hold the steering wheel at times.

Stoltenberg accepted the foregoing recommendations, which would shortly thereafter be put to the test. The Force Commander, General Cot, decided to have a series of test runs and he would send cables to the Special Representative, often in the middle of negotiations, on which John Wilson and I would have to scramble to make a recommendation to Stoltenberg for his decision. It was often inconvenient but we respected the process and always arranged for a response to be sent back within the hour.

On one occasion, the Yugoslav leaders were locked deep in negotiations in the Palais des Nations in Geneva in the search for peace in Bosnia-Herzegovina. In came an urgent cable from General Cot, a simulation: A number of United Nations peacekeepers were pinned down by hostile forces and unless the planes were called in they would surely be killed. John Wilson and I huddled and came up with a recommendation. We could not let several United Nations peacekeepers be killed. We therefore advised Stoltenberg to accept the recommendation for the planes to be called in. We asked Stoltenberg to step out of the room where the parties were deep in discussions and we met with him in an adjoining room. We gave him a draft cable by which he would agree to send forward, in simulation mode, a recommendation to the Secretary-General to call in the planes.

Stoltenberg was a seasoned player. He had been a Minister of Defence in Norway, as well as Foreign Minister. He looked at John Wilson and me in the eyes and said: "Next door I have the Yugoslav leaders locked in discussions for peace. If I authorize the use of the planes it will surely mean that the talks will be aborted, the fighting will continue for months before they get together again, and thousands more will die. I am afraid I cannot allow that and therefore cannot agree to send forward a recommendation to the Secretary-General to call in NATO planes."

John Wilson and I had been convinced that there was only one course possible: protect the peacekeepers. But here was a man who had the bigger picture in his mind and had the strength to make a tough decision. Wilson and I both learned something important that day. In peacekeeping and in peacemaking tough choices had to be made sometimes. This was one such occasion. We swallowed hard, but we respected the guts of Stoltenberg. Fortunately, it was only a simulation!

The practical difficulties of operating the procedure of close air support were felt on the ground. In mid-November, 1994 a Danish Army Lt. Col, the deputy commanding officer of the Nordic battalion in the safe area of Tuzla called for close air support when his forces came under deliberate Bosnian Serb shelling. A US Air Force plane, with which he was in communication, locked on to a

Serb tank firing on his troops but did not complete the action because authorization for the use of close air support had not been not forthcoming. The Danish commanding officer was quite critical of what he considered the failure of the leadership of the UN Forces to authorize close air support. However UN spokesmen in Zagreb replied that there had not been not enough time to call in the planes because by the time the Serb attack came to their attention it was nearly finished. A UN spokesman said that close air support had been initiated but by then the Serb firing had stopped. The procedure, according to the spokesman was that the attack had to be in progress for the planes to strike. United Nations representatives acknowledged that a US Air Force plane had locked on to the Serb tank but that UNPROFOR had not authorized the strike.

There were those arguing vehemently for air strikes against the Bosnian Serbs. The UNPROFOR Force Commander, General Cot, was one of them. For those engaged in the peacemaking process the consequences of such strikes on the negotiations could be incalculable. So dangerous was the situation that, over Christmas, 1993, Stoltenberg decided to be in Zagreb so that he could be on the spot to manage things personally should the Force Commander decide to opt for air strikes over the holiday period, when people were dispersed. Stoltenberg and I spent Christmas Day and Christmas week that year in the Intercontinental Hotel in Zagreb. The Hotel staff, knowledgeable of Norwegian customs, prepared for his Christmas meal salted Cod, 'bacalau' in the recipe traditionally prepared in Norway around Christmas. We spent a week in Zagreb watching over the situation first hand. Stoltenberg, as a United Nations representative, supported the safe areas regime introduced by the Security Council. He wanted, however, objectivity and wisdom to be brought to bear upon its implementation. The dangers of trigger-happiness troubled him greatly.

If I may be allowed a personal observation, in my three and a half years on the Yugoslav peace journey I saw and did a great deal. The Christmas week in Zagreb stands out in my memory. It was a dangerous time, and as Dayton would show eventually, peace would have to be negotiated in the final analysis.

Conclusion

From the foregoing, it will be seen that Stoltenberg's experience as the first ever wartime Special Representative of the Secretary-General holds great historical significance because of the range of issues that had to be dealt with, and also because it was the first instance in which the concept of political leadership of a large UN peace operation would be applied. Stoltenberg handed over to his successor a working system for leading the largest operation in the history of UN peacekeeping and humanitarian activities.

Conclusion

The UN Served Magnificently in Practising the Art of the Possible

As I write this book the international community is observing the sixteenth anniversary of the massacres in Srebrenica. This gives cause for deep introspection. Shortly after the Bosnian Serb army moved in on Srebrenica the then Secretary-General of the United Nations, Boutros Boutros-Ghali, asked his trusted representative, Thorvald Stoltenberg, the United Nations negotiator on the conflict, to visit the Bosnian Serb headquarter of Pale to use his influence to obtain Red Cross access to the men in Bosnian Serb detention. I had accompanied Stoltenberg and his partner Lord Owen to many parts of the world in the search for peace in the former Yugoslavia and had previously done the overland route from Belgrade to Pale with him and Lord Owen to meet the Bosnian Serb leaders there. I accompanied Stoltenberg on this mission as well and proceeded with him to Belgrade.

By way of background, let me say that the lead negotiators for the International Conference on the Former Yugoslavia, Cyrus Vance and Lord Owen, and then Thorvald Stoltenberg and Lord Owen (succeeded in the closing stages by Carl Bildt), had worked indefatigably for three years to help stop the conflict. They could not succeed because, rightly or wrongly, the United States preferred the lifting of the arms embargo so that the Bosniacs could secure arms to avenge their losses against the Bosnian Serbs and the Germans had their favourites in the Croats. Russia had its sympathies with the Serbs, but it was a weak power at the time. Carl Bildt, who had succeeded Lord Owen as the European Union negotiator alongside Thorvald Stoltenberg representing the United Nations, had decided to work closely with the Americans. His hunting pack became the Contact Group established by the United States to lead the negotiations.

There are many questions directed at the responsibility of the United Nations regarding the situation in Srebrenica and the United Nations has been quite open in letting the facts come out. But few questions have been asked of the Contact Group and its responsibility for dealing with the situation. At the meeting in the American Embassy in Belgrade, General Rupert Smith was in attendance. He reported that he had been in contact with the Bosnian Serb General Ratko Mladic. Political Representatives present at the meeting said that they had been in contact with the Serb leadership. There was not a hint that the men were already dead but it is hard to believe that those with the satellite intelligence capability were not aware of this.

 | DOI 10.1163/9789004245907_022

The principals went off for a meeting at President Milosevic's villa in Belgrade. The political people met Milosevic. General Smith met Ratko Mladic. When they came back General Smith reported that he had met with General Mladic who had promised Red Cross access to the detained men from Srebrenica. He said that during the next week they would work out the details. I have never seen a report about what happened during that week but, as we now know, the men were already dead.

This is what we, on the United Nations side, had to put up with in our search for peace in the Former Yugoslavia: lack of information, governments pursuing their own agendas, and unclean hands on all sides of the conflict in Bosnia – even though, admittedly, some hands were dirtier than others.

Propaganda raged on all sides and good men had their names dragged in the dirt: Cyrus Vance, Lord Owen, Thorvald Stoltenberg, and Yasushi Akashi. This was, alas, the name of the game. Let me take the case of Cy Vance briefly. If there was one thing that characterized him it was 'honour'. He and Lord Owen were determined to help roll back the Bosnian Serb gains in Bosnia. This was the motive driving the Vance-Owen plan.

Many were and remain critical of the plan, and I have no difficulty with that. But what I do object to are those who wrote that Vance and Owen accepted and sought to ratify ethnic cleansing. I worked closely with these two good men and nothing can be further from the truth. In fact, they deliberately took the side of the Bosniacs against the Bosnian Serbs and the Bosnian Croats.

It was Vance who pursued a personal crusade that the victims of the massacre at Vukovar hospital should not be forgotten. He asked me to work personally on arranging a forensic investigation of the mass grave site at Ovcara, near Vukovar. I liaised with the Dutch Chairman of the UN Committee of Experts gathering information on atrocities, Professor Frits Kalshoven, and with Physicians for Human Rights. Without Vance that forensic investigation would never have gotten off the ground. Later, Stoltenberg, as SRSG in charge of the peacekeeping forces in the Former Yugoslavia, arranged for UN peacekeepers to guard the site over many, many months! I was Director of Stoltenberg's Office as SRSG and I also worked on this.

After the publication of the Vance-Owen plan its authors received tongue-lashings from many quarters, including from leading figures in the Clinton Administration. Vance felt so betrayed, and let down, particularly by his erstwhile Deputy, Warren Christopher. Vance was a former Secretary of State. I have never seen the daily intelligence brief the US authorities provided to him but he repeatedly told me that they had little in them. He was in a position to judge. He felt he got no support in his peacemaking effort from the Clinton Administration.

To the contrary, I personally worked on the brief Vance sent to Christopher following Clinton's victory in the elections. We provided detailed explanations of the goals of the negotiators and also the accompanying documents. Vance met at his New York appartment with incoming National Security Adviser Sandy Berger for the better part of a Saturday. I had also worked on the brief for that meeting. Vance was convinced that Christopher paid no attention to his submissions but, instead, was irresponsibly critical.

At one stage in the negotiations Vance and Owen had moved the process to New York, in the spring of 1993. Vance came to work early in the morning. As Director of the International Conference on the Former Yugoslavia and adviser to our negotiators, I also came in early. One early morning, Vance and I were alone and he was obviously pained by the stance of Christopher. This extraordinarily self-controlled man rarely showed his feelings. But on this occasion his pain over what he considered Christopher's betrayals overcame him.

Christopher's handling of the issue of the American hostages in Teheran, which had led to Vance's resignation as US Secretary of State caused Vance great pain. Suffice it to say that he found Christopher's behaviour then inexplicable, to say the least. Closer to our subject matter, Vance felt that Christopher was deliberately condescending and duplicitious when he could have been supportive. I have carefully considered whether I should write these words. I have met Christopher in passing on one or two occasions when I happened to be accompanying principals. I have no view of my own on him. But I have referred to this matter to illustrate the difficulties of the peace negotiators trying to bring the conflicts in the Former Yugoslavia to an end. For the peace negotiators this was a lonely business.

I was involved in the peace processes for three and a half years. During this time I did not take a single day off, weekends included. We criss-crossed the world in the search for peace. For one of these years Stoltenberg doubled as mediator and SRSG in charge of all United Nations operations in the Former Yugoslavia, including the largest-ever peacekeeping operation in the history of the United Nations, UNPROFOR. I was Director of his Office as SRSG. I saw it all and stayed with it all. I was the only UN official on the scene at Dayton, not a part of the process, but present. The lot of the peacemaker is a lonely one. So is the lot their principal aides; so was my lot. There is so much that I can write about the Yugoslav peace journey. In this work I have tried to provide some impressions. I have numerous notes and papers on our efforts over these three and a half years. I shall have, in the future, to consider how I make these available to researchers.

There were numerous legal and human rights issues at the heart of the peace negotiations in the former Yugoslavia. The points that came up included the following: How does one deal with interlocutors / negotiators against whom there were allegations of war crimes and crimes against humanity? How does one deal with claims to peoplehood and statehood? How did one grapple with the Yugoslav experience with peoples, nationalities and minorities? How did this relate to concepts in international law? How did one seek to insert human rights provisions in the peace agreements – which were the most extensive ever inserted in draft peace agreements? How did one tackle succession issues? How could one draw upon the concept of international guarantees of an agreement. Could one draw upon the concept of internationalized cities or internationally administered cities? How did one seek to grapple with competing claims of justice and peace? Should there have been a standing working group on human rights issues as an integral part of the negotiating architecture?

Other issues raised ranged from self-determination, territorial rights, rights of succession, the rights of peoples and minorities and issues of respect for the norms of human rights and humanitarian law. I was involved in all aspects of these negotiations from the day the International Conference installed itself in Geneva on 2 September 1992 to the day the Conference was dissolved at the end of April 1996.

I helped helped prepare many of the draft agreements and drafted every single report submitted by the Co-Chairman to the Security Council during this period. I was also, for a year, simultaneously Director of ICFY and Director in the Office of the Special Representative of the Secretary-General for the Former Yugoslavia, in charge of all Peace-Keeping and Humanitarian Operations in the Former Yugoslavia. UNPROFOR was the largest Peace-Keeping Operation in the history of the United Nations, with some 44,000 troops, and I was directly involved in questions touching on the use of air support in defence of the peace-keeping troops during this period, as well as the protection of the safe areas. I thus had unique vantage points into the peace-making, peace-keeping and humanitarian processes during these conflicts. I offer below some additional impressions on key issues that arose during the Yugoslav peace negotiations.

A The Interlocutors

One of the questions that came up repeatedly during the peace-negotiations was whether the mediators were justified in negotiating with interlocutors accused of war crimes and crimes against humanity, such as Radovan Karadzic and Ratko Mladic. This was essentially a political issue but, in today's world, it could very well be a legal issue, namely, should one negotiate with a person who has been accused of war crimes and crimes against humanity?

For most of the period of the International Conference on the Former Yugoslavia, there were allegations of war crimes and crimes against humanity against Bosniac Serb, and Bosniac Croat, negotiators, but there were no formal indictments against them until late in the process. Human rights groups kept making the point that the peace mediators should be dealing with well-meaning civic and political leaders who could take the country forward on the basis of internationally recognized values. There might have been a case to consult such leaders in a parallel process. But the fact of the matter was that the leaders of the Bosniac, Croat and Serb factions were the ones who had the military power on the ground and if one were to have any hope of stopping the conflict, it was by negotiating with them.

Having regard to contemporary attitudes on the role of human rights in peace negotiations, one would need to pose the question to international lawyers: should peace negotiators refrain from dealing with those accused of war crimes and crimes against humanity? Can they?

B The Requirements of Statehood

As the Former Yugoslavia was breaking up, the European Community (now the European Union) asked the Badinter Commission to look into the question of the requirements for statehood of the former constituent republics and the Commission laid down such criteria, including: a commitment to democracy, the rule of law and respect for human rights, as well as guarantees for the protection of minority rights. When the International Conference on the Former Yugoslavia came to the scene it had to grapple with claims to statehood by the Bosnian Serb Republika Srpska and a similar Croatian Serb self-professed republic. Each entity had a population, defined territory and the ability to govern itself and to conduct external relations. At no time, however, did the peace mediators of the International Conference on the Former Yugoslavia ever entertain the idea of recognition of these two entities. In both cases, the mediators insisted on the sovereignty and territorial integrity of both Bosnia and Herzegovina and Croatia.

C Peoples, Nations, Nationalities and Minorities

Throughout the Peace Negotiations on the Former Yugoslavia, one came across constantly the concept of peoples, nations, nationalities and minorities. In the Yugoslav practice, in the days of President Tito, a people was a constituent element of the Federal Republic. A nationality was a distinct group within a people while a minority was viewed in the sense of a smaller grouping different from the people or nationality in question. In general international law, one was conversant with the terms 'peoples and minorities', which had distinctive meanings; however the juxtaposition of peoples, nationalities, and minorities led to complex political negotiations. The Serb population of Croatia, for example, was used to being recognized as a people in the Croatian Constitution within the Former Socialist Federal Republic of Yugoslavia. However, after the breakup of the Former Yugoslavia and the establishment of the Croatian State, the Croatian Government considered the Serb population a minority and sought to give it that status. The Serb population resisted this and this lay at the root of a great part of the conflict in that country. For the Serbs, recognition as a people was important.

The situation in the Former Yugoslav Republic of Macedonia was particularly complex. There, were Macedonians, Albanians, Serbs and other nationalities to be reckoned with. They wished to be recognized as constituent peoples while, at the same time, the international regime for the protection of minorities was clearly relevant for protection on the ground. Regardless of aggregate populations within the State, there were many instances where they broke down into majorities and minorities in particular localities. In the International Conference on the Former Yugoslavia, we sought to develop rules of coexistence nationally on subjects such as: education and media outlets in the Albanian language. We also sought to foster an inter-ethnic and inter-party dialogue on the basis of the international standards for the protection of minorities. It was recognized by centrist leaders in the Former Yugoslav Republic of Macedonia that the international norms for the protection of minorities could provide the basis for coexistence among the different peoples in the country.

D Human Rights Provisions

Previous peace negotiations have had human rights provisions, as in the case of the peace accords on El Salvador – where there had also been an important Verification regime. In the El Salvadorian negotiations, what was important were the arrangements for the protection of human rights. In the peace negotiations in the Former Yugoslavia, human rights concepts, as we saw above, were central to the construction of the peace. The concepts incorporated in the accords had to wrestle, as we saw above, with notions such as peoples, nationalities, and minorities. Religious rights were also of central importance. At the outset of the Bosnian peace negotiations in September 2003, the Yugoslav peace mediators spent weeks going over with the leadership of the three Bosnian factions the basic international norms on human rights so that they would be conversant with them and would understand them when the agreements came to be worked upon. For nearly 50 meetings, we went over the basic international instruments on human rights with the Bosnian factions.

When it came to the Croatian theatre, we had to wrestle with the concept of autonomy and respect for minority rights within a regime of autonomy and we spent several months going over these issues in seeking to craft an agreement for autonomy for the Croatian Serb parts of the country.

In Serbia itself, there were Hungarian minorities to be protected and our working group on ethnic communities and nationalities engaged in discussions for months to try to work out understandings on the protection of the Hungarian minorities.

In Kosovo and in the Former Yugoslav Republic of Macedonia, the issues of language, education, schools, and culture were tackled. In the case of the Former Yugoslav Republic of Macedonia, important understandings were reached on the provision of education and TV programmes in the Albanian language.

The right of refugees to return was a wrenching issue. I drafted the framework of the first peace agreement for Bosnia and Herzegovina put down by the International Conference on the Former Yugoslavia and inserted in it a provision on the rights of refugees to return to their territory, which made its way eventually into the Dayton Peace Agreements. Sadly, this right, as has happened elsewhere, was more easily asserted than implemented.

E Succession Issues

A situation involving the breakup of the Former Yugoslavia into the sovereign States of Slovenia, Croatia, Bosnia-Herzegovina, the Former Yugoslav Republic of Macedonia, and Serbia and Montenegro gave rise to complex issues of State succession. The International Conference on the Former Yugoslavia had a working group that met periodically to look into these succession issues and a draft agreement was worked upon during the Conference. This draft agreement would eventually be built upon by the successor states in working out practical succession arrangements.

F Autonomous Territories

In the midst of the conflict in Croatia, the Serb people, as we have seen above, insisted on being recognized as a people and wanted to break away from

Croatia. In the end, they did not achieve this, but were in fact expelled *en masse* from the country. The peace mediators in the International Conference on the Former Yugoslavia worked for months on a plan called the Zagreb-Four (Z-4) plan, which would have given the status of autonomous territories within the Croatian State to the principal Serb areas. Unfortunately it proved hard to sell this concept, but the document itself, the Z-4 document, was one of the most advanced pieces of work on the concept of autonomy.

G International Guarantees

We came across the issue of international guarantees when we worked on the Z-4 plan. This was an agreement that was meant to provide a regime of autonomy for the Serb population in Croatia. The question arose: Could one get the agreement internationally guaranteed? We explored the meaning of this concept in international law, but in the end, however, the major powers were not willing to participate in such a guarantee and the issue was not pressed.

H Internationalized Cities

We had very thorny issues to deal with when it came to the status of Sarajevo and Mostar. Sarajevo was bitterly contested between the Bosniacs and the Serbs. Mostar was bitterly contested between the Bosniacs and the Croats. We worked extensively on the concept of an international city in the case of Sarajevo, but, in the end, this concept did not go forward. We did succeed, however, in placing Mostar under international administration for a period of years. The idea was Lord Owen's. He deserves credit for it.

J Justice and Peace Negotiations

It is a wrenching issue that a peace negotiator has to deal with sometimes, namely, how to end the war and, at the same time, provide for a minimum of justice in the outcome of the peace negotiations. At one stage in the negotiations, the mediators worked on the concept of three constituent peoples for Bosnia, each with their own constituent State. The Serbs and the Croats, because of the external support they received, had largely succeeded in carving out for themselves extensive areas of Bosnia and Herzegovina. What, then, would be the land territory of a constituent State for the Bosniacs? The mediators, Lord Owen and Thorvald, Stoltenberg, developed the concept of a contiguous State with access to the Sava River and the Adriatic Sea. The mediators insisted that this criterion be met, otherwise they would not be associated with any peace agreement.

Legal and human rights questions were central to the peace negotiations in the Former Yugoslavia under the auspices of the International Conference on the Former Yugoslavia. If there is one impression that forms in the mind of the author a decade and a half later, it is probably that the peace negotiations should have built in a forum for addressing human rights issues on a standing basis. The International Conference on the Former Yugoslavia had a structure that consisted of: the Co-Chairmen, a Standing Committee of the principal countries participating in the Conference, and six working groups on the following topics: Bosnia and Herzegovina, humanitarian issues, succession issues, ethnic communities, nationalities and minorities, and economic issues. In our submission there should have been a seventh working group on human rights issues, which would have provided a framework for addressing human rights questions throughout the duration of the Conference and subsequently. The Humanitarian Issues Working Group, under the inspiring leadership of Mrs. Ogata, valiantly wrestled with the humanitarian challenges in a conflict that lasted more than five years. The Humanitarian Issues Working Group was attentive to human rights issues but, in the nature of things, had to focus on helping people rather than taking up the wrenching protection issues. A human rights working group might have permitted the Conference to do better on this score.

I have many memories of meetings with historic figures in Yugoslavia. One of them was Milovan Djilas. Stoltenberg, who had been a diplomat posted in Belgrade, knew Djilas well and sought a meeting with him, which he graciously granted. On Wednesday 18 May, 1994, from 12 noon to 1.15 pm, I accompanied Stoltenberg and Owen as they met Djilas in his modest Belgrade apartment. The great man was in his senior years but was in good spirits and his mind was sharp. The walls of his apartment were lined with books.

Stoltenberg and Owen were interested in Djilas's views on the peace process and how he saw the position of the Serbs at that time. Stoltenberg began the conversation by telling Djilas that the situation in Bosnia and Herzegovina was at a difficult, critical stage. If there were no peace agreement soon, one could be in a Lebanon-type situation, even though the major nations had moved closer in their policies towards Bosnia and Herzegovina. The Co-Chairmen therefore sought Djilas's evaluation of the prevailing situation and how he saw the future.

Djilas began by dealing with the situation in Serbia. The strongest political leader in Serbia, he said, was Milosevic. The rest were "not up to him – or worse." Among the opposition leaders Draskovic was the best. But he had no political concept. In the last two years there had been some modest democratic evolution in Serbia. The Fascists such as Seselj, were weaker. There was the beginning of Parliamentary life. Communications were free even though there was some manipulation by the government. One could say that in Serbia there was an "authoritarian democracy."

Turning to the situation in Bosnia and Herzegovina he said that it was on the verge towards peace or to more war. The Geneva Ministerial Meeting on 13 May had taken good decisions, but there had been so many good plans before. It was important that the countries which met in Geneva strongly insist on their proposed formula for the borders (51/49%). Then all problems would be open to resolution. The pressure should be put not only on the Serbs but on the Moslems to adopt the 51/49 formula.

The Northern corridor was important for all three sides. He did not see any alternatives to the corridor unless one contemplated United Nations protection. For the Serbs there had to be a connection between Eastern and Western Bosnia. He thought that one could consider the possibility of giving the Serbs a small part along the Sava River while allowing the Muslims to come to Brcko. One could have bridge connections…He emphasized "for Serbs as I see, they must have some passage along the Sava or there will always be trouble." He added, "the alternative is that the United Nations send a lot of troops – but this is not realistic. Some form of United Nations protection must exist even after peace."

Djilas returned to the territorial formula and stated: "Everybody agrees that there will be more war if there is not energetic action to enforce the 51/49% formula."

Commenting on the proposed federation between Muslims and Croats in Bosnia and Herzegovina Djilas commented: "The Federation will not last. It is an artificial creation to bring about an alliance against the Serbs. It will not last. No federation in Bosnia and Herzegovina will last. The Serbs will reunite with Serbia and the Croats with Croatia. I see a Muslim state in Bosnia and Herzegovina. It is too late to save Bosnia. The Federation will separate on the first occasion. It is an artificial entity."

Commenting on prevailing currents in the area Djilas said that the West did not understand the Nationalistic movements in Bosnia and Herzegovina: "They are nationalists, not fascists; but their methods do not differ." Milosevic, he said, was not dictatorial: he was authoritarian. The regime of Tudjman was different to the regime of the Croats in Bosnia and Herzegovina. The latter were anti-democratic – Ustashas.

There had never, Djilas continued, been democracy in the region. Nationalism had been the ruling ideology in central and southern Europe in the nineteenth century. Communism was a short-lived interlude. He, Djilas, did not believe in Yugoslavia as a state. He saw the emergence of small states that will need to work together. He saw eventually a separate Muslim state with the Bosnian Serbs joined to Serbia and the Bosnian Croats joined to Croatia. The Muslims, he added, must have a state or the nationalistic movements would massacre them. He saw the Muslim state in central Bosnia.

According to Djilas, Milosevic did not insist on uniting with the Bosnian Serbs at once but stage by stage. "Milosevic is a man of power. He wants to play a great historical role in the life of Serbia – the one who brought the different areas with Serbs together."

On the relationship between Karadicz and Milosevic he said that one could differentiate but not separate them. Karadicz was a transitional figurė for the Chetniks. Karadicz was in the tradition of the Mihailovic movement. Draskovic also used the memory of Mihailovic.

Dealing with the situation in Kossovo, Djilas said that while Yugoslavia existed he had been against its separation. But the Serbs had done so many things there with the result that Albanian consciousness had moved far from autonomy. The Albanians now had a para-state with their own police and schools. The Albanians saw time working on their side. There was no uprising because the Albanians were working with the Americans, who were quietening them down. The American idea was to give them autonomy. They would agree to this as a stage towards eventual independence.

Asked whether he saw a link between the way Kosovo is treated and the Krajina is treated Djilas said that a lot depended on what happened in Bosnia and Herzegovina. If Bosnia and Herzegovina were solved then the Krajina would be solved. Milosevic would not go to war over the Krajina because the people in Serbia did not want war. Milosevic's economic poicy was oriented against war. He, Djilas, thought that in the Krajina if the Croats were to get Slavonia the Serbs must be given some territory around Baranja. Djilas's assessment was that it was not difficult for Milosevic and Tudjman to come to an agreement. The difficulty was with the Serbs in the Krajina.

On internal developments within Croatia, Djilas thought that Tudjman's split with Msic was a positive thing. Tudjman was authoritarian. Msic was a younger and more "liberal" man. On the word liberal Djilas commented: "Here 'liberal' has its own shade."

Asked why Tito had recognised Muslims as a nation Djilas replied that after the war the Communists had always distinguished Muslims from Serbs and Croats. There was in Bosnia not only a Muslim religion but also a kind of Muslim ruling class. Between the first and second world wars the Muslim elites were really elements of a feudal ruling class. Between the two world wars they were always united in the MJO – the Muslim Jugoslav Organisation. After WWII they developed a strong intellectual class that is now ruling in Bosnia. Tito had recognised this and had noticed their cohesiveness so he recognised them as a nation so that they could be a balancing entity. The Muslims, Djilas continued, are now established as a distinct entity.

The Serbs liked to call them Turks but the Muslims considered themselves higher than Turks. They had rarely married Turks. There were never many Turks in Bosnia. In the Croat consciousness Muslims are Croats. However, the Muslims will separate from the federation when they are strong. The Muslim majority in Bosnia and Herzegovina would have given them hegemony over Serbs and Croats. Since the latter have Serbia and Croatia they would never accept Muslim hegemony. He was not sure the Croats would ever make the Muslim-Croat Federation workable. They would find some pretext to slip out of the Federation.

Asked about disputed areas in Bosnia and Herzegovina, Djilas thought that the Muslims must eventually have Visegrad. Foca would probably stay with Serbia or Montenegro and eventually Zvornik may be part of Serbian territory. He thought it a difficult proposition that the Serbs would even give Sanskai Most to "Turks."

Concluding the conversation Djilas thought that Bosnia and Herzegovina had started a change of the whole international order including the Helsinki principles and principles of human rights. Because of developments in Bosnia, nationalism was now permitted everywhere. He cautioned: "This is the nucleus of a new crisis that must be stopped or everything will be lost."

He ended the conversation with the thought: "Utopia is the human mind. Without it we can do nothing."

I have reproduced this conversation for its historical significance. The detailed references to people and places will be understood by people familiar with the conflict. For others, the flow of the thinking of the great author will be of importance. It provides a good backdrop to the complexities of the Former Yugoslavia. Suffice it to say that one met few utopias of the mind among the Yugoslav protagonists along the journey.

International Mediators and Governmental Mediators

I came away from three and a half years of full-time, total involvement in the search for peace in the Former Yugoslavia convinced that it made a difference if one were an international mediator or a governmental mediator, especially a mediator from a powerful government. I had been alongside Vance, Owen, and Stoltenberg from the beginning of September, 1992, until the end of April, 1996, and had seen them give their guts for peace in Bosnia and Herzegovina but they just could not pull it off. I am confident that peace plans we put on the table were superior to that of Dayton but they could not stick because of the lack of sincerity of one or more of parties, or because powerful governments, especially that of the United States of America, had ranged themselves on the side of one or other party and obstructed the search for peace.

When the Vance/Owen plan was put on the table everyone sat on his haunches. When the Owen-Stoltenberg plan was put on the table all three parties supported it but the Government of the United States sabotaged it. When the Owen-Stoltenberg-European Union plan was put on the table it was as good as the Bosniacs could get but the United States continued to obstruct it because they were set on a course of arming the Bosniacs and letting them fight it out.

What caused this to change was the approaching Presidential elections in the United States. President Clinton was up for re-election in 1996 and he wanted the Bosnian conflict off the table so that it could not be used against him in the campaign. Then entered American mediators, with the full panoply of the economic and military power of the United States of America. People could be given economic and military inducements to follow the American line, the USA could nudge NATO into military action, and the parties at Dayton could be pressurized into submission – something no international mediator without powerful governmental backing could pull off.

I watched the signing of the Dayton Peace Accords with mixed emotions. I was pleased that the conflict might finally be coming to an end. But I knew within me that we had better peace agreements a year, two years before, but could not make them stick, because we lacked the power behind us to bring the parties to book.

Cy Vance had a distinguished record as an American statesman and peace negotiator. He had served in many government positions, including that of Secretary of State. He had been involved in numerous negotiations, openly and discreetly. He had led the human rights foreign policy under the Carter Administration. He had helped the United Nations Secretary-General defuse dangerous crises, including in South Africa and the former Yugoslavia. He had provided the blueprint for bringing the conflict in Croatia to an end and had helped design the blueprint for UNPROFOR, a United Nations protection force in the Serb enclaves in Croatia.

When he began his stint as the UN Co-Chairman of the International Conference on the Former Yugoslavia the Bush Administration was still in power. Larry Eagleberger became the Acting Secretary-of-State and attended a meeting of the Steering Committee of the Conference in December of 1992 when he called for the prosecution and trial of Serb war criminals in the conflict in Bosnia-Herzegovina. I have the impression that the Bush I administration extended to Vance the respect and support he deserved as a senior American statesman doing his best in his mid-seventies, to help bring a disastrous conflict to an end.

Unfortunately, that changed with the arrival of the Clinton Administration. There were policy and personality reasons for this. I accept that the Clinton Administration, especially Vice-President Albert Gore, were revolted by Bosnian Serb atrocities against the Bosniacs and wished to arm the Bosniacs so that they could avenge their losses against the Serbs. What was sad about this, however, was that this was done in stealth, while allowing the mediators of the International Conference on the Former Yugoslavia to press on with their efforts at the same time as the US Government was telling President Izetbegovic that they would re-arm him and help him to fight on.

In the spring of 1993 Secretary-of-State Warren Christopher went on a mission to Europe to persuade European partners to follow a policy of lifting the arms embargo and striking at the Bosnian Serbs (life and strike). When he could not persuade his European partners to adopt this policy he returned to the USA and the USA refrained from lifting a finger to help the international mediators while they proceeded to provide arms supplies to the Bosniacs. Some of their close partners, such as Turkey, also clandestinely armed the Bosniacs. The USA was also aware that Iran was providing arms to the Bosniacs. It was known that foreign mujahiddeens were in Bosnia, including the infamous Osama bin Laden! The poor mediators had to pursue their quest for peace while this potent brew simmered in Bosnia.

Bibliography

A International Peace Conferences

F. Adcock and D.J. Mosley, Diplomacy in Ancient Greece. New York, St. Martin's Press, 1975.

A. Adolf, Peace. A World History. Cambridge, Polity Press, 2009.

R. Aron, Peace and War. A Theory of International Relations. New York, 1966.

G.J. Bass, Stay the Hand of Vengeance. The Politics of War Crimes Tribunals. Princeton, Princeton University Press, 2000.

A.C.F. Beales, The History of Peace. A Short Account of the Organized Movements for International Peace. New York, 1931.

J. Child, The Central American Peace Process. Sheathing Swords, Building Confidence. Boulder, Lynne Rienner, 1992.

R. Cohen and S. Cohen, Peace Conferences: The Formal Aspects. Jerusalem Papers on Peace Problems, No. 1. Hebrew University, Jerusalem, 1974.

R. Dallek, The Lost Peace. Leadership in a Time of Horror and Hope, 1945–1953. New York, Harper Collins, 2010.

J.G. Dickinson, The Congress of Arras, 1435. A Study in Medieval Diplomacy. New York, Biblio and Tannen, 1972.

R. Hoffman and P.J. Albert (Eds.), Peace and the Peacemakers. The Treaty of 1783. Charlottesville, The University of Virgina Press, 1986.

K.J. Holsti, Peace and War: Armed Conflicts and International Order 1648–1989. Cambridge, Cambridge University Press, 1991.

M. Howard, The Invention of Peace. Reflections on War and International Order. New Haven and London, Yale University Press, 2000.

J. Keegan, A History of Warfare. New York, Random House, 1994.

D. King, Vienna, 1814. New York, Harmony Books, 2008.

H. Kissinger, A World Restored. Metternich, Castlereah and the Problems of Peace 1812–22. Boston, Houghton, Mifflin, 1987.

C.R. Mark, The Geneva Conference on Laos, 1961–62. Published by the Reference Service of the US Library of Congress, 1968.

G. Mattingly, Renaissance Diplomacy. London, Jonathan Cape, 1955.

M. McMillan, Peacemakers. Six Months that Changed the World. The Paris Conference of 1919 and its Attempt to End War. London, John Murray, 2001.

W.N. Medlicott, The Congress of Berlin and After. A Diplomatic History of the Near Eastern Settlement, 1878–1880, 1963.

W. Murray and J. Lacey (Eds.), The Making of Peace. Rulers, States, and the Aftermath of War. Cambridge, Cambridge University Press, 2009.

H. Nicholson, The Congress of Vienna. A Study of Allied Unity 1812–1822. London, Constable and Co., 1946.

H. Nicholson, Peacemaking 1919. New York, Grosset and Dunlap, 1965.

A. Osiander, The States System of Europe, 1640–1990. Peacemaking and the Conditions of International Stability. Oxford, Clarendon Press, 1994.

P.R. Pilar, Negotiating Peace. War Termination as a Bargaining Process. Princeton, Princeton University Press, 1983.

J.G. Russel, Peacemaking in the Renaissance Philadelphia, University of Pennsylvania Press, 1986.

J.B. Scott, The Hague Peace Conferences of 1899 and 1907, 1909.

J. Wheeler-Bennett and A. Nicholls, The Semblance of Peace. The Political Settlement after the Second World War. London, St. Martin's Press, 1972.

Quincy Wright, A Study of War. 2 vols. Chicago, University of Chicago Press, 1942.

P.H. Wilson, The Thirty Years War. Europe's Tragedy. Cambridge, MA, Harvard University Press, 2011 (Previously published by Penguin, 2009).

M.H. Yavuz and P. Sluglet (Eds.), War and Diplomacy: The Russo-Turkish War of 1877–1878 and the Treaty of Berlin. University of Utah Press, 2012.

B Yugoslavia

Martti Ahtisaari, by F.P. Miller et al., 2010.

C. Bell, On the Law of Peace: Peace Agreements and the Lex Pacificatoria. Cambridge, Cambridge University Press, 2008.

C. Bildt, Peace Journey. The Struggle for Peace in Bosnia. London, Weidenfeld and Nicolson, 1998.

R. Caplan, Europe and the Recognition of New States in Yugoslavia, 2005.

J. Cutileiro, Vida e Morte dos Outros – A communidade internacional e o fin da Jugoslavia. Lisboa, Imprensa de Ciencias Sociais, 2003. (Life and death of others. The International Community and the end of Yugoslavia. – English version available at the Princeton University Library.)

M. Goulding, Peacemonger, London, John Murray, 2002.

R. Holbrook, To End a War. New York, Random House, 1998.

S. Ogata, The Turbulent Decade. Confronting the Refugee Crises of the 1990s. New York, W.W. Norton, 2005.

D. Owen, Balkan Odyssey. Victor Gollancz, 1995.

J. Pettifer and M. Vickers, The Albanian Question. Reshaping the Balkans. London, I.B. Tauris, 2007.

J. Phillips, Macedonia. Warlords and Rebels in the Balkans. London, I.B. Tauris, 2004.

B.G. Ramcharan (Ed.), The International Conference on the Former Yugoslavia. Official Papers. Martinus Nijhoff, 1997, 2 Vols.

M. Rose, Fighting for Peace. London, The Harvill Press, 1998.

G. Salvesen, Thorvald's Verden. Oslo, Chr. Schibsteda Forlag A/S, 1996.

J.R. Schindler, Unholy Terror. St Paul, Minnesota, Zenith Press, 2007.

R. Smith, The Utility of Force: The Art of War in the Modern World. 2008.

H. Sokalski, An Ounce of Prevention: Macedonia and the UN Experience in Preventive Diplomacy. Washington, DC, US Institute for Peace, 2003.

T. Stoltenberg, De tusen dagen: Fredsmedlere pa Balkan, 1996. (Memoirs on his efforts as a peacemaker and peacekeeper in the Balkans).

S. Touval, Mediation in the Yugoslav Wars. The Critical Years, 1990–1995. London, Palgrave, 2002.

C. Vance, Hard Choices. Critical Years in American Foreign Policy. 1983.

A. William, Preventing War: The UN and Macedonia. Lanham, MD: Rowman &Littlefield, 2000.

S. Woodward, Balkan Tragedy, Washington, DC, Brookings, 1995.

Index

www.ingramcontent.com/pod-product-compliance
Lightning Source LLC
LaVergne TN
LVHW102226300926
849160LV00005B/43
* 9 7 8 9 0 0 4 2 4 5 8 9 1 *